# Ethnic Enterprise in America

# Ethnic Enterprise in America

# Business and Welfare Among Chinese, Japanese, and Blacks

# IVAN H. LIGHT

University of California Press
Berkeley, Los Angeles, London 1972

University of California Press
Berkeley and Los Angeles, California
University of California Press, Ltd.
London, England

Copyright © 1972, by
The Regents of the University of California
ISBN: 0-520-01738-2
Library of Congress Catalog Card Number: 77-121189
Designed by Steve Reoutt
Printed in the United States of America

to Mumpo

# Contents

Acknowledgments    ix

1. Ethnic Enterprise in American Cities    1
2. Rotating Credit Associations    19
3. Rotating Credit and Banking    45
4. *Kenjin* and Kinsmen    62
5. Immigrant Brotherhood in Chinatown    81
6. Urban League and Business League    101
7. Church, Sect, and Father Divine    127
8. From Mutual Aid to Insurance Enterprise    152
9. Voluntary Association and Immigrant Brotherhood    170
   Appendix    191
   Works Cited    193
   Index    201

# Acknowledgments

So many people have lent me ideas and stimulation that I am unable to single out for appreciation everyone who merits it. Nonetheless, I want to acknowledge particularly the advice and assistance of Martin Trow and Reinhard Bendix. In addition, John Stewart, Samuel J. Surace, Sheila Henry, and Lucy Hirata were kind enough to give me their professional evaluation of some chapters. Joan Z. Clayton, Josephine Hower, and Shaw Sin-ming read my drafts with a critical eye in the office of friendship. Although vastly grateful for the help of these and so many others, I bear exclusive responsibility for any errors of fact or interpretation.

The most excellent helper of all was my wife, Leah, who helped me to remember that voluntary association is not the be-all and end-all of life.

Most of the research was conducted under a grant from the Manpower Administration, U.S. Department of Labor under the authority of Title I of the Manpower Development and Training Act of 1962. Researchers undertaking such projects under government sponsorship are encouraged to express freely their professional judgment. Therefore, points of view or opinions stated in this work do not necessarily represent the official position or policy of the Department of Labor.

# Ethnic Enterprise in American Cities

# 1

One evening in mid-August 1965, a sullen group of blacks watched helmeted Los Angeles police subdue a local mother whom they accused of having spat upon a white officer. The housewife cursed them hysterically as they dragged her, manacled, to their squad car. When the police had departed, the angry spectators began to throw rocks and bottles at passing white motorists, overturning and burning any vehicles that stopped. In the racially tense atmosphere, news of these incidents circulated quickly through the Watts district.

Thirty hours later, an angry crowd of black residents had gathered on Avalon Boulevard in the business district of Watts. Small retail stores lined both sides of this central shopping street. Most of these stores belonged to whites, and the crowd was in a mood to "get whitey." Blacks pried off the iron gates protecting storefronts, smashed plate glass windows, and began to loot retail stores of their merchandise. After the shelves had been emptied, homemade gasoline incendiary bombs were left behind to complete the revenge.

Emboldened by the night's successes, a much larger crowd returned to Avalon Boulevard the next morning. Smashing, looting, and burning took on epic dimensions. Women and children from adjacent housing projects joined in the looting, each taking home as much as he could handle and then returning for another load of merchandise. Black store owners hastened to post "soul brother" or "Negro owned" placards in their display windows. Although some black owners lost their businesses despite this precaution, the people of Watts generally spared stores displaying these placards. Most of the looted and burned small businesses belonged to whites.

The Watts disorder of 1965 was a harbinger of others similar to it. In 1966 American cities experienced forty-three disorders and riots in black neighborhoods. The National Advisory Commission

on Civil Disorders listed 164 black riots in the first nine months of
1967. Of this number, eight were major disorders involving numerous fires, intensive looting, sniping, two or more days of violence,
sizable crowds, and the use of National Guard or army units in the
suppression of the riots. The single most serious riot occurred in
Detroit, Michigan, where forty-three persons were killed between
July 25 and July 27, 1967. Thirty of the forty-three who died were
shot to death by police, National Guardsmen, or store owners
defending their merchandise.[1]

Although the various riots differed in intensity and duration,
wherever they occurred they usually involved attacks by local blacks
on white-owned stores in their neighborhoods. Looting and burning
of retail stores was the basic scenario of nearly every riot, disturbance,
and uprising. Typically, there was no dramatic precipitating event
to call down black wrath upon the retail proprietors in the neighborhood. As in Watts, black complaints of police brutality provoked
the mood in which the local people revenged themselves on white-
owned retail businesses. Although owned disproportionately by Jews
and by foreign-born whites, the alien businesses symbolized the
"white power structure" to resentful blacks. Moreover, in Watts,
Detroit, Newark, and the hundreds of other cities where looting occurred, white proprietors controlled or even monopolized the retailing of clothing, furniture, appliances, liquor, and groceries in black
neighborhoods.[2] Few blacks owned stores in which this attractive,
readily portable merchandise was on display; such black-owned
businesses as did exist tended to specialize in barbering, beauty
culture, television repair, and other services. Under these circumstances, the white-owned retail stores were obvious, convenient, and
rewarding targets of black anger.

Had all small businesses in Watts been black owned, then popular
anger about police misconduct or white racism would not have seized

[1] *Report of the National Advisory Commission on Civil Disorders*, ch. 1. Con-
cerning the Watts riots, see Robert Conot, *Rivers of Blood, Years of Darkness* (New
York: Bantam Books, 1967); Jerry Cohen and William S. Murphy, *Burn, Baby,
Burn!* (New York: Avon Books, 1966).

[2] *Report of the National Advisory Commission*, pp. 139–40; Richard Berk,
"Doing Business in the Ghetto: Retail Merchants," in *Racial Attitudes in American
Cities*, pp. 125–26.

upon the local business district for a racial revenge. Also, if all retail businesses in Watts and in the other riot struck cities had been owned by blacks, the local residents would have harbored no grudges against gouging white merchants. To be sure, many looters were simply interested in obtaining free merchandise and did not really care about the color or malpractices of the owner from whom they liberated it. For such people, "getting whitey" was only a hypocritical justification for "getting mine." Nonetheless, the undeniable presence of such individuals ought not to obscure the popular legitimations which made it possible for anyone to loot at all; nor should these legitimations obscure the conditions which called them forth. After all, black people will not legitimate the burning and looting of black-owned stores as a protest of white exploitation. In this limited but obvious sense, the whites' hegemony over retail districts was a specific precipitant of the burning and looting which visited their stores. The white-owned stores certainly did not cause basic racial unrest. But there are, after all, many ways for basic unrest to express itself other than by burning and looting of small businesses in the neighborhood.

## THE INVISIBLE MAN

In this scenario of American rioting, the conspicuously missing figure is the black retail proprietor who does business in a black neighborhood and specializes in appliances, furniture, clothing, liquor, or groceries. In fact, this figure is missing because few black people operate such retail stores. In every large black neighborhood in the United States, white proprietors virtually monopolize local retail trade.[3] It is difficult to explain why blacks, unlike other ethnic minorities, have relied on white outsiders to supply their retail needs. Indeed, blacks have, for several decades, loudly and repeatedly complained that white merchants exploit and rob them at every turn, and they have grounds for complaint. Yet these vocal complaints

[3] See Theodore L. Cross, *Black Capitalism* (New York: Atheneum, 1969), p. 100; Alex Poinsett, "The Economics of Liberation," *Ebony* 24 (August 1969): 150–52; Jules Abend, "U.S. Negroes Gain Ground in Business," *International Management* 23 (March 1968): 33; Eugene P. Foley, "The Negro Businessman: In Search of a Tradition," pp. 112–15; John Z. DeLorean, "The Problem," in the American Assembly, eds., *Black Economic Development*, (Englewood Cliffs, N.J., 1969), pp. 7–20.

notwithstanding, few black retailers have emerged to challenge the exploiters.

It is hardly surprising that black people would like to own the retail stores located in their own neighborhoods. Retail proprietorship is, after all, a classic avenue of upward social mobility for the disadvantaged, and a "symbol of opportunity" in the Horatio Alger tradition. Indeed, as late as 1940, two serious American sociologists could refer to retail trade as "the age-old field of opportunity by which a person of humble origin and circumstance may hope to become an owner, secure profits, and achieve a measure of personal security against the hazards of life."[4] The archaic ring of this flowery tribute notwithstanding, self-employment has still an undeniable appeal to the unskilled, the unemployed—indeed to anyone disadvantaged in the general labor market. Making a decent living in retail trade is certainly harder nowadays when small businessmen have to compete with immense corporate enterprises. Those with advantageous educational and color credentials can normally do better by working for the A & P than by working against it. Hence, only the disadvantaged now have an economically rational motive for operating retail stores in competition with the A & P or any other retail giant. Because blacks are so disadvantaged, their want of a proprietary class is more anomalous today than it was a half century ago.

In view of the importance of the small proprietor in other American minorities, the "complete absence of a business class" among blacks is especially perplexing.[5] As Mabel Newcomer has observed, the persistent overrepresentation of the foreign born in businesses is not a testimony to the entrepreneurial drive of the foreign born, nor an invidious commentary upon the lethargy of native-born Americans. Compared to the native born, the foreign born have received less schooling and hold less impressive educational credentials. They possess fewer high-priced salable skills. They experience discrimina-

[4] H. Dewey Anderson and Percy E. Davidson, *Occupational Trends in the United States* (Stanford: Stanford University Press, 1940), p. 450. Also see Kurt Mayer, "Business Enterprise: Traditional Symbol of Opportunity," *British Journal of Sociology* 4 (1953): 160–80.

[5] Nathan Glazer and Daniel P. Moynihan, *Beyond the Melting Pot*, p. 30. Cf. also Max Weber, *The Protestant Ethic and the Spirit of Capitalism*, p. 39.

tion because of their accents and ethnicity. Hence, the foreign born find in self-employment relatively better income and status rewards than do native-born persons who have advantages in the labor market.[6]

Of course, as many writers have noted, the comparison of blacks and foreign-born whites is often misleading because the latter experienced milder discrimination than did American blacks. They have also had the enormous advantage of a colorless skin.[7] Simply because of their visibility, black people were easier to spot and, therefore, to discriminate against than were Irish, Italians, Poles, or Jews, however unpopular those categories may have been. No matter how much education or gentility he pumped into his black skin, a black American constantly encountered powerful whites who wanted to treat him like a field hand and to exclude him from prestigious or remunerative positions. These cruel disadvantages explain many differences between blacks and foreign-born whites, but they do not explain why the latter have been regularly active in business proprietorships (even in black neighborhoods) whereas the blacks themselves have not. On the contrary, the extra disadvantages of blacks ought, strictly speaking, to have stimulated them to more extensive self-employment than the foreign-born whites.

These deductions aside, the social histories of Americans of Chinese and Japanese descent offer empirical illustration of the manner in which poverty, discrimination, and ethnic visibility stimulated business proprietorship among some disadvantaged immigrants. The illustration is analytical because, even in California where they are most numerous, Chinese and Japanese together make up only 2 percent of the state's population. On the other hand, the Asian immigrants were poor and visibly non-European and were subject to racial discrimination on that account. These very qualities tended to force the Chinese and Japanese into the classic small

[6] Mabel Newcomer, "The Little Businessman: A Study of Business Proprietors in Poughkeepsie, N.Y.," *Business History Review* 35 (winter 1961): 478. Also see Orvis E. Collins et al., *The Enterprising Man* (East Lansing: Michigan State University Press, 1964), p. 241.

[7] Roger Daniels and Harry H. L. Kitano, *American Racism: Exploration of the Nature of Prejudice* (Englewood Cliffs, N.J.: Prentice-Hall, 1970), p. 121; *Report of the National Advisory Commission*, p. 144.

business occupations with which they have now become identified in the popular mind. But since they shared these practical disadvantages with black Americans, the logic of Asian-American business development raises questions about the absence of parallel developments among American blacks—and about a social theory whose expectations are incongruent with observations.

### DEVELOPMENT OF CHINESE BUSINESS

Chinese immigration to the United States began in 1848. During the Gold Rush, most Chinese laborers worked with pick and shovel in all-Chinese gangs. They were not popular with the European and American miners who forced the Celestials to occupy worked-out, inferior diggings. After the Gold Rush, the pick and shovel employment of the Chinese continued since their labor was in demand for the construction of the transcontinental railroad. Again the Chinese worked in labor gangs; this time, however, they worked as employees of the railroads. They remained highly unpopular with white laborers who complained of their inexpensive dietary habits and deleterious effect on the wage rate for unskilled labor.[8]

Nineteenth-century Americans harbored no patronizing attitudes toward the resident Chinese. In the 1870s and 1880s, whites occasionally burned and pillaged West Coast and Rocky Mountain Chinatowns, wantonly slaying the wretched inhabitants. On "China steamer days," San Francisco hoodlums made a sport of greeting and escorting to Chinatown the disembarking sojourners. This greeting and escort service took the form of taunts, beatings, brick-bats, and hurling of overripened fruit in an atmosphere of drunken Irish hilarity. Such abusive treatment provoked the indignation only of a few, Protestant divines who observed that, whatever their depravity and filthiness, the Chinese were potential converts to Christianity. These pleas notwithstanding, "the feeling against the Chinaman" on the part of American workingmen remained "more bitter and intolerant than that against the Negro."[9]

[8] Concerning the early history of the Chinese in the United States, see Gunther Barth, *Bitter Strength*; Stanford M. Lyman, "The Structure of Chinese Society in Nineteenth-Century America"; Mary Roberts Coolidge, *Chinese Immigration.*
[9] Rev. Ira M. Condit, *The Chinaman as We See Him*, p. 21. Coolidge, *Chinese Immigration*, pp. 77–78; Herbert Asbury, *The Barbary Coast* (New York: Alfred

Anti-Chinese agitation ultimately forced passage of the Chinese Exclusion Act in 1882. Thereafter, the immigration of Chinese declined, but the hostility of white labor to the resident Chinese persisted. Chinese experienced discrimination in hiring. They were forced out of manufacturing employments in white-owned firms. Even Chinese-owned cigar and garment manufactories experienced public pressure to cease operations in economic competition with white firms. Whites took steps to exclude Chinese labor from employment and Chinese firms from the market. These pressures left resident Chinese with few opportunities for earning a livelihood.

For employment, Chinese had principally to look to domestic service, laundry work, restaurants, and small retail stores catering principally to other Chinese. Whites did not object to Chinese in domestic service. They raised no barrier to Chinese in the laundry trade, since this occupation was not one in which white males cared to engage. Chinese-owned restaurants were also tolerated. Serving cheap, appetizing meals, they were able, in the frontier period, to win the patronage of the white working class. For the Chinese in the United States, obtaining a livelihood was a question of scraping the bottom of the barrel after the whites had helped themselves.

By 1900 the familiar outline of the Chinese economy in the United States was coalescing. On the one hand, Chinese in the general labor market were occupied as domestic servants, cooks, and gardeners (Table 1). On the other hand, self-employed Chinese operated laundries, restaurants, import outlets, and groceries. By 1920 more than 50 percent of the Chinese in the United States were employed or self-employed in restaurants or laundries with the majority of the rest still, but in declining proportions, occupied as domestic servants.[10]

The Chinese did not "by nature" gravitate into laundry and restaurant businesses. These operations required very long hours of work at low rates of remuneration. When higher paying wage or

Knopf, 1933), ch. 7; Alexander Saxton, *The Indispensable Enemy: Labor and the Anti-Chinese Movement in California* (Berkeley and Los Angeles: University of California Press, 1971).

[10] D. Y. Yuan, "Voluntary Segregation: A Study of New York Chinatown," in *Minorities in a Changing World*, ed. Milton L. Barron (New York: Alfred Knopf, 1967), p. 267.

TABLE 1

*Distribution of Gainfully Employed Males by Race and Occupational Group for the United States, 1900 (in percent)*

|                                      | All U.S. Males | Negro     | Oriental[a] |
|--------------------------------------|---------------:|----------:|------------:|
| Agricultural pursuits                | 39.5           | 58.3      | 16.3        |
| Professional service                 | 3.4            | 1.1       | 0.7         |
| Domestic and personal service        | 14.6           | 23.7      | 57.2        |
| Trade and transportation             | 17.9           | 7.6       | 15.2        |
| Manufacturing and mechanical pursuits| 24.3           | 9.0       | 10.5        |
| Percentage Total                     | 99.7           | 99.6      | 99.9        |
| Number                               | 23,753,836     | 2,675,497 | 103,943     |

SOURCE: U.S. Department of Commerce and Labor, Bureau of the Census, *Twelfth Census of the United States: Special Reports, Occupations* (Washington, D.C.: Government Printing Office, 1904), Table 37, p. cxiv.

a Chinese and Japanese only.

salary jobs became available, they took them. The Chinese preference for high wages was indicated by the alacrity with which they abandoned Chinatown occupations when the labor shortages of World War II opened new employment opportunities for them.[11] Since World War II, salaried white collar jobs have become increasingly available to college-educated Chinese-Americans who prefer these jobs to self-employment in restaurants, curio stores, or laundries.[12] But prior to 1940, discrimination in employment virtually eliminated opportunities for Chinese in the general labor market. The classic small businesses of prewar Chinese were, in this sense, monuments to the discrimination that had created them.

### DEVELOPMENT OF JAPANESE BUSINESS

Japanese immigration to the United States began about 1900, nearly a generation after the peak of Chinese immigration. Japanese settlements were more restricted to the Pacific Coast states than were Chinese enclaves. The Japanese were also substantially more rural than were the Chinese (Table 2). Like the Chinese, Japanese im-

[11] Rose Hum Lee, "Chinese in the United States Today," *Survey Graphic* 31 (October 1942): 419; idem, "The Decline of Chinatowns in the United States," *American Journal of Sociology* 54 (March 1949): 422–32.

[12] Beulah Ong Kwoh, "The Occupational Status of American-Born Chinese Male College Graduates," *American Journal of Sociology* 53 (November 1947): 192–200; D. Y. Yuan, "Division of Labor Between Native-Born and Foreign-Born Chinese in the United States: A Study of Their Traditional Employments," *Phylon* 30 (summer 1969): 160–69.

TABLE 2

*apanese and Chinese in the United States and in California, and Percentage Urban, 1910–1930*

|  | 1910 | | 1920 | | 1930 | |
|---|---|---|---|---|---|---|
|  | Population | % Urban | Population | % Urban | Population | % Urban |
| *apanese* | | | | | | |
| United States | 72,157 | 46.7 | 111,010 | 48.5 | 138,834 | 53.8 |
| California | 41,356 | 45.0 | 71,952 | 45.6 | 97,456 | 54.6 |
| *Chinese* | | | | | | |
| United States | 71,531 | 76.5 | 61,639 | 81.1 | 74,954 | 87.3 |
| California | 36,248 | 66.9 | 28,812 | 72.5 | 37,361 | 80.9 |

SOURCE: Stanford M. Lyman, *The Asian in the West*, pp. 71–72.

migrants began as wage earners and gravitated thereafter into self-employment. One of the earliest pursuits of Japanese immigrants was strikebreaking in coal mines of Colorado and Utah where "they replaced Greeks striking for higher wages in 1907."[13] In the early period, Japanese were, however, principally occupied as agricultural laborers in California, a task for which the resident Chinese population had become too old and infirm. Other Japanese were employed as railroad and construction workers, cannery hands, lumber mill and logging laborers, and domestic servants.[14]

So long as the Japanese remained willing to perform agricultural labor at low wages, they remained popular with California ranchers. But even before 1910, the Japanese farmhands began to demand higher wages and to employ what the ranchers regarded as unscrupulous tactics in order to obtain them. Worse, many Japanese began to lease and buy agricultural land for farming on their own account. This enterprise had the twofold result of creating Japanese competition in the produce field and decreasing the number of Japanese farmhands available to perform wage labor. California's Alien Land Laws attempted to prevent the Japanese from acquiring land on their own account. The first of these laws was passed in 1913. By 1921 the Alien Land Laws had been perfected, and they began to interfere seriously with Japanese agriculture.

The land laws tended to drive the Japanese into urban areas

[13] Minako Kurokawa, "Social Mobility Among Japanese Businessmen in San Francisco" (M.A. thesis, University of California, Berkeley, 1962), p. 34.
[14] Masakazu Iwata, "The Japanese Immigrants in California Agriculture," p. 27; Harry H. L. Kitano, *Japanese Americans*, p. 15.

where they might become troublesome competition for working class whites. Under the banner of the Asiatic Exclusion League, organized (white) labor attempted to forestall this possibility by forcing the curtailment of Japanese immigration and the exclusion of Japanese from the general labor market.[15] Squeezed off the land and deprived of nonmenial wage and salary employment opportunities, what were the Japanese to do for a living? Confronting this question, California's Board of Control anticipated that "the Oriental, if crowded out of the agricultural field, will rapidly increase his commercial activities."[16] Urban self-employment absorbed the energies of Japanese men who faced discriminatory barriers in agriculture and in the urban labor market. By 1919, for example, 47 percent of hotels and 25 percent of grocery stores in Seattle were Japanese owned. The census of 1940 reported that 40 percent of Japanese men in Los Angeles were self-employed. Although a culturally derived preference for self-employment clearly supported this development, the Japanese interest in commercial self-employment was also a plain response to a discriminatory opportunity structure which precluded wage or salary employment at nonmenial levels.

SPECIAL CONSUMER DEMANDS

Since northern blacks were visibly non-European and were subject on that account to discrimination in the labor market, they had the Orientals' objective motive for opening small businesses. The blacks' repeated affirmation of their desire to own the retail stores in their own neighborhoods indicates that the objective motive was also a conscious one. Nonetheless, by 1929 there were enormous and anomalous differences between the business development of Chinese and Japanese and that of blacks (Table 3). On the one hand, Oriental retail stores were not only proportionately more numerous than those of the whites, their stores also reported larger payrolls and net sales than did the white-owned proprietorships. To a large extent

[15] Carey McWilliams, *Prejudice* (Boston: Little, Brown, 1944), p. 20; Roger Daniels, *The Politics of Prejudice*, pp. 16–30.
[16] State Board of Control of California, *California and the Oriental*, p. 104. See also T. Iyenaga and Kenoske Sato, *Japan and the California Problem* (New York: G. P. Putnam's Sons, 1921), p. 171; Yamato Ichihashi, *Japanese in the United States*, p. 121.

TABLE 3

*Index Numbers of Stores, Personnel, Payroll, Stocks, and Sales of
Retail Proprietorships in the United States by Race or Color of Proprietor, 1929*
*(100 = expected)*

|  | Oriental[a] | Negro |
|---|---|---|
| Stores | 142 | 27 |
| Proprietors | 203 | 26 |
| Full-time employees | 248 | 10 |
| Total payroll | 207 | 6 |
| Stocks on hand (end of year) | 124 | 4 |
| Net sales (1929) | 168 | 6 |

SOURCE: U.S. Department of Commerce, Bureau of the Census, *Fifteenth Census of the United States, 1930*, vol. 1, *Distribution*, pt. 1, "Retail Distribution" (Washington, D.C.: U.S. Government Printing Office, 1933), Table 12–A, p. 89. These results exclude retail corporations so that only proprietorships are compared.
a Chinese and Japanese only.

this white-Oriental difference was attributable to the noteworthy tendency of Chinese and Japanese to operate partnerships with more than one owner. Also, Chinese and Japanese stores were apparently soaking up unemployment by squeezing in more owners and employees per sales dollar than did white-owned stores. On the other hand, Negro-owned retail proprietorships were, in proportion to population, only one-fourth as numerous as those of the whites. This handful of black-owned retail stores provided only one-tenth as much employment as did white retail proprietorships. Most of the black stores were solo proprietorships employing no hired labor.

R. H. Kinzer and E. Sagarin have offered the best explanation of this anomalous difference. Their now widely accepted view emphasizes the inhibiting effects of white retailers in black neighborhoods.[17] White businessmen have traded with blacks because they sold what the blacks wanted to buy; hence, blacks who wanted to become retail tradesmen had to compete with white retailers. Foreign-born immigrants, however, did not face this competition. Unlike American blacks, foreign-born peoples had special consumer demands which outside tradesmen were unable to satisfy: "Since the immigrants spoke little English and had their own ethnic culture, they needed stores to supply them with ethnic foods and other ser-

[17] Robert H. Kinzer and Edward Sagarin, *The Negro in American Business*, pp. 144–45. Also see Daniels, *Politics*, p. 12.

vices."[18] The special demands of ethnic consumers (for example, lasagna noodles, kosher pickles, won ton soup) created protected markets for ethnic tradesmen who knew about the things their countrymen wanted. For instance, Chinese grocery stores feature exotic vegetables which most Americans cannot even identify. It is, therefore, no accident that only Chinese operate Chinatown grocery stores where exotic Chinese vegetables are sold. Only a Polish Jew can distinguish the grades of kosher pickles most appealing to other Polish Jews. Outside competition was, in this sense, the exclusive curse of the urban blacks.

From this perspective, the rank order of population segments in retail trade ought to be viewed as mirroring the culturally derived consumer demands of each section in terms of their uniqueness. Overrepresentation of Japanese and Chinese in retail trade would, then, be explained in terms of the special consumer demands of Oriental consumers. Underrepresentation of urban blacks would be similarly explained by the lack of special consumer demands and the consequent presence of inhibiting white competition. This argument explains why Negroes, a disadvantaged ethnic minority, should have ranked persistently lower in retail business proprietorships than foreign-born minorities.

Such census data as are available are at least congruent with this consumer-demand explanation. In six large cities of the North between 1900 and 1920, the groups with presumably the most unique consumer demands were (rho = .80) also the groups with the greatest proportion of retail dealers (Table 4). Edwards reported the same rank orders in his selection of thirteen large cities in 1930.[19] On the whole, there tended to be a higher proportion of Oriental retail dealers than foreign-born white ones. The latter, in turn, were more frequently retail dealers than were native-born whites of foreign or mixed parentage. And this last group was regularly occupied as retail proprietors in greater proportion than the native whites of native parentage. Presumably, the native-born white had the most

---

[18] *Report of the National Advisory Commission*, p. 144.

[19] Alba M. Edwards, *A Social-Economic Grouping of the Gainful Workers of the United States* (Washington, D.C.: U.S. Department of Commerce, Bureau of the Census, 1938), pp. 269–79.

TABLE 4

*Retail Merchants and Dealers as a Percentage of Employed Males Ten Years of Age or Older by Nativity and Race or Color for Six Cities: 1900, 1910, and 1920*

| | 1900[a] | 1910[b] | 1920[c] |
|---|---|---|---|
| **Chicago** | | | |
| Negro | 1.1 | 1.2 | 1.1 |
| Native white, native parents | 3.7 | 3.3 | 3.1 |
| Native white, foreign or mixed parent(s) | 3.7 | 3.6 | 3.3 |
| Foreign-born white | 4.7 | 5.7 | 6.2 |
| Indians, Chinese, Japanese, etc.[d] | 13.7 | 9.0 | 6.9 |
| **Los Angeles** | | | |
| Negro | 2.1 | 1.3 | 1.5 |
| Native white, native parents | 6.5 | 1.3 | 4.4 |
| Native white, foreign or mixed parent(s) | 6.6 | 5.8 | 5.2 |
| Foreign-born white | 8.2 | 7.9 | 7.7 |
| Indians, Chinese, Japanese, etc.[d] | 8.4 | 12.0 | 12.2 |
| **New York** | | | |
| Negro | 0.7 | 0.8 | 0.6 |
| Native white, native parents | 4.9 | 3.4 | 2.6 |
| Native white, foreign or mixed parent(s) | 4.8 | 4.4 | 3.8 |
| Foreign-born white | 7.5 | 9.3 | 9.2 |
| Indians, Chinese, Japanese, etc.[d] | 12.0 | 8.3 | 2.8 |
| **Oakland** | | | |
| Negro | 1.4 | 1.6 | 0.9 |
| Native white, native parents | 5.5 | 4.9 | 3.8 |
| Native white, foreign or mixed parent(s) | 4.7 | 5.6 | 4.8 |
| Foreign-born white | 7.1 | 6.7 | 5.9 |
| Indians, Chinese, Japanese, etc.[d] | 8.1 | 10.1 | 11.8 |
| **Philadelphia** | | | |
| Negro | 1.4 | 2.1 | 1.4 |
| Native white, native parents | 5.7 | 4.9 | 3.7 |
| Native white, foreign or mixed parent(s) | 5.1 | 5.0 | 4.3 |
| Foreign-born white | 6.1 | 8.2 | 9.0 |
| Indians, Chinese, Japanese, etc.[d] | 5.3 | 8.7 | 5.4 |
| **San Francisco** | | | |
| Negro | 1.1 | 0.8 | 1.3 |
| Native white, native parents | 3.9 | 3.4 | 3.2 |
| Native white, foreign or mixed parent(s) | 4.5 | 6.0 | 5.0 |
| Foreign-born white | 7.6 | 7.0 | 6.2 |
| Indians, Chinese, Japanese, etc.[d] | 10.9 | 8.3 | 7.7 |

[a] U.S. Department of Commerce and Labor, Bureau of the Census, *Twelfth Census of the United States: Special Reports, Occupations* (Washington, D.C.: Government Printing Office, 1904), pp. 516 ff.

[b] U.S. Department of Commerce, Bureau of the Census, *Thirteenth Census of the United States*, vol. 4, *Population, 1910, Occupational Statistics* (Washington, D.C.: U.S. Government Printing Office, 1914), pp. 545 ff.

[c] *Ibid., Fourteenth Census of the United States, 1920*, vol. 4, *Population, 1920, Occupations* (Washington, D.C., 1923), p. 1078.

[d] Excludes Mexicans.

ordinary consumer demands. Unfortunately, these data are not decisive because, except for the Negro, the rank order of population segments in retail dealerships also agrees closely (rho = .80) with relative social disadvantage.

One indirect proof of the consumer-demands explanation hangs on a comparison of black-owned proprietorships in services and in retail trades. The service proprietorships are usually conducted within the black neighborhoods in the form of barbering and beauty shops, mortuaries, drayage, and various repair services. The margin of black underrepresentation has historically been substantially smaller in service proprietorships than in retail proprietorships.[20]

The consistently much stronger representation of blacks in service proprietorships is usually attributed to the absence of white competition in service trades. Whites have, for example, been unwilling to operate barber shops or beauty parlors in black neighborhoods. This unwillingness provided black barbers and beauticians with a monopoly of these trades in black neighborhoods. On the other hand, the whites have always been anxious to sell food, clothing, appliances, and liquor in black areas. The relative success of black-owned service establishments suggests that black-owned retail trade would have been comparably stronger had it too been protected from outside competition as were the retail trades of the foreign born.

Among both Chinese and Japanese immigrants, there was also a marked tendency for small businesses to depend at first on an exclusively ethnic clientele and only later to branch out to a wider trade. In part, this tendency mirrored the cultural assimilation of Oriental immigrants who learned to want things American stores sold. For example, in 1932 Helen V. Cather noted than San Francisco Chinese were "learning to use American canned goods and to patronize the chain stores. Also, they buy much of their clothing in American department stores. This is hard on the merchants of Chinatown for almost all of their goods are sold to their own people."[21] An

[20] Andrew F. Brimmer and Henry S. Terrell, "The Economic Potential of Black Capitalism," pp. 10–11; St. Clair Drake and Horace R. Cayton, *Black Metropolis*, 2: 456, 460; Allan H. Spear, *Black Chicago*, p. 112.

[21] Helen Virginia Cather, "History of San Francisco's Chinatown," p. 82. Also see Edward K. Strong, Jr., *The Second Generation Japanese Problem* (Stanford, Calif.: Stanford University Press, 1934), pp. 233–34; idem, *Japanese in California*

official survey of Japanese retail business in 1909 also concluded that 63 percent of their retail trade in California was conducted with other Japanese. Commenting on Japanese retail trade, John Modell noted that by 1910 the various Little Tokyos were able to supply virtually all the goods needed by fellow Japanese; but in businesses like American-style clothing, the Japanese found themselves at a distinct disadvantage and were yet unable to supply themselves with these articles. According to W. T. Kataoka, the "Japanese trade" exceeded "American trade" in the Japanese-owned stores until 1924. Thereafter, the "American trade" became ever more important.[22]

The distribution of Chinese and Japanese retail trade in California in 1929 provides additional evidence of the beneficial commercial effects of their customers' exotic tastes. Oriental retail stores were generally overrepresented in retail trade (Table 5), but performance varied pronouncedly by line of trade. Chinese and Japanese operated more than their share of food stores, general stores, general merchandise stores, and cheap restaurants. But few Orientals were running automotive stores, lumber yards, apparel stores, or household-furnishing establishments. The retail strength of Chinese and Japanese commerce clearly lay in those sectors in which the Oriental merchants had the maximum advantage of their customers' "unusual" demands. Either the Orientals were not buying automobiles, lumber, clothing, and furnishings, or they were buying them from whites.

INADEQUACIES OF THE CONSUMER-DEMANDS EXPLANATION

Although the special demands of Chinese and Japanese consumers had pronounced and beneficial effects on Oriental-owned retail trade, ethnic consumer demands do not explain the trade that Orientals conducted with non-Orientals. This trade was extensive. For example, Chinese restaurants and Chinese-operated groceries derived important support from non-Chinese customers: "Aside from the

---

(Stanford, Calif.: Stanford University Press, 1933), p. 127; McWilliams, *Prejudice*, p. 88.

[22] California Bureau of Labor Statistics, *Fifteenth Biennial Report, 1911–12* (Sacramento: State Printing Office, 1912), p. 604; John Modell, "The Japanese of Los Angeles," pp. 61, 288; W. T. Kataoka, "Occupations of Japanese in Los Angeles," p. 56.

TABLE 5

*Oriental Retail Trade in California and Negro Retail Trade in Illinois:*
*Index Numbers of Stores and Sales for 1929*
*(100 = expected)*

|  | Oriental[a] (California) | | Negro (Illinois) | |
|---|---|---|---|---|
|  | Stores | Sales | Stores | Sales |
| All stores | 131 | 75 | 21 | 3 |
| Food group | 198 | 196 | 19 | 4 |
| General stores | 242 | 144 | 25 | 2 |
| General merchandise | 187 | 28 | 8 | b |
| Automotive | b | b | 7 | 1 |
| Apparel | 67 | 31 | 13 | 3 |
| Furniture and household | 22 | 11 | 6 | 3 |
| Restaurants, etc. | 311 | 207 | 58 | 11 |
| Lumber and building | 3 | b | 5 | b |
| Other retail | 138 | 79 | 23 | 6 |
| Second hand | 28 | 30 | 144 | 31 |

SOURCE: U.S. Department of Commerce, Bureau of the Census, *Fifteenth Census of the United States, 1930,* vol. 1, *Distribution,* pt. 2, "Retail Distribution" (Washington, D. C.: U.S. Government Printing Office, 1934), Table 12–C, p. 180, and Table 12–B, p. 615. Includes corporations.

a Chinese and Japanese only.

b Less than one-half of 1 percent of expected number.

Chinese grocery stores, there are another hundred and ten Chinese-operated American grocery stores scattered in white neighborhoods [in Los Angeles]. These groceries carry regular grocery supplies; many of them also have a meat department. The customers are mostly white."[23] Chinese-owned laundries and garment manufactories derived their exclusive support from non-Chinese.[24] Some proportion of the retail trade conducted by Oriental general stores and general merchandise stores was derived from the tourist trade in Chinatowns. Japanese-American business pivoted around distribution of produce grown on Japanese farms. Some of these vegetables were exotically Japanese, but most were not. In 1919 the market value of Japanese crops in California was more than 10 percent of the total value of all California crops.[25] The Japanese themselves could hardly have

23 Wen-Hui Chung Chen, "Changing Socio-Cultural Patterns of the Chinese Community in Los Angeles," p. 348.

24 California Department of Industrial Relations, *First Biennial Report, 1927–30* (Sacramento: State Printing Office, 1931), p. 153.

25 Daniels, *Politics,* p. 10; Iwata, "Japanese Immigrants," p. 25.

consumed all of the produce they sold. Many Japanese-owned produce outlets conducted their trade exclusively with non-Japanese. In
1929 Kataoka located 746 such establishments in Los Angeles.[26] In
addition, the Japanese operated dry-cleaning establishments, fisheries, cheap hotels, and lunch counters that derived exclusive or
important support from non-Japanese.

Oriental grocery stores retailed 4.1 percent of all food products
sold in California in 1929. Yet in 1930 Chinese and Japanese numbered only 2.3 percent of the total population of California. Chinese
and Japanese could not themselves have consumed 4.1 percent of all
food products retailed in California without consuming on the average and as individuals twice as much food as other Californians. On
this reckoning roughly one-half of food commodities retailed by
Orientals must have been consumed by non-Orientals. The estimated
cash value of these foodstuffs in 1929 was $11,978,000. Unless
Chinese and Japanese purchased more dry goods than other Californians, about one-quarter of their general stores' retail sales must
have been to non-Orientals. The estimated cash value of this one-
quarter was $486,000 in 1929. It is equally unlikely that this Asiatic
2.3 percent of the California population consumed the 4.3 percent
of restaurant meals which they sold. Apparently, non-Orientals consumed about one-half of these restaurant meals, the estimated cash
value of which came to $3,891,000 in 1929. In sum, food, dry goods,
and restaurant meals consumed by non-Orientals accounted for at
least $16,355,000, or 32.3 percent, of all Chinese and Japanese
retail sales in 1929. This figure is a conservative estimate of the proportion of Oriental retail commerce which was conducted with
non-Orientals in California.

The cash value ($16.4 million) of Oriental commerce conducted
only with non-Orientals in California was more than twice that ($6.5
million) of *all* retail business transacted by Negroes in Illinois in
1929.[27] Yet in 1930 there were 304,036 urban Negroes in Illinois
and 84,615 urban Chinese and Japanese in California. Thus, relative

[26] Kataoka, "Occupations," p. 56.
[27] See U.S. Bureau of the Census, *Fifteenth Census of the United States, 1930*,
vol. 1, *Distribution*, pt. 2, "Retail Distribution" (Washington, D.C.: U.S. Government Printing Office, 1934), Table 12–C, p. 180, and Table 12–B, p. 615.

to the urban population, Chinese and Japanese in California transacted nearly eight times more cash business with non-Orientals alone than did all Negro-owned retail business in Illinois. Hence, the special consumer demands of the Chinese and Japanese populations obviously do not completely account for the Orientals' margin of retail sales superiority in 1929.

The still popular consumer-demands argument assumes that apart from their culturally determined preferences for chop suey or pork chops, there were no culturally-derived differences in the economic behavior of foreign-born Orientals and native-born blacks. This assumption is harmonious with the notion of an underlying economic man but is otherwise demonstrably inadequate. It would have been surprising indeed if Chinese, for example, had brought to the Gold Mountain only an interest in Chinese commodities and had left behind Chinese styles of economic organization. In fact, the Chinese brought with them both their culturally derived consumer preferences and their culturally preferred style of economic organization. One such preference was a penchant for partnerships rather than solo entrepreneurships. Preferences such as this have economic consequences. But the consumer-demands theory ignores culturally derived differences in economic organization even though it pays ample attention to culturally derived consumer preferences. In sum, the consumer-demands explanation is correct but inadequate; it is but one part of a larger, sociological explanation.

# Rotating Credit Associations

# 2

The single most prominent argument advanced to explain the black American's underrepresentation in small business has fastened on his special difficulty in securing business loans from institutional lenders, especially from banks. This explanation is 200 years old.[1] It asserts that, because of poverty, lack of capital, and inability to borrow, blacks have been unable to finance business ventures. In its most straightforward form, this argument holds that black business failed to develop because prejudiced white bankers were unwilling to make business loans to black applicants at all or were willing to make loans but only on terms very much less favorable than those extended to white borrowers with equivalent business credentials. In a more sophisticated version, the argument maintains that black borrowers were relatively disadvantaged in the capital market simply by virtue of their impoverishment and the marginal status of their businesses. Impecunious blacks opening solo proprietorships were objectively higher risks than were the typically wealthier whites operating larger businesses. Hence, quite apart from discriminatory treatment at the hands of white bankers, blacks did not receive loans at all or received them only at a higher price than did whites. The humble stature of black business implicated borrowers in a vicious cycle of smallness, credit difficulties, smallness.

However, the discrimination-in-lending theory has lately lost the preeminent place it formerly occupied among explanations of Negro business retardation. In the first place, studies of small businessmen have shown that, contrary to expectation, loans from institutions have been relatively insignificant among the financial resources actually employed by proprietors in the capitalization of small firms. Only a small percentage of proprietors have reported seeking or obtaining bank loans in order to open a small business; by far the

[1] Abram L. Harris, *The Negro as Capitalist*, p. 22; John Hope Franklin, *From Slavery to Freedom*, 2d ed. (New York: Alfred Knopf, 1963), p. 309.

greater percentage rely entirely on their personal resources, especially their own savings, and loans from kin and friends: "Small new enterprises are financed primarily by owners, their relatives and friends, and by suppliers of materials and equipment. Banking institutions extend only slight accommodation to small new businesses."[2] These findings do not support the familiar argument that institutional discrimination in lending produced black difficulties in small business. On the contrary, these findings suggest that even had racial discrimination been exceptionally severe in commercial lending, it could have had only a minor impact. Since bank credit has been so insignificant a resource for new proprietors in general, even complete denial of bank credit could hardly account for the Negro's singular difficulties in small business.[3]

Reviewing the relevant arguments, Gunnar Myrdal observed that "the credit situation has certainly been one of the major obstacles barring the way for the Negro businessman." Yet Myrdal also complained that the credit theory appeared highly inadequate when the Negro's actual involvement in small business was contrasted with that of foreign-born whites, and especially with that of Americans of Japanese or Chinese descent.[4] If discrimination in lending accounted for black underrepresentation in business, then the Orientals ought also to have been underrepresented relative to more advantaged foreign-born whites. In turn, one would expect the foreign-born whites to have been underrepresented relative to native-born whites. If smallness or poverty accounted for the Negro's difficulties in securing commercial loans, then smallness ought to have interfered with foreign-born whites and Orientals as well. But, in fact, both foreign-born whites and Orientals were overrepresented in business relative to native whites, who presumably suffered no discrimination in lending. If Orientals and foreign-born whites were able to over-

[2] Alfred R. Oxenfeldt, *New Firms and Free Enterprise* (Washington, D.C.: American Council on Public Affairs, 1943), pp. 146, 160. Also see Kurt B. Mayer and Sidney Goldstein, *The First Two Years* (Washington, D.C.: U.S. Small Business Administration, 1961), p. 53; Joseph A. Pierce, *Negro Business and Business Education*, pp. 187–88.

[3] Eugene P. Foley, *The Achieving Ghetto* (Washington, D.C.: National Press, 1968), pp. 136–40.

[4] Gunnar Myrdal, *An American Dilemma*, 1:308, 314.

come these handicaps, then why were black Americans not also able to surmount them?

Accounting for these anomalies has necessitated a reconsideration of black business history in which the emphasis has shifted from financial to social causes. E. Franklin Frazier's "tradition-of-enterprise" hypothesis stands out as the general paradigm for research in this area: "Although no systematic study has been undertaken of the social causes of the failure of the Negro to achieve success as a businessman, it appears from what we know of the social and cultural history of the Negro that it is the result largely of the lack of traditions in the field of business enterprise."[5] "Experience in buying and selling" was apparently the tradition Frazier thought relevant, for he explicitly deemphasized the role played by "such economic factors as . . . availability of capital," evidently because of Myrdal's earlier discussion.

In his discussion of Negro business, Eugene Foley has followed Frazier's lead in interpreting Negro business from the perspective of traditions; however, Foley singled out a different tradition: "In the final analysis, the fundamental reason that Negroes have not advanced in business is the lack of business success symbols available to them."[6] Foley's theory has an advantage of concreteness relative to Frazier. However, Foley's view of the relevant traditions is flimsy and probably incorrect, for there is a very old tradition of successful Negro businessmen in the United States. This tradition is, to be sure, one of successful individuals, rather than one based on collective experience. But it is withal a tradition that offers "business success symbols" to Negroes. Around the turn of the century Booker T. Washington undertook an energetic campaign to bring these black entrepreneurs to popular attention. But the subsequent decline of Negro business despite the vigorous turn-of-the-century popularization of business success symbols suggests that the problems of Negro business were independent of popularized success symbols.

---

[5] E. Franklin Frazier, *The Negro in the United States*, pp. 410–11.

[6] Eugene P. Foley, "The Negro Businessman: In Search of a Tradition," p. 124. Cf. Booker T. Washington, *The Negro in Business* (Boston: Hertel, Jenkins, 1907), *passim*.

ROTATING CREDIT ASSOCIATIONS

Regarding questions of finance as purely economic and, therefore, beyond the pale of sociological analysis, Frazier failed to follow up lines of inquiry suggested by his own conclusion. That is, Frazier did not inquire into cultural traditions relevant to the capitalization of small business even though he had himself singled out "tradition" as of overriding importance in accounting for Negro underrepresentation in business. Recent anthropological studies of economic development have generated renewed scholarly interest in traditions of informal financial cooperation in many areas of the non-Western world. Although these are practical economic traditions, they are a part of functioning cultures. Hence they are of sociological as well as of economic interest. These informal methods of financial cooperation are of considerable importance in fulfilling Frazier's program of research, because they constitute concrete traditions relevant to the financing of small business enterprises.

Although the details of such financial cooperation differ by region, Clifford Geertz has shown that a basic model can be extracted from the manifest diversity of ethnic customs. This basic model he has appropriately labeled the "rotating credit association."[7] In a comprehensive review of rotating credit associations throughout the world, Shirley Ardener has agreed with Geertz that basic principles of rotating credit can be extracted from the diversity of customs, but she has slightly restated the formula for expressing the essential rotating credit idea. She defines it as "an association formed upon a core of participants who agree to make regular contributions to a fund which is given, in whole or in part, to each contributor in rotation."[8] Within the limits of the rotating credit association as defined, Ardener was also able to specify the axes of variation which distinguish local customs from one another. That is, local rotating credit associations frequently differ with regard to membership size and criteria of membership, organization of the association, types of funds, transferability of funds, deductions from the fund, and sanc-

---

[7] Clifford Geertz, "The Rotating Credit Association: A 'Middle Rung' in Development," p. 213.

[8] Shirley Ardener, "The Comparative Study of Rotating Credit Associations," p. 201. Italicized in original.

tions imposed on members. But despite variations in these important respects, the rotating credit association may be taken as a generic type of cooperative financial institution. In many parts of the non-Western world, this type of association serves or has served many of the functions of Western banks. Such associations are, above all, credit institutions which lend lump sums of money to members. In this activity, rotating credit associations are found frequently to "assist in small scale capital formation."[9]

Of especial importance to this discussion are the rotating credit associations of southern China, Japan, and West Africa. Immigrants to the United States from southern China and Japan employed traditional rotating credit associations as their principal device for capitalizing small business. West Indian blacks brought the West African rotating credit association to the United States; they too used this traditional practice to finance small businesses. American-born Negroes apparently did not employ a similar institution. Hence, the rotating credit association suggests itself as a specific tradition in the field of business which accounts, in some measure, for the differential business success of American-born Negroes, West Indian Negroes, and Orientals.

### HUI IN CHINA AND IN THE UNITED STATES

The generic term for the Cantonese rotating credit association is *hui*, which means simply "association" or "club." Several variants of hui existed in China, but the rotating credit principle was everywhere strongly pronounced. Such associations are thought to be about 800 years old in China.

D. H. Kulp described a simple form of hui used in southern China.[10] Greatly more complex variants of hui also existed; but the simple lottery scheme described by Kulp illustrates the basic principle of the Cantonese hui. A person in need of a lump sum of money would take the initiative in organizing a hui by securing from friends or relatives an agreement to pay a stipulated sum of money—say,

[9] *Ibid.*, p. 217.

[10] Daniel H. Kulp, *Country Life in South China*, 1:190ff.; also see Kenneth Scott Latourette, *The Chinese: Their History and Culture*, 3rd ed. (New York: Macmillan, 1946), p. 593; Max Weber, *The Religion of China*, p. 99; Gideon Sjoberg, *The Preindustrial City* (Glencoe, Ill.: Free Press, 1960), p. 215.

$5—every month into a common pool. In a hui of ten members, the organizer himself received the first lump sum created, or $50, which he employed as he pleased. A month later the organizer held a feast in his home for the ten contributors. At the feast the ten members again contributed $5 each to create a fund of $50. A lottery determined which member (excluding the organizer) would receive the lump sum. Since a member could receive the lump sum only once, at each subsequent feast the pool of members still in the lottery narrowed until, finally, at the tenth feast the outstanding member automatically received the lump sum of $50. The organizer never contributed to the money pool; his repayment was exclusively in the form of the ten feasts, each of which was supposed to have cost him $5. At the conclusion of the ten feasts, each member would have dribbled away $55 in cash and would have received one lump sum of $50 and ten 50-cent feasts. Also, the organizer of the hui had received the interest-free use of $50 when he needed it, eight of the ten members had received an advance on their contribution (credit), and all of the participants had enjoyed ten sumptuous feasts in convivial company.

If the membership chose, a hui could be organized on less benevolent lines. Instead of a lottery to determine which member of the club would take the pot, each eligible member might submit a sealed bid indicating how much interest he was prepared to pay to have the use of the money.[11] The high bidder received the pot. This system of hui operation placed a clear premium on not needing the money. Those who wanted the money in the early rounds of the hui would have to compete and pay a high interest. On the other hand, wealthier members who were not in need of money could collect the high interest paid by members who needed the use of their surplus. This form of hui created an investment opportunity for the wealthy and tended to enlist the profit motive in the extension of credit. Of course, even in this more capitalistic form of mutual aid, the interest actually paid by members in need of money tended to be less than what they would have paid for equivalent funds obtained from the town moneylender.

[11] Hsiao-tung Fei, *Peasant Life in China*, pp. 273ff.

Cantonese in the United States employed the hui as a means of acquiring capital for business purposes.[12] The extent of the practice is impossible to ascertain with precision, but the evidence suggests that the traditional hui was widely used and of first importance in the funding of small business enterprises. An early reference to what was probably a hui is found in Helen Clark's discussion of Chinese in New York City;[13] however, the earliest discovered reference to what was certainly a Cantonese hui appears in Helen Cather's history of the Chinese in San Francisco:

> The Chinese have a peculiar method of obtaining funds without going to commercial banks. If a responsible Chinaman needs an amount of money, he will organize an association, each member of which will promise to pay a certain amount on a specified day of each month for a given length of time. For instance, if the organizer wants $1,300 he may ask 12 others to join with him and each will promise to pay $100 each month for 13 months. The organizer has the use of the $1,300 the first month. When the date of the meeting comes around again, the members assemble and each pays his $100, including the organizer. All but the organizer, who has had the use of the money, bid for the pool. The man paying the highest bid pays the amount of the bid to each of the others and has the money. This continues for 13 months. Each man makes his payment each month but those who have already used the money cannot bid for it again. By the end of the 13-month period, each will have paid in $1,300 and have had the use of the whole amount.[14]

Cather did not name the institution she described, but it was clearly a Cantonese hui of the bidding type. In regard to the origins of the practice, she learned from informants that "This is a very old Chinese custom and is still [1932] practiced by the Chinese in San Francisco. Since a man may belong to several of these associations at one time, it is not hard for a Chinaman to secure funds on short notice, for he

[12] Chinese immigrants in Britain have also employed the device for this purpose. See Maurice Broady, "The Chinese in Great Britain," in *Colloquium on Overseas Chinese*, ed. Morton H. Fried (New York: Institute of Pacific Relations, 1958), p. 32.

[13] Helen F. Clark, "The Chinese of New York Contrasted with Their Foreign Neighbors," *Century* 53 (November 1896): 110.

[14] Helen Virginia Cather, "The History of San Francisco's Chinatown" (1932), pp. 60–61.

can estimate from past bids about how much he must bid to secure the money."[15]

In his history of San Francisco's Chinatown, Richard Dare mentions the *yueh-woey* custom which was frequently used to secure business capital.[16] Like the institution described by Cather, Dare's yueh-woey was of the bidding and interest-paying type. In New York City's Chinatown, Virginia Heyer also found a bidding type of hui in operation. Memberships were usually limited to persons from the same village in China:

> Sometimes members of small associations form loan societies to provide capital for fellow members who hope to start businesses. Each member contributes a fixed amount of money to a common fund. The one who offers the highest rate of interest in secret bid gets to borrow the whole fund, though first he must repay the full interest. . . . This method of financing business ventures was frequent in the past, but in recent years [1953] it is said to have been less common.[17]

Betty Lee Sung has recently described a hui of the bidding type which was popular among the Chinese in New York before 1950. One hundred members of the hui (all of the same clan) paid $10 a week for 100 weeks. Each week members bid for the $1,000 pot. If there were no bidders, a lottery among the outstanding members determined which one would receive the total fund subscribed at a stipulated low rate of interest. The hui described by Sung did not include conviviality, and the number of members greatly exceeded that characteristic of the hui in South China. In American Chinatowns, the hui had evidently become more commercial and less fraternal: "The *hui* in effect served as a systematic savings method for the thrifty and as a source of credit for those who needed a lump sum in cash for business or other reasons. Few Chinese utilized American banks."[18] The economic importance of the hui in the

[15] *Ibid.*, p. 61.
[16] Richard Kock Dare, "The Economic and Social Adjustment of the San Francisco Chinese for the Past Fifty Years" (M. A. thesis, University of California, Berkeley, 1959), pp. 12–13.
[17] Virginia Heyer, "Patterns of Social Organization in New York City's Chinatown" pp. 60–61.
[18] Betty Lee Sung, *Mountain of Gold*, pp. 141–42.

Chinese-American small business economy was emphasized by Gor Yun Leong, who observed that, "without such societies, very few businesses could be started."[19]

### KO IN JAPAN AND IN THE UNITED STATES

Variously called *ko, tanomoshi,* or *mujin,* the Japanese form of the rotating credit association was probably adapted in the thirteenth century from the Chinese institution.[20] In Japan, ko clubs among rural villagers included from twenty to fifty persons, whereas, according to Hsiao-tung Fei, the Chinese hui normally included only eight to fourteen persons. Unlike the hui, the Japanese institution sometimes included unrelated persons. Ko clubs met twice yearly, but the hui met monthly. Since the ko typically included more members than the hui, the Japanese clubs sometimes carried on as long as twenty years before each of the participants had received his portion. Ko was an extremely popular financial institution in rural Japan as late as the 1930s. According to John Embree, richer villagers and those in special need of funds belonged to several clubs. More of the villagers' money was tied up in ko than in commercial banks, credit unions, or postal savings.

Both a bidding system and a lottery system of ko were practiced.[21] Only the bidding system provided for the payment of interest by early drawers to late drawers. Under the rules of the bidding system, an organizer would receive the first portion. Meetings were held at the organizer's residence where refreshments were served and business was combined with sociability. At the second meeting, bidders

---

[19] Gor Yun Leong, *Chinatown Inside Out* (New York: Barrows Mussey, 1936), pp. 177–78; also see Paul C. P. Siu, "The Chinese Laundryman: A Study of Social Isolation" (Ph.D. diss., University of Chicago, 1953), pp. 112, 116–17. For a novelist's treatment of *hui* among immigrant Chinese in New York City, see Lin Yutang, *Chinatown Family* (New York: John Day, 1948), pp. 249–50.

[20] John F. Embree, *Suye Mura,* pp. 138ff.; Koichi Hosono, "Outline of Small Business Financing in Japan," in *Small Business in Japan,* ed. Tokutaro Yamanaka (Tokyo: Japan Times, 1960), pp. 339–40. Also see Hugh T. Patrick, "Japan, 1868–1914," in *Banking in the Early Stages of Industrialization,* ed. Rondo Cameron et al. (New York: Oxford University Press, 1967), p. 245.

[21] Sometimes the bidding and lottery forms were combined so that half of the pots were allocated on the basis of bidding and half on a lottery basis. See Guenther Stein, "Made in Japan—I," *Forum* 94 (November 1935): 290–94.

for the combined fund indicated the amount of payment they were willing to receive from the other participants. The lowest bidder received the fund thus created. Having once received the fund, persons were obligated to pay back at the regular meetings the full stipulated contribution. Thus, as the ko wore on, fewer and fewer persons were bidding for the fund and fewer and fewer could be released by a low bid from the necessity of paying back the stipulated rate.

In the United States the memberships of ko associations were usually composed of immigrants from the same prefecture or village in Japan. Religious organizations, Buddhist and Christian alike, also organized clubs for the benefit of their congregants. But congruent with the Japanese traditions of neighborliness, neighborhood and friendship groups also started clubs. Although the larger ko clubs required each member to furnish guarantors, the meetings of the clubs were social as well as financial occasions. Sake was served before dinner and members entertained one another with friendly conversation. Interest payments were tendered as gifts rather than as payments for the use of money.[22]

In Hawaii, northern California, and the Pacific Northwest, Japanese settlers referred to the rotating credit associations as *tanomoshi*. In southern California the term *mujin* prevailed. Exactly how extensively these clubs were used is difficult to ascertain, but Fumiko Fukuoka referred to the mujin as "a common and popular form of mutual financial aid association among the Japanese in Southern California." She observes that this "ancient form of mutual aid association" had been "brought to America by the Japanese immigrants."[23] Of foreign-born Japanese sampled in California in the course of a 1965–66 survey, almost one-half reported having participated in some form of economic combination involving the pooling of money. Of the participating half, 90 percent had taken part in a tanomoshi.[24] According to Embree, Hawaiian Japanese

[22] Bradford Smith, *Americans from Japan* (Philadelphia: J. B. Lippincott, 1948), p. 58; Shotaro Frank Miyamoto, *Social Solidarity Among the Japanese in Seattle*, pp. 75–76.
[23] Fumiko Fukuoka, "Mutual Life and Aid Among the Japanese of Southern California," p. 33.
[24] John Modell, "The Japanese of Los Angeles," p. 95.

organized tanomoshi which met monthly rather than biannually as in Japan and in which larger sums were invested.[25]

In 1922 Schichiro Matsui charged that white-owned banks in California discriminated against Japanese businessmen and farmers. Nonetheless, the tanomoshi permitted Japanese to capitalize business enterprises on their own. "Very popular among the Japanese in every line of trade," the tanomoshi was helpful because "a merchant without security may thus obtain credit."[26] Two decades later S. F. Miyamoto also stressed the economic importance of tanomoshi among Japanese in Seattle:

> Few [Japanese] . . . were able to expand their business individually to any great extent. Possibly without a system of cooperative financing the Japanese would not have developed the economic structure that they did. Fortunately, they met their needs through adaptations of Japanese customs, such as the money-pool known as the *tanomoshi.* . . . It is difficult to ascertain the extent to which such pools were used by the Japanese immigrants . . . but from the wide-spread recognition of its use, it was probably no inconsequential part of their financing practices. The largest hotel ever attempted by the Japanese, a transaction involving some $90,000, . . . was financed on the basis of a *tanomoshi.*[27]

Commentators agreed that the rotating credit associations were more popular with Japanese of the immigrant generation than with their American-born offspring, the nisei, especially those with college degrees. For purposes of financing business operations, the nisei preferred the impersonal credit union or savings and loan association.[28] According to a nisei informant, Japanese in the San Francisco Bay region no longer employ the tanomoshi for purposes of business capitalization. However, the custom survives. Its purposes

[25] John F. Embree, "Acculturation Among the Japanese of Kona, Hawaii," *Memoirs of the American Anthropological Association* 59 (1941): 91.

[26] Schichiro Matsui, "Economic Aspects of the Japanese Situation in California," pp. 86–87.

[27] Miyamoto, *Social Solidarity,* p. 75; also see Harry H. L. Kitano, *Japanese Americans,* pp. 19–20.

[28] Ruth Masuda, "The Japanese Tanomoshi," *Social Process in Hawaii* 3 (May 1937): 19; Smith, *Americans,* p. 58; Modell, "The Japanese," p. 96.

are now social, and only small sums are invested. This information agrees with the findings of Minako Kurokawa's recent study of Japanese small businessmen in San Francisco. She noted that, as a source of business capitalization, "the traditional institution of mutual aid [tanomoshi] . . . was not mentioned by respondents."[29] On the other hand, a nisei informant in Los Angeles claims to be personally involved in an on-going tanomoshi, the members of which are still principally interested in securing capital for business purposes. According to this informant, the custom remains very widespread among Japanese in Los Angeles and retains its business significance.

### ESUSU IN AFRICA, BRITAIN, AND THE AMERICAS

Anthropological research has documented the existence of rotating credit associations in many parts of Africa, including West Africa from which the progenitors of American Negroes were abducted as slaves. Although the details of administration and organization differ substantially among African regions and peoples, the essential rotating credit principle is virtually ubiquitous. However, one such rotating credit institution, the Nigerian *esusu*, is of especial importance here because of its historical influence on Negro business in the Americas. The esusu developed in southeastern Nigeria among the Yoruba people. Among the Yoruba's northern neighbors, the Nupe, the rotating credit institution is known as *dashi*, but the Nupe's custom differs little from the Yoruba's.[30] The antiquity of the esusu has not yet been finally established, but researchers are of the opinion that the custom was indigenously African. Certainly the Yoruba esusu existed as early as 1843, for it is mentioned in a Yoruba vocabulary of that date. In Sierra Leone, thrift clubs of some sort existed as early as 1794, but they cannot be positively identified as organized on the rotating credit principle.[31]

In his discussion of Yoruba associations, A. K. Ajisafe provides

[29] Minako Kurokawa, "Occupational Mobility Among Japanese Businessmen in San Francisco" (M.A. thesis, University of California, Berkeley, 1962), p. 70.

[30] S. F. Nadel, *A Black Byzantium* (New York: Oxford University Press, 1942), pp. 371–73; also see P. C. Lloyd, "The Yoruba of Nigeria," in *Peoples of Africa*, ed. James L. Gibbs (New York: Holt, Rinehart, and Winston, 1965), p. 559; Kenneth Little, *West African Urbanization*, p. 51; Michael Banton, *West African City* (London: Oxford University Press, 1957), pp. 187–88.

[31] Ardener, "Comparative Study," p. 209.

a statement of the esusu institution which summarizes its formal operation:

> There is a certain society called Esusu. This society deals with monetary matters only, and it helps its members to save and raise money thus: Every member shall pay a certain fixed sum of money regularly at a fixed time (say every fifth or ninth day). And one of the subscribing members shall take the total amount thus subscribed for his or her own personal use. The next subscription shall be taken by another member; this shall so continue rotationally until every member has taken.[32]

In the principle of pooling funds and rotating the pot among the membership, the Yoruba esusu does not differ from either of its Oriental counterparts; however, in common practice, it exhibits some idiosyncracies. As W. R. Bascom observed, "anyone who wishes to do so may found an *esusu* group, provided that others are willing to entrust their money to him."[33] But the organizer or president of the esusu needed only to be known; he did not need to know all of the members personally. Once an organizer had announced his intention to sponsor an esusu, persons willing to entrust their money to him indicated a willingness to join. Such personal acquaintances of the organizer, if accepted, became in turn heads of "roads." There were as many separate roads as there were persons who had directly contacted the organizer and had been scrutinized and accepted by him. As heads of roads, these personal acquaintances of the organizer were entitled to contact their own friends and kin concerning membership in the esusu. Heads of the roads normally were responsible for "collecting the contributions and making the disbursements within their subgroups which consist of members who have applied to them rather than to the founder for admission." In this manner the Yoruba esusu delegated responsibility for the integrity of all members from the original organizer to managers known and appointed by and accountable to him.

The Yoruba esusu was apparently carried to the Americas by African slaves. Indeed Bascom bases his argument for the indigenous

[32] A. K. Ajisafe, *Laws and Customs of the Yoruba People* (London: George Routledge, 1924), pp. 48–49.
[33] William R. Bascom, "The *Esusu*: A Credit Institution of the Yoruba," p. 64.

African origins of the esusu on the persistence in the West Indies of
the same custom among the descendants of slaves. An early reference
mentions the practice of *asu* in the British Bahamas in 1910:

> Another method of promoting thrift is apparently of Yoruban origin.
> Little associations called "Asu" are formed of one or two dozen people
> who agree to contribute weekly a small sum toward a common fund.
> Every month (?) the amount thus pooled is handed to a member, in
> order of seniority of admission, and makes a little nest-egg for in-
> vestment or relief. These "Asu" have no written statutes or regula-
> tions, no regular officers, but carry on their affairs without fraud or
> miscalculation.[34]

In the Trinidad village studied by M. J. Herskovits, residents referred
to their rotating credit association as *susu*. As Herskovits observed,
the term is clearly a corruption of the Yoruba word esusu. Trinidadians originally from Barbados and Guiana told Herskovits of the
form of the susu in their birthplaces. In Barbados the rotating credit
association was commonly known as "the meeting" and in Guiana
as "boxi money."[35] According to Herskovits, the Trinidadian susu
"takes the form of a cooperative pooling of earnings by those in the
group, so that each member may benefit by obtaining in turn, and
at one time, all the money paid in by the entire group on a given
date. Members may contribute the same amount. The total of the
weekly contribution . . . is called 'a hand.' "[36]

Jamaicans refer to their rotating credit association as "partners."
The partners in Jamaica is headed by a "banker" and the membership is composed of "throwers." In operation the club is apparently
identical to the susu of Trinidad. In the Jamaican setting, however,
members apparently used their partnership portions for business
capitalization, whereas rural Trinidadians appear to have made use
of the fund only for consumption purposes. Many Jamaican petty
traders used their partnership "draw" to restock their stalls with
imported goods for which they were required to pay cash. The part-

[34] Harry H. Johnston, *The Negro in the New World* (New York: Macmillan,
1910), p. 303.
[35] Melville J. Herskovits, *Trinidad Village*, p. 292.
[36] *Ibid.*, p. 76.

nership constituted the "most important source of capital for petty traders."[37]

West Indian migration to the United States commenced around 1900 and continued until 1924. In 1920, at the peak of the immigration, foreign-born Negroes, almost exclusively West Indians, numbered 73,803, of whom 36,613 resided in New York City. Most of these migrants came from the British West Indies. West Indians in Harlem distinguished themselves from native-born Negroes by their remarkable propensity to operate small business enterprises.[38] The West Indians, W. A. Domingo observed, "are forever launching out in business, and such retail businesses as are in the hands of Negroes in Harlem are largely in the control of the foreign-born."[39] Moreover, the West Indians were more aggressive than the native-born Negroes in their choice of self-employment enterprises. Whereas native-born Negroes tended only to open noncompetitive service enterprises, the West Indians operated grocery stores, tailor shops, jewelry stores, and fruit vending and real estate operations in which they undertook direct competition with whites doing business in the ghetto. Only the Bajan, it was said, could withstand the competition of the Jew.

The thriftiness of the West Indians provoked resentment on the part of American-born Negroes who regarded the West Indians as stingy and grasping. Some of the West Indians' thrift expressed itself in patronage of orthodox savings institutions, especially the postal savings. However, the West Indians in Harlem also employed the traditional susu credit institution as a savings device. According to Amy Jacques Garvey, higher status West Indian migrants of urban origin "acquired the habit of accumulating capital" through the part-

[37] Margaret Katzin, " 'Partners': An Informal Savings Institution in Jamaica," pp. 436–40.

[38] This difference was persistently noted so long as West Indians remained a distinctive part of the Harlem population. See George Edmund Haynes, *The Negro at Work in New York City* (New York: Columbia University Press, 1912), p. 101; Gary Ward Moore, "A Study of a Group of West Indian Negroes in New York City" (M.A. thesis, Columbia University, 1923), p. 26; Ira De A. Reid, *The Negro Immigrant*, pp. 120–21; Claude McKay, *Harlem: Negro Metropolis*, pp. 92–93; Roi Ottley, *New World A-Coming* (New York: World, 1943), p. 46; Gilbert Osofsky, *Harlem: The Making of a Ghetto* (New York: Harper and Row, 1963), p. 133.

[39] W. A. Domingo, "The Tropics in New York," *Survey* 53 (March 1, 1925): 648–50.

ners system from enforced contact with lower status West Indians of
rural origins. Mrs. Garvey adds that in Harlem, "Women were mostly
active in running the [partners] system—being bankers and collec-
tors. Some 'threw a regular hand' for their husbands or brothers to
enable them to operate small businesses. Later, the West Indian shop-
keepers, barbers, etc. operated bigger 'pools' for setting up or capitalizing existing small business, or buying homes."[40] The partners
draw also permitted a West Indian to purchase passage for relatives
to the United States and to finance the secondary education of their
children in the islands. As to the extensiveness of the practice of partners in Harlem, Mrs. Garvey observes that "the 'partners' system was
fairly widespread in the 1920's and 1930's, but the Depression
lessened its usage."

The significance of the partners as a factor in West Indian saving
is further illustrated by postwar British West Indian migration to
Britain. As in Harlem during the first several decades of the century,
West Indians in Britain attracted attention because of their extraordinary frugality. Observers noted that West Indian migrants tended
to "economize to a much greater extent than comparable English
income groups." Investigating the savings habits of London's Jamaicans, Hyndman reported that the traditional partners played the
leading role:

> Methods of saving vary, but the most prevalent is the friendly co-
> operative effort normally referred to by Jamaicans as "partner." Other
> names for similar systems in the Eastern group of islands are "Sou-
> sou," "chitty," "syndicate." This is a simple method based on mutual
> trust between friends and relations, and complete confidence in the
> man or woman who is organizer—fifteen or twenty people pay a
> weekly sum of between one pound and five pounds to the organizers.
> Either by drawing lots or by prior arrangement, the total amount at
> the end of each week goes to one of the twenty. . . . In some instances
> the weekly payments necessitate a strenuous savings effort, but in most
> cases the "partners" is carried on time and again with satisfaction on
> all sides.[41]

[40] Personal communication of February 12, 1968. For a novelist's treatment of
West Indian life in Harlem, see Paule Marshall, *Brown Girl, Brownstones*, (New
York: Random House, 1959).
[41] Albert Hyndman, "The West Indian in London," p. 74.

R. B. Davison's sample of Jamaican migrants in Britain also disclosed the persistence of the partners custom. At the end of the first year after arrival, 25 percent of Jamaicans sampled reported that they were presently involved in a partners or had recently been so involved. Other Jamaicans reported that they would participate in partners if only they could find an on-going group with a reliable membership and banker. One Jamaican claimed to be still participating by mail in a partners in Jamaica. "The urge to engage in some form of cooperative savings," observed Davison, "is strong among at least a substantial minority of the Jamaican community."[42]

As in the United States, West Indians in Britain evinced a strong interest in real estate investment. In providing financial resources for such investment, the partners played a major role. Hyndman found that, by means of continuous participation in the partners, Jamaicans became able to "command a large sum of ready cash," which often provided "the initial payment on a house" or the passage to Britain of a family member. Racial discrimination in housing rentals apparently influenced the Jamaicans' schedule of priorities. West Indians scrimped in order "to achieve property ownership because of the difficulties experienced in providing adequate accommodation" for themselves and their families. Jamaicans came to own a substantial amount of real property in a relatively short time, especially in view of their impoverished origins. Of Davison's sample of Jamaicans, 75 percent were residing in houses "as tenants of Jamaican landlords."[43] Jamaican-owned housing thus clearly encompassed almost enough units to house the entire Jamaican population. Virtually all of this real estate had, of course, been purchased since 1945.

### ROTATING CREDIT AS A TRADITION OF ENTERPRISE

The employment of the esusu by West Indian migrants in Harlem and again in Britain illustrates the manner in which a traditional economic custom encouraged the business activities of immigrants. The process was much the same among Chinese, Japanese, and West

[42] R. B. Davison, *West Indian Migrants*, pp. 95–96, 102–03.
[43] The extent of business self-employment among West Indians in Britain is, however, less clear. Hyndman reported a few "one man or family businesses" ("West Indian," pp. 71–72). But Davison's sample turned up only one "successful, self-employed immigrant" (*West Indian*, p. 110).

Indians. But unlike any of these immigrant groups, American-born Negroes in the United States did not employ any rotating credit institution, apparently because this African economic custom had vanished from their cultural repertoire. Since ethnographic accounts of black life in the United States did not consciously investigate the persistence of the Yoruba esusu or its variants, only negative evidence for this proposition exists. That is, lack of reference to rotating credit associations among Negroes in the United States may be taken as prima facie evidence that such practices were not, in fact, employed.[44] Students of this question have thus far been unable to locate any instance of rotating credit practices among American-born Negroes. Even Herskovits made no mention of rotating credit associations in the United States, although his own research in Trinidad had awakened him to the persistence of this Africanism.[45]

The persistence of the rotating credit associations among Chinese, Japanese, and West Indians provides tangible support for E. F. Frazier's contention that tradition played a critical role in the business success of "other alien groups" and that a lack of traditions inhibited Negro-owned business in the United States. Moreover, it makes possible an understanding of why racial discrimination in lending affected American-born Negroes more deleteriously than it did Orientals and foreign-born Negroes. Unlike the Chinese, Japanese, and West Indians, American-born Negroes did not have the rotating credit tradition to fall back on as a source of capital for small business enterprises. Hence, they were especially dependent on banks and lending companies for credit; and when such credit was for one reason or another denied, they possessed no traditional resources for making do on their own.

SLAVERY AND EMANCIPATION IN THE BRITISH WEST INDIES
AND IN THE UNITED STATES

The absence of the rotating credit association among American-born Negroes probably involves a cultural disappearance in that the custom was very likely known to blacks brought as slaves to North America. Strongly prevailing scholarly opinion does maintain that

---

44 Ardener, "Comparative Study," p. 208.
45 Melville J. Herskovits, *The Myth of the Negro Past*, p. 165.

Yoruba slaves brought the custom of esusu to the West Indies, but the possibility cannot be ruled out that free African laborers imported the custom after emancipation in 1838. Moreover, in the present state of knowledge, it cannot positively be asserted that rotating credit institutions existed on the western coast of Africa prior to 1834, although they probably did. Since most slave trading was conducted prior to 1834, the supposition that African slaves carried the esusu with them to the New World depends on the existence of the custom in West Africa during the slaving period.[46]

If, however, slaves did carry the esusu with them to the New World, then the nonexistence of the rotating credit institution among blacks in the United States suggests a genuine cultural disappearance. West Indian and American slaves did not differ in the African regions from which they were abducted.[47] Indeed, the West Indies served as a "seasoning" place for slaves ultimately sold in the American South. The West Indian or American destination of abducted blacks was, in effect, random in respect to region of African origin. Whatever the tribal and ethnic mélange of blacks in North America, a similar distribution doubtless characterized the West Indian blacks.[48] Accordingly, social conditions in the British West Indies and in the southern portion of the United States presumably account for the persistence of the esusu only in the islands.

In accounting for the survival of the esusu in the Caribbean and its apparent demise in the United States, the "bedrock" facts are those of demography. Throughout the slavery period the black population of the Caribbean islands dramatically exceeded the white population. "West Indian planters," remarks W. D. Jordan, "were lost not so much in the Caribbean as in a sea of blacks."[49] This demographic situation in the Indies contrasted vividly with that in

[46] Ardener, "Comparative Study," pp. 204, 209.

[47] Herskovits, *Myth*, p. 43. Moreover, rotating credit institutions are found widely in West Africa today. If the institution were equally ubiquitous during the slaving period, then all slaves would presumably have known the custom, regardless of specific tribal affiliations or regional origins.

[48] James P. Comer, "The Social Power of the Negro," *Scientific American*, 216 (April 1967): 21–27.

[49] Winthrop D. Jordan, *White over Black* (Chapel Hill: University of North Carolina Press, 1968), pp. 141, 175–76; Franklin, *From Slavery*, p. 65 (see n. 1 above); Frank Tannenbaum, *Slave and Citizen* (New York: Random House, 1946), pp. 6–7.

the United States, where Africans were a numerical minority. To be sure, blacks in the United States occasionally constituted a local majority; yet the numerical preponderance which they everywhere enjoyed in the Indies was rarely matched in the United States. All-black Caribbean islands were hospitable to the perpetuation of African cultural traditions such as the esusu. The outnumbered and subdued blacks in the southern portion of the United States confronted much more formidable barriers to the perpetuation of African culture traits.

Administrative necessity, furthermore, induced the West Indian slaveholders to institutionalize the operation of a slaves' economy. This indulgence reflected the shortage of whites which deprived West Indian slaveholders of the administrators necessary to supervise subsistence farming as an organized function of the plantation. These activities had, in consequence, to be left to the initiative of the blacks. To support themselves, slaves were customarily and typically provided with plots of land on which to grow their own subsistence. Alternate Saturdays and Sundays were made available to permit slaves to attend to their cultivation. Slaves also kept stock and had recognized grazing rights on the plantation grounds. In the British Caribbean, these informal expectations were elevated to the status of statutory law by the Consolidated Slave Acts of 1820 which required owners to provide slaves with "rights" in land and in the free time to cultivate it.[50] Since the sugar estates made little organized provision for their own subsistence, the white plantation overlords were themselves economically dependent on the slaves' economy for their own provisioning. By the mid-eighteenth century, for example, the entire population of Jamaica was completely dependent on the black economy for its subsistence.[51] The economic dependence of the whites and their well-justified fears of insurrection tended, of course, to inhibit them from interfering with the economic activities which

[50] M. G. Smith, *The Plural Society in the British West Indies* (Berkeley and Los Angeles: University of California Press, 1965), p. 104; idem, "Slavery and Emancipation in Two Societies," *Social and Economic Studies* 3 (December 1954): 248; Xenophon F. Ferguson, "The Old Plantation Regime in Jamaica, 1655–1834" (M.A. thesis, University of California, Berkeley, 1933), pp. 161–63; W. J. Gardner, *A History of Jamaica* (New York: D. Appleton, 1909), pp. 387–90.

[51] Orlando Patterson, *The Sociology of Slavery* (London: Macgibbon and Kee, 1967), p. 216.

the slaves claimed as "rights." Thus, the slave's economy of the West
Indies acquired not only a traditional and then statutory legitimacy;
it also acquired in the course of time a porcupine coat of protective
sanctions.

Although Caribbean slaves were entitled to plots and to time off
for cultivating them, not all slaves opted to be cultivators. Some
slaves devoted their free time to trade and to crafts. Division of labor
encouraged the exchange of commodities and the formation of markets for that purpose.[52] Both blacks and whites attended these weekly
markets. Slaves successful in commerce could employ their proceeds
for the purchase of manumission. The peculium of the slaves enjoyed
recognition in custom and later in law such that slaves were entitled
to alienate or to inherit property, and to accumulate without hin-
drance the wherewithal for their own manumission.[53] Through this
participation in the slave-operated subeconomy of the Indies, some
few blacks even attained substantial wealth.

The great leeway accorded the slaves in the organization of their
subsistence economy reduced the external obstacles to the maintenance of African economic traditions. Such traditions of production
had an everyday significance in that, even under slavery, provisioning
remained a daily concern of every slave: "The production of a per
capita agricultural surplus within the internal economy under slavery
facilitated . . . the development of a strong marketing pattern which
probably rested on the foundations of the African cultural heritage
of the slaves."[54] Part of this heritage, it is reasonable to suppose, was
the esusu.

American slaveholders generally preferred to provision their blacks
from plantation storehouses, and subsistence farming was organized
as a regular function of the plantation. To be sure, many slaveholders
in the United States supplied small plots and time off for the slaves
as useful incentives. Some masters even permitted slaves thus re-
warded to sell their produce in town rather than to the plantation.

[52] Douglas Hall, "Slaves and Slavery in the British West Indies," *Social and
Economic Studies* 11 (December 1962): 314.

[53] Smith, *Plural Society*, pp. 104, 128. The Hispanic colonies were more liberal
than the British West Indies in this regard. See Tannenbaum, *Slave*, pp. 65–66.

[54] Sidney W. Mintz, "The Jamaican Internal Marketing Pattern: Some Notes and
Hypotheses," *Social and Economic Studies* 4 (March 1955): 99.

But even where the small-plot-and-free-time system prevailed, they were only incentives.[55] American slaves never achieved the consensually, not to mention legally, validated rights to self-maintenance that Caribbean blacks enjoyed. Where such activities were tolerated, they depended on the *bon plaisir* of the slaveholders. Since the peculium of the slave did not achieve a consensually or legally validated status in the United States—with rights of alienation, inheritance, and manumission—the legal and moral basis of the slave-operated economy was absent.

Trade among slaves or between slaves and whites was, in the United States, an irregular, sporadic occurrence. The *licet* of the slaveholders intervened between slaves and commerce; and slaveholders in the United States were of divided opinion concerning the desirability of such trade. This situation contrasts rather starkly with the weekly markets in the major towns of the West Indies. Hence, it is inappropriate to speak of a slave-operated subsistence economy in the United States. Since such an economy was clearly relevant to the survival of cooperative African economic customs, the lack of slave self-maintenance and markets in the United States would tend to account for the disappearance of such customs among American blacks.

In the South, nonslaveholders and smaller slave plantations grew food and feed crops for their own maintenance and for local sale. This source of supply was routinely available to any slaveholding plantations that did not make their own provision for subsistence agriculture.[56] In a crisis, such as unruliness among the slaves, even the self-provisioning plantations could purchase supplies from local whites. Such provisioning would tide the owners over the period of discontent, while deprivation would, on the other hand, help to bring insubordinate blacks to their senses. Such relief was unavailable to West Indian cultivators who became, accordingly, more dependent on the private economic activities of their own blacks. The small white freeholders in the southern United States also provided a militia

[55] Kenneth M. Stampp, *The Peculiar Institution* (New York: Alfred Knopf, 1955), pp. 164–65; Roy S. Bryce-Laporte, "The Conceptualization of the American Slave Plantation as a Total Institution" (Ph.D. diss., University of California, Los Angeles, 1968), p. 108.

[56] Stampp, *Peculiar Institution*, pp. 51–53.

capable of suppressing black insurrection. The support of these armed whites further strengthened the hand of the American slaveowner against his own slaves. Equivalent local military assistance was unavailable to West Indian plantation managers, who found it doubly expedient to refrain from interfering with the slaves' "rightful" economic activities.

The great size of the West Indian sugar plantations and the practice of absentee ownership also contributed to the survival of African customs and culture among the slaves. Immense West Indian sugar plantations employed hundreds of slaves in the cane fields. Hired white administrators oversaw the administration of plantation work. The owners of the plantations typically preferred to reside in the comfort of London where they could most comfortably enjoy the proceeds of the diligent labor of their distant blacks. Overseers were poor whites who viewed their position in the Indies as a temporary exile from which they hoped to return to England as wealthy men. Absentee owners naturally viewed their West Indian enterprises in purely financial terms. "Kindliness and comfort, cruelty and hardship were rated at balance-sheet value."[57]

In the United States, even the larger cotton plantations were small when compared to the norm of Indies sugar plantations. Moreover, many small- and medium-sized southern farms held from one to twenty slaves who were accordingly dispersed in small clusters throughout the region. By 1860, somewhat less than one-half of all slaves in the United States lived on farms which employed no more than twenty slaves.[58] The smaller size of the holdings brought slaves into personal contact with their owners. Indeed, on the smallest farms, owner and slave worked side by side in the fields, although whites resorted to common field work only from necessity. Larger plantations employed poor whites to oversee production. As in the West Indies, overseers were transient and faithless. Absentee ownership, however, was exceptional in the United States. Plantation owners preferred to live on their lands where they occupied the main

[57] Ulrich Bonnell Phillips, *American Negro Slavery* (New York: D. Appleton, 1918), p. 52; also see Jordan, *White over Black*, p. 142; Hall, "Slaves and *Slavery*," p. 315.
[58] Stampp, *Peculiar Institution*, pp. 31–32.

roost in a collonaded white mansion overlooking the shanties of their blacks. These conditions were propitious for the creation of a patriarchal relationship between a planter and his Negroes. Certainly southern conditions were more conducive to such a development than were West Indian conditions, where blacks in great numbers confronted an absentee owner or corporation only through the written reports of transient administrators. Compared to his West Indian counterpart, the southern Negro was well situated to absorb the culture of the slaveholders. Whatever the other implications of this relationship, it can hardly have induced a conservative attitude in the slaves concerning the desirability of retaining or practicing African customs.[59]

Postemancipation conditions in the West Indies were also more conducive to the survival of African economic customs than were postemancipation conditions in the United States. In the British Caribbean, with the exception of Barbados, the emancipation of the slaves was followed by the widespread withdrawal of the freedmen from wage labor on the sugar plantations. The freedmen retreated to the interior of the islands where there remained extensive tracts of unsettled Crown lands available for squatting. Here the freedmen founded free villages and subsistence farming communities of their own—greatly to the inconvenience of the sugar plantation owners who desired their participation as "free" laborers on the plantations.[60] Subsistence farming in the backwoods was not a profitable way of life, but those who followed it remained free of the domination of the large estates. In the isolated inland communities, African economic customs were readily applicable to the everyday tasks of production.

In contrast, emancipation in the American South did not release the freedmen from the domination of the plantation system. Since

[59] *Ibid.*, pp. 325, 362–64; Charles S. Johnson, *Shadow of the Plantation* (Chicago: University of Chicago Press, 1934), pp. 22–23; Bernard Magubane, "The American Negro's Conception of Africa: A Study in the Ideology of Pride and Prejudice" (Ph.D. diss., University of California, Los Angeles, 1967).

[60] G. E. Cumper, "Labour Demand and Supply in the Jamaican Sugar Industry, 1830–1950," *Social and Economic Studies* 2 (March 1954): 49; Eric Williams, *History of the People of Trinidad and Tobago* (Port-of-Spain, Trinidad: People's National Movement, 1962), pp. 86–101; see also Robert Austin Warner, *New Haven Negroes* (New Haven: Yale University Press, 1940), pp. 143ff.

unsettled tracts of public lands were unavailable to them, blacks could not retreat from the cotton-dominated plantation economy to subsistence farming on their own account. Hence, the American plantation system resurrected itself upon titularly "free" labor in the form of sharecropping agreements between white owners and freedmen. For political reasons, the "forty acres and a mule" promised the freedmen did not materialize. Yet precisely this land reform would have been necessary to duplicate through political intervention the subsistence farming, freeholding Negro communities which sprang up in the West Indies without political intervention. It may be that by 1865 African economic customs had already disappeared from the cultural repertoire of American blacks. In any event, tenant farming and debt peonage were unfavorable conditions for the operation of cooperative African economic practices. In the West Indies, on the other hand, the postemancipation social situation of Negroes encouraged continued reliance on cooperative economic customs.

In the broad view, these considerations suggest a causal chain ultimately linking the eradication of African economic customs under the North American slavery regime to the subsequent disadvantages of American-born Negroes in the field of business credit in the urban North. On the other hand, pre- and postemancipation social conditions in the British West Indies permitted the intergenerational continuity of African customs. In the hands of the West Indian descendants of slaves in Harlem, the perpetuated African economic customs encouraged and facilitated the business activities of the immigrants. These suppositions are congruent with the accepted scholarly belief that African customs, in particular the esusu, were part of the cultural heritage of slaves in both the United States and in the West Indies. Insofar as an environmental explanation can account for the manifest lack of the rotating credit association among American-born blacks but not among West Indian blacks, the environmental explanation tends to buttress the supposition that esusu disappeared from the cultural repertoire of American blacks.

Every step of this historic process is not equally in focus at this time. It remains to be documented, for example, that rotating credit was actually employed by slaves in the operation of their separate subsistence economy in the West Indies. Hence, there is only a speculative case for the supposition that social conditions in the United States extirpated the esusu from the cultural repertoire of blacks in this country, whereas social conditions in the West Indies encouraged their persistence. All conjectures as to causality must, naturally, come to grips with the manifest fact that American-born Negroes did not employ esusu in the twentieth century, whereas West Indian Negroes did.

# Rotating Credit and Banking

# 3

In evaluating the contribution of rotating credit to Oriental commerce, it is helpful to compare this informal financial system with more rationalized operations such as banks. Banks provided an obvious alternative to rotating credit associations in that the financial services actually provided by rotating credit clubs might alternatively have been provided by banks. Most students would simply assume that rationalized financial institutions would provide a more efficient and satisfactory financial structure than an old-fashioned money pool. This premise leads to the corollary supposition that Chinese and Japanese small business would have been better served had the Orientals been more active in banking and less active in *hui* and *tanomoshi*.

But the dismal histories of Oriental- and Negro-owned banks offer little support for such a view. Both Negroes and Orientals opened banks of their own in the first third of this century. The Negro banks and their problems have received substantial attention; Chinese and Japanese banks have not. The experience of Orientals in banking is of considerable importance for the interpretation of Negro banking history since it suggests a standard of comparison. This standard permits the assessment of the relative success that blacks attained in banking as well as an evaluation of the advantages and disadvantages of banking and of rotating credit as alternative types of lending institutions.

### BANKS AND BANK FAILURES

The earliest Negro-owned banks appeared in the South between 1888 and 1900. Fraternal orders created the financial institutions to serve as repositories for their funds. The banks thus established bore the name of the parent fraternal, for example, Knights of Honor

Savings Bank.[1] In the North, on the other hand, the first bank did not appear until 1908. The banks of the North were fewer in number than those of the South and were usually nonfraternal in origin. Two Chicago banks, the Binga State Bank and the Douglass National Bank, achieved exceptional size in the world of Negro banking. The combined resources of these two nonfraternal banks amounted to 36 percent of those of all twenty-one Negro banks in existence in 1929.[2]

Between 1884 and 1935, Negroes organized no fewer than 134 banking institutions in the United States. This sum does not include the numerous credit unions, industrial loan associations, and building and loan associations which blacks also organized in this period.[3] Unfortunately, many of the 134 banks thus hopefully established later failed, a few in default of obligations. By 1929, only twenty-one Negro-owned banks still survived, and the Depression reduced this number to twelve in 1936. Eleven of these remained active in 1945.[4] Thus, of the 134 banks founded, 92 percent were closed, liquidated, or suspended within a half-century. Since these bank closings took place before federal deposit insurance, the depositors lost their money.

Discouraging though this record was, Negro banks in this period were actually more successful than Oriental banks in California, among which the mortality rate was 100 percent. Japanese and Chinese opened ten state-chartered banks in California between 1900 and 1910. Of this number, six closed before the decade was out, victims of the California Banking Act of 1910. One bank survived until 1912, and three others limped along until the mid-1920s. Characteristically, Japanese banking was more decentralized than was Chinese. The Chinese opened only one bank; the remaining nine were all opened by Japanese residents of California. However,

[1] Booker T. Washington, *The Story of the Negro*, 2 vols. (New York: Doubleday, Page, 1909), 2:218.

[2] Abram L. Harris, *The Negro as Capitalist*, p. 163.

[3] E. Franklin Frazier, *The Negro in the United States*, p. 395; Joseph A. Pierce, *Negro Business and Business Education*, pp. 150–63.

[4] Pierce, *Negro Business*, p. 152; Harris, *Negro*, p. 48; also see Monroe N. Work, "The Negro in Business and the Professions," *Annals* 140, no. 229 (November 1928): 142–43; Robert H. Kinzer and Edward Sagarin, *The Negro in American Business*, p. 102.

the Chinese-Americans' Canton Bank was substantially larger than any of the more numerous Japanese institutions and also was longer-lived. In 1920 the California superintendent of banks reported the net assets of the Canton Bank as $4.2 million, whereas in the same year the assets of the two surviving Japanese banks totaled only $1.3 million. Foreign exchange constituted the bulk of the Canton Bank's business, at least in its later years.[5] Probably only the Nippon Bank and the Industrial Bank of Fresno made a systematic business of extending credit to Japanese farmers in California. The contribution of the Canton Bank to the Chinese-American economy was probably not, on balance, any greater than that of the Nippon Bank and Industrial Bank of Fresno to the Japanese-American economy despite its greater size. When the Canton Bank was suspended in 1926, the Industrial Bank of Fresno and the Nippon Bank had already expired. These failures put an end to prewar efforts of California's Orientals to operate banking institutions on their own account.[6]

To be sure, American branches of Asian banks persisted despite the failure of the resident Orientals' state banks. The Bank of Canton, Ltd. and the Hong Kong and Shanghai Banking Corporation did business in San Francisco throughout most of this period. However, the Hong Kong and Shanghai Bank was an English institution, and the Bank of Canton was owned by mainland Chinese. These two banks were exclusively interested in foreign exchange. Their deposits were not available for the commercial purposes of resident Chinese. Similarly, the Yokohama Specie Bank and Sumitomo Bank, both incorporated in Japan, had overseas branches in San Francisco, Los Angeles, and Sacramento. In its 1920 report, the California Board of Control erroneously enumerated seven banks in California supposedly owned by Japanese-Americans, as well as two branches of the Yokohama Specie Bank. According to the board of control, the Yokohama Bank was also interested in foreign exchange, but it

---

[5] State of California, *Eleventh Annual Report of the Superintendent of Banks* (1920); Elbert W. Davis, "Liquidation of the Canton Bank," *California State Banking Department Bulletin* 2 (January 1928): 4–6. Net assets of about 30 Negro-owned banks in the early 1920s were estimated to be $13 million. Frazier, *Negro*, p. 396.

[6] The Cathay Bank of Los Angeles is currently the only state-chartered bank owned by resident Chinese in California. This bank began operations in 1962.

added that "all the Japanese banks are engaged principally in extending credit to Japanese merchants and farmers." The Chinese were thought to finance themselves from their own resources. Evidently the San Francisco Chinese shared the board's belief in some measure, for Helen Cather reported that they were of the opinion that Japanese-Americans experienced less difficulty in securing bank loans than did Chinese, because the Yokohama Bank was willing to underwrite their loans on practically no collateral. On the other hand, Schichiro Matsui claimed that both the Yokohama Bank and the Sumitomo Bank were interested exclusively in foreign exchange. Indeed, this lack of support was, in his opinion, partially responsible for the Japanese-Americans' extensive resort to tanomoshi.[7]

This unhappy record of persistent bank failure offers little preliminary ground for supposing that these institutions were dependable sources of credit for personal or commercial purposes. But the causes of these repetitious bank failures are also instructive. The causes were not random. The banks established by these immigrant minorities were plagued by recurrent problems that tended systematically to bring down the institutions. These recurrent difficulties are of considerable analytical importance, because the rotating credit associations "happened" to be immune to them. This immunity from the problems characteristically afflicting formal banking institutions suggests the advantageousness of rotating credit as a financial system for the small commercial purposes of these immigrants.

### PROBLEMS OF ADMINISTRATION

The Negro-owned banks experienced a chronic inability to recruit highly trained and qualified officials. This difficulty reflected the very low educational level of the entire Negro population and, of course, the inferior educational institutions which perpetuated the prevailing inequality of training and skill. However, the problem was exacerbated by the marked propensity of the best trained Negroes to enter the professions. Banking tended to recruit the uneducated or the less

[7] State Board of Control of California, *California and the Oriental*, p. 80; Helen Virginia Cather, "History of San Francisco's Chinatown," pp. 83–84; Schichiro Matsui, "Economic Aspects of the Japanese Situation in California," p. 84. See also Fumiko Fukuoka, "Mutual Life and Aid Among the Japanese of Southern California," pp. 31–32.

competent graduates of inferior educational institutions (Table 6). Consequently, "abject ignorance of elementary banking principles" among officials of Negro-owned banks was closer to the norm than

TABLE 6

*Education, Occupation, and Residence of Selected Negro Elite, 1915*

| | Occupation | | | |
|---|---|---|---|---|
| | Insurance Official | Banker | Realtor | All Listed Persons[a] |
| Percent of listed Indicating B.A. or Higher Degree | 36.2 | 50.0 | 21.1 | 64.3 |
| Percent of Listed Residing in the North[b] | 36.3 | 10.0 | 66.6 | 39.2 |
| Number | 11 | 10 | 33 | 1270 |

SOURCE: F. L. Mather, ed., *Who's Who of the Colored Race* (Chicago, 1915). Content analysis of 1270 biographical entries.

[a] Includes only native-born persons resident in the United States.

[b] The South was defined as the Confederate states plus Oklahoma and Washington, D.C. All other places were defined as in the North.

the exception. Indeed, even today, the outstanding problem facing Negro banks is the "severe shortage of management talent."[8] Lack of training and incompetence on the part of the Negro bankers was especially unfortunate in view of the small size and restricted investment opportunities of the Negro-owned banks. Other things being equal, these small banks had a heavier burden to bear than the larger white banks in simply engineering their survival. Only the best trained Negro bankers had a fighting chance of averting the destruction which stalked their miniscule institutions at every turn. There was less room for blunderers in Negro banking than in banking in general, but the Negro banks had more than their share of incompetents.

In both fraternal and nonfraternal Negro banks, official venality and misappropriation of funds proved another recurrent problem.[9]

[8] Harris, *Negro*, p. 73; Andrew F. Brimmer, "The Banking System and Urban Economic Development," p. 13. See also Lawrence Johnson and Wendell Smith, "Black Managers," pp. 112–25 in the American Assembly, eds., *Black Economic Development* (Englewood Cliffs, N.J., 1969); Joseph R. Houchins, "Causes of Negro Insurance Company Failures," pp. 2–3.

[9] Arnett G. Lindsay, "The Negro in Banking," *Journal of Negro History* 14

Because of the pervasive incompetence of most bank officials, the line between incompetence and venality is hard to draw in practice. But official venality undoubtedly figured in the fall of important banks like the Binga Bank, the Douglass Bank, the Capitol Savings Bank, and the True Reformers' Bank. Embezzlement was all the harder to detect because of the prevailing incompetence of bankers and auditors and lax state regulation. Faulty and inadequate records encouraged unscrupulous officials to appropriate institutional funds in the expectation that embezzlements would go undetected. Usually a bank crisis was necessary to provoke the inquiries which led to detection of the unscrupulous officials. But such crises were also associated with the fall of the bank, so that the belated discovery of fraudulent officials proved cold comfort to uninsured depositors.

The allied problems of mismanagement and official venality that repetitiously plagued Negro-owned banks also afflicted the banks operated by Chinese and Japanese in California. According to the California state superintendent of banks, the single most frequent cause of Oriental bank suspensions was mismanagement. Seven of the ten Oriental state-chartered banks in California were suspended at one time or another, and one (the Nippon Bank) was suspended three times before being finally liquidated. In all seven of these cases of involuntary bank suspension, mismanagement was given as a cause of suspension; and in half of these cases, "official defalcation" was also listed as a cause of suspension. According to the 1910 report of the California superintendent of banks, "The Japanese banks now in liquidation . . . are in very bad condition. . . . Their affairs show that they were simply looted."[10] Criminal prosecutions of bank officials were balked by the incompleteness of records (kept in Japanese) and by the fact that most of the malfeasant acts were committed before the Bank Act of 1910 declared them criminal acts.

These problems of administration did not, however, affect Oriental rotating credit. *Hui* and *ko* did not require the services of educated, technically skilled administrators. Indeed, there were no paid officials

(April 1929): 172–73; Harris, *Negro*, p. 173; Gunnar Myrdal, *An American Dilemma*, 1:315.

[10] State of California, *Twenty-second Annual Report of the Superintendent of Banks* (1931), p. 22; idem, *First Annual Report of the Superintendent of Banks* (1910), p. 6.

at all in the rotating credit associations. The "administration" of hui or ko amounted only to opening sealed bids and announcing the results. Since the collected funds simply rotated among the members, tellers did not have to manage the fund. Hence, the problem of financial expertise which recurrently dogged Oriental and the Negro efforts in formal banking did not affect the Oriental rotating credit associations. Lack of a technically skilled officialdom became a problem only when these poor immigrants attempted to operate a Western-style bank.

Official venality was also a problem which emerged only when formal banking institutions were operated. Since hui and ko did not require the institutional management of collected funds, these rotating credit associations offered scant opportunity for official venality. Moreover, each serial collection required a full public "accounting." No teller could pocket a contribution without prompt detection by other participants. Quite a different situation prevailed in banks whose officials could expect successfully to hoodwink depositors by fancy financial manipulations. Unlike Western banks, rotating credit associations were tamper-proof with respect to official defalcation. In an era of very lax state regulation, this advantage of rotating credit was especially valuable.

### PROBLEMS OF INVESTMENT

In addition to the administrative problems of incompetence, mismanagement, and official venality, Negro banks also suffered from purely economic difficulties. Indeed, A. L. Harris regarded the administrative problems as epiphenomenal; in his view, insoluble economic contradictions would have condemned the banks to failure even had they been managed with exceptional skill instead of exceptional ineptitude. The unavoidable weakness of all Negro banking, according to Harris, was the eternal need to find profitable employment for capital and the chronic inability of the banks to do so because of the inability of black communities to support that capital.[11]

Because of the contradiction between the banks' need for profitable investments and the lack of investment opportunity in the

[11] Harris, *Negro*, p. 172; cf. Brimmer, "Banking System," p. 22.

ghettos, Negro-owned banks were driven to make systematically unsound investments in ghetto real estate, faltering fraternal orders, unmarketable securities of fly-by-night enterprises, and unsecured loans to individuals. These investments temporarily propped up the tottering banks at the same time that they virtually guaranteed ultimate failure. In this manner the basic structural weaknesses produced a suicidal investment policy.

Northern banking suicide began with the heavy channeling of capital into real estate investments in the overcrowded ghettos. In prosperous times and periods of population influx, real property values in the black ghettos regularly increased. Overcrowded, deteriorating slums appeared to offer viable investment opportunities for banks and realtors. Hence, realty and real-estate-oriented banking were important business activities among northern blacks.[12] Speculation in slum tenements was a distinctly northern form of entrepreneurial social mobility open to ambitious blacks lacking educational credentials (Table 6, p. 49).

Although these heavy real estate investments appeared profitable, they ultimately involved disastrous illiquidities. These illiquidities reared their heads in periods of business decline, when white banks grew unwilling to rediscount ghetto housing and slum dwellers lacked the means to purchase it.[13] Chicago's Binga Bank exemplified the "riches-to-rags" cycle inherent in this chronic banking problem. The boss and namesake of the bank, Jesse Binga, had begun his business career as a pedlar, but by dint of shrewd real estate investments had founded what became the largest Negro-owned bank in the nation. Like many self-made tycoons, Binga took advantage of his financial prominence and publicly sneered at the incompetence of better educated but less successful bankers. In 1930 Binga's gloating received its reward when his southside real estate empire collapsed. His money now gone, Binga himself was convicted of embezzlement in 1931 and incarcerated for nine years in the penitentiary.

In the South, the banks' self-destruction began in the halls of fraternal congregation. The fraternal orders had "collected from the

---

[12] John Daniels, *In Freedom's Birthplace* (New York: Houghton Mifflin, 1914), pp. 366–67.

[13] Harris, *Negro*, pp. 163–64; Gunnar Myrdal, *An American Dilemma*, 1:315.

masses of the colored people large amounts of money that would not otherwise have been saved."[14] Lodge officials and brothers were of the opinion that these monies could best be employed to capitalize race-conscious banking institutions which would, in turn, stimulate business development. Thus, the many fraternally sponsored banks of the South came into existence in response to a popular clamor for Negro business development rather than in response to a concrete economic demand for banking services.

As a result, the newly established, fraternally sponsored banks found themselves in the position of having to stimulate black business in order to develop investment opportunities for themselves. In the most successful ventures, this contingency had been anticipated by plans for the development of fraternally sponsored business enterprises. In this planned development, the fraternally sponsored bank was to serve as the strongbox for the simultaneous establishment of fraternally sponsored businesses. In this manner the economic rationale of the bank was planned for it by the many-sided expansion of fraternally sponsored businesses. The business these schemes envisioned was centralized, cooperative, and of medium to large scale.

The syndrome typical of the best fraternally sponsored ventures is illustrated by the True Reformers' Savings Bank, the first of the fraternally sponsored banks. Between 1888 and 1910 it was the most illustrious of such banks and was everywhere hailed as a glorious example of successful Negro banking. Its collapse in 1910 provoked widespread dismay. The founder of the order, the Rev. W. W. Browne envisioned the bank as only a first step in the ultimate creation of an interlocking network of fraternally sponsored businesses. In fulfillment of this plan, the fraternal order established a True Reformers' Old Folks Home, the Reformers' Mercantile and Industrial Association (a grocery chain), the *Reformer* newspaper, the Reformer Printing Company, the Reformer Hotel in Richmond, Virginia, the Reformer Building and Loan Association, and the Reformers' Real Estate Department. These "affiliated by-products" of fraternalism were centrally controlled and staffed with hired managers and em-

[14] Washington, *Story of the Negro*, 2:168–69.

ployees. The True Reformers fraternal order was the hub around which the various enterprises rotated; the Reformers' Savings Bank was the financial core of the network.[15]

Since all the auxiliary corporations were coordinated by the fraternal order, the decisive managerial positions were in the hands of officers of the fraternal order. Operating the network of enterprises, including the bank, was a monumental endeavor whose success depended to a great degree on sophisticated business skills. Such skills were especially relevant in view of the order's decision to subsidize its less successful endeavors from the surpluses of more successful ones. This decision subordinated the balance sheets of the individual operations to that of the syndicate as a whole. Moreover, the fraternal order subordinated the interest of the True Reformers' Savings Bank to that of the order and its plan for business development. But officers were incompetent, and a few were dishonest. These fatal connections set the stage for the collapse of the bank. When the bank closed, the receivers discovered that the fraternal order and its subsidiary enterprises were heavily in debt to the savings bank and had taken out constantly renewed loans from the bank without intending to liquidate them at maturity. "Because of the Order's power over the bank, its subsidiary enterprises continued to hold title to the property which under ordinary banking conditions should have been taken over by the bank for liquidation."[16] These unwise departures from sound banking practices so weakened the bank that, in the words of the receivers, "the Order wrecked the bank."

In view of the distress of the fraternal order and its subordinate businesses, and the venality of some administrators, the wisest course for the True Reformers' Bank might have been, as Harris recommended, to have severed its fraternal relationship with the order and to have dealt with the parent organization on exclusively commercial terms. Had this course been followed, the floundering fraternal order would have been unable to have dragged down the bank, and the True Reformers' Bank might have survived the True Reformers'

15 See William T. Thom, "The True Reformers," U.S. Department of Labor *Bulletin* 41 (July 1902): 807–14; Harris, *Negro*, pp. 62ff.; Albert L. DeMonde, Jr., *Certain Aspects of the Economic Development of the American Negro, 1867–1900* (Washington, D.C.: Catholic University of America, 1945), pp. 82ff.

16 Harris, *Negro*, pp. 67–68.

fraternal order. However, this conventional wisdom overlooks the circumstances under which the savings bank appeared in the first place. The True Reformers' Savings Bank depended on the order's ancillary business enterprises for investment opportunity. If these failed to develop, the bank lost its economic raison d'être. Hence, quite apart from incompetence, undue influences, or official venality, bank officers had no choice but to sink the bank's funds into the tottering business ventures of the fraternal order. Mismanagement made excellent sense.

It would be incorrect to conclude from the sad experience of the fraternally sponsored banks that fraternalism as such had no place in finance. After all, the Orientals' rotating credit system of finance was also a kind of "fraternal" institution. Ties of region and of kinship created the operating nuclei of the rotating credit associations, just as the fraternal ties of lodge brothers and sisters gave rise to the Negro-owned banks. But the structure of the rotating credit associations precluded the economic difficulties which everywhere precipitated the downfall of the fraternally sponsored banks.

First of all, the rotating credit associations did not arise in response to a centrally directed plan for business growth as did the fraternally sponsored banks. Decentralized operations obviated the necessity of a technically skilled administration, but expert administration was vital to the success of the planned, interlocking business operations which the fraternal orders attempted to stimulate. The "experts" actually charged with making these decisions turned out to be lodge moguls, doctors of divinity, and incompetent officials. Financial expertise was quite unnecessary to the success of rotating credit associations, which relied on market opportunities rather than managerial planning as the locus of investment decision making.

The rock on which the fraternally sponsored banks ultimately floundered was the lack of concrete investment opportunities in Negro business. This crisis had been precipitated by the unwise creation of the banks in response to a popularly experienced subjective need for black-owned banks rather than a hard-headed analysis of local investment opportunities. The "fraternalism" of the rotating credit associations was, however, free of this difficulty which recurrently plagued the fraternally sponsored banks. The rotating credit institutions came into existence only when specific investors experienced a practical need for funds. Thus, Oriental "fraternalism" was never in danger of losing sight of economic realities. Rotating credit provided no means whereby a popular clamor for business or credit could actualize itself in an expensive financial institution which lacked economic merit as indicated by the price system. This safeguard prohibited the disastrous mistakes that overcame the zealous but ineffectual efforts of the fraternal orders to stimulate business by opening banks.

Moreover, the banks' survival need for profit was not shared by the tanomoshi or hui. The rotating credit associations had no outstanding obligations to depositors which necessitated profitability. There were no operating costs. In interest-paying variants of tanomoshi or hui, depositors could estimate the probable cost of taking a portion sooner or later. However, depositors could not anticipate a stipulated rate of return, nor was interest "owed" to a depositor who chose to delay his turn in order to secure a higher return. When business conditions deteriorated in the course of an ongoing hui or tanomoshi, some takers benefited and others suffered; but no one had been deprived of an obligation if his money ceased to command interest. Nor did any member of the association need to make profitable use of funds offered. Hence, the hui or tanomoshi lacked a survival need for profit and could not generate systematically unsound investments. If the contradiction between survival needs for profit and lack of profitable opportunity was the Achilles heel of Negro banking, this difficulty was singularly lacking in the rotating credit associations.

To be sure, had Negro-owned business been greatly stronger than it was, banks would have experienced less of a chronic problem in locating investment opportunities. That the banks did experience such a difficulty is evidence that black banking was developed entirely out of proportion to black business. But the experience of the Negro banks also suggests that formal banking could not antedate business development. An important justification of Negro banking was the development of Negro business. However, in practice the Negro banks' record of failure indicates that banks could not create a business structure to support themselves. On the other hand, of course, business could not emerge so long as credit was unavailable.

This vicious cycle suggests that rotating credit filled a role in the Oriental economies which Western banking was chronically unable to do for Negroes. The rotating credit associations broke the cycle of underdevelopment which mutually inhibited Negro business and finance.

Moreover, in their loans to individuals, the black banks customarily required no security other than the integrity of the borrower. Borrowers were too impoverished to furnish security. In hard times the proportion of unredeemable loans was very high and greatly contributed to the difficulties of the banks. Even today "most of the Negro banks spend a substantial amount of time and effort (not always with success) trying to collect on defaulted or delinquent loans."[17] In hui and ko, loans were also made without security other than the good name of a borrower; however, a group of friends or fellow villagers was in a vastly better position than a bank official to evaluate the reliability of borrowers and to collect outstanding loans. In assessing the personal reliability of loan applicants, bank officials had to act in a formal, bureaucratic context, typically without informal social knowledge of the borrower. Moreover, in case of default banks could compel payment only through expensive, lengthy, and frequently ineffective litigation. In a similar situation, members of a rotating credit association could bring informal pressures to bear on a defaulting participant. These pressures were free, immediate, and unrelenting. They involved not only social disgrace, but also banishment from the informal economic structure. In the last resort, a hui or ko could secure compensation from the responsible kinsmen of an insolvent or absconding member. Such compensation was naturally unavailable to the bank in the dunning situation.

Yet because of their desperate need for investment outlets, the Negro banks needed perforce to rely heavily on individual borrowers to absorb a substantial proportion of their working capital. Hence, the Negro banker could less afford to be selective in his loan policy than could a rotating credit association which stood under no similar compulsion to lend. The Negro banks, then, were less able to evaluate the personal reliability of loan applicants, less able to collect from defaulters, and more impelled to take risks than were the rotating

[17] Brimmer, "Banking System," p. 13.

credit associations. Clearly, if funds were to be lent without security on the basis of individual honesty, the rotating credit association was subject to less irregularity than the banking institution.

The lugubrious history of Oriental and Negro banking offers scant ground for supposing that banks of their own provided viable financial resources for small business development. The bank failures resulted from weaknesses of investment and administration to which rotating credit associations happened to be immune. Given the concrete socioeconomic reality of these migrant groups and apart from abstract or theoretical preferences, these considerations suggest that rotating credit associations were better suited to the small business purposes of immigrants than were banks.

Happily for the Chinese and Japanese, the advantageous solution was the one which they actually employed. Although their banks were unsuccessful, the Orientals had always the option of falling back on rotating credit, which, apart from its advantageousness, they preferred on cultural grounds. Unfortunately for him, the black American did not have this option. If his banks failed, the black American had to open new banks or to forego the enjoyment of credit. Since rotating credit had dropped out of his cultural repertoire, the black had perforce to make do with the less desirable rationalized institutions with which he had become familiar. What was remarkable about the Negro's efforts to finance himself was not the systematic bank failures which frustrated his efforts, but the lack of a traditional alternative.

SOCIOLOGICAL UNDERPINNINGS OF ORIENTAL CREDIT

The advantages of rotating credit depended entirely on the mutual trust of members of the clubs; without such mutual trust, neither hui nor ko could have functioned at all. The rotating fund could be no safer than the least honest of its members, and this situation produced the intense moral scrutiny to which candidates for admission were subject by the members at large. Moreover, the advantages of rotating credit depended on widespread mutual confidence. Only widespread, institutionalized mutual confidence in the community at large could permit the ready formation of rotating credit associations in response to spontaneous individual needs; and only widespread mutual confidence could encompass enough persons to render the rotating fund large enough to fill commercial needs. If confidence were restricted to very small groups, then the rotating credit associations could not attain great flexibility in formation nor sufficient size to render commercially useful portions.

Risk is inherent in lending. A borrower may always die or become insolvent. Such risks exist even when lenders and borrowers completely trust one another's honesty. Rotating credit clubs did not possess any magical means of eliminating the risks of lending, which in Western practice are offset by collateral assignments. The ability of the hui and ko routinely to provide credit without requiring collateral depended, in the last analysis, on the strong, informal, and moralistic social relations of lenders and borrowers. These purely social relations served as an alternative form of security against the pure risks of lending. The rotating credit associations also required members to have confidence in the honesty of those of any individual member's close circle who stood moral surety for him. This confidence extended beyond the limits of the membership circle. These extended lines of social trust offset purely objective and unavoidable risks of lending and permitted the Oriental rotating credit associations routinely to carry on their activities. That the Chinese and the Japanese were able to mobilize the extensive social trust required to operate these informal lending institutions was not a result of chance. Building and maintaining it required more or less continuous attention to the punctilio of decorum, honor, and especially of family reputation.

In the Chinese and Japanese rotating credit associations, the unavoidable risks of lending were borne by nonmembers of the club who were morally and "legally" obligated to make good the debts of a member. Should a member default, die, or prove unable to repay his debts, his kin were expected to make good the obligation.[18] Hence, the credit of every participant in the rotating credit association

---

[18] See J. M. Scanland, "Chinese Business Methods in San Francisco," pp. 1079–80; S. S. Huebner, "Insurance in China," p. 108; William Carlson Smith, *Americans in Process* (Ann Arbor: University of Michigan Press, 1937), p. 272.

was guaranteed by his family. Under these circumstances a family reputation for honesty was naturally a matter of capital importance. A person could secure membership in a hui or ko only if the other members were confident that the applicant's family would stand surety for him in good faith. Hence, many rotating credit associations were able routinely to lend money without requiring collateral assignments.

Among both Chinese and Japanese, trustworthiness resided in ascriptively defined subcommunities of region and kinship. Regional and kinship ties had moral significance, in that persons thus linked together were ethically bound to behave honorably in financial transactions. Since all Chinese and Japanese were organized into such ascriptively bordered moral communities, the two Oriental communities could depend on extensive social trust in the community at large. This social trust enabled the rotating credit associations to attain the flexibility in formation and the large size necessary to commercially useful credit agencies. Had the Oriental communities been composed of isolated individuals, they would not have been able to employ rotating credit, since isolated individuals lack the necessary social trust. Since, however, both the Chinese and Japanese communities were subordered on the basis of ascriptive ties infused with moral significance, the proportion of social isolates was quite low.

On the other hand, the Orientals' solution to the problem of social trust unavoidably linked their rotating credit clubs to ascriptively bounded groups of restricted size. The ascriptively bounded subgroups could raise only modest sums of capital. When it is necessary to create massive sums of capital, banks are much more satisfactory organizations than rotating credit associations. Banks can raise a massive capital because they are voluntary associations. As such, they are able to collect deposits from ascriptively unrelated persons who have no standing reason to trust one another. Hence, they are able to collect deposits from much wider sectors of society and so to piece together much larger capital sums than can rotating credit associations.

This important advantage of banking refers, however, to a stage of industrial development which the immigrant generation never attained. Hui and tanomoshi were capable of providing sufficient capital for the small businesses which Chinese and Japanese operated. Banks were unable to provide equally efficient service to Negro-owned small business, and Negro-owned big business did not develop for obvious reasons. In fact, the large sums of money amassed by Negro banks proved decisive liabilities since they generated the unsound investments which brought down the banks and further impoverished the hopeful depositors.

# Kenjin and Kinsmen

# 4

Among the Japanese settlers in America the decisive community ties were those created by *ken* affiliations. The *kenjinkai* were social organizations based on the provincial origins of immigrants. Immigrants from Hiroshima prefecture in Japan affiliated with the Hiroshima kenjinkai, and so forth. Since 89 percent of Japanese emigrated from eleven southern prefectures, virtually all Japanese settlers were eligible for membership in some ken organization.[1] People from the same ken referred to one another as *kenjin* ("fellow ken people") even when not active members in a prefectural club. Kenjin were said to differ in respect to basic personality traits. Ken endogamy was preferred. Dialectal differences also distinguished the different ken groups. Ken-consciousness was, however, characteristic only of overseas Japanese. In Japan, ken ties had not counted for much in daily life.[2]

The manifest purposes of the kenjinkai were social and benevolent. The prefectural clubs sponsored festival occasions when the membership came together for fellowship and recreation. Observance of Japanese and American holidays was normally in the province of the prefectural clubs, and kenjin made a point of attending these occasions: "We have a store which is run by my family. We are poor, busy, and have many children. We cannot go out like other families. But we have never missed a kenjinkai picnic; it is the only occasion when we can meet many friends. . . . We eat, drink, and chat in our native dialect."[3] In addition to these recreational functions

[1] Stanford M. Lyman, "The Structure of Chinese Society in Nineteenth-Century America," pp. 48–71; Yasaburo Yoshida, "Sources and Causes of Japanese Emigration," *Annals* 34 (September 1909): 377–87. Also see Harry H. L. Kitano, *Japanese Americans*, p. 10.

[2] Shotaro Frank Miyamoto, *Social Solidarity Among the Japanese in Seattle*, pp. 117–18; cf. Yukiko Kimura, "Locality Clubs as Basic Units of the Social Organization of the Okinawans in Hawaii," *Phylon* 29 (winter 1968): 333–35.

[3] Fumiko Fukuoka, "Mutual Life and Aid Among the Japanese in Southern California," p. 17.

the kenjinkai also played a leading role in overseeing the social and economic welfare of the immigrants. The kenjinkai published newspapers, offered legal advice to members, sponsored the tanomoshi, and served as employment agencies.[4] Prefectual contacts were critical sources of influence in business and politics. Kenjinkai provided direct welfare assistance to destitute or needy members, buried the indigent, and paid medical bills. Because of these varied prefectural services, Japanese thought that membership in a large *kai* was a distinct advantage. Some unfortunates were from kens that did not have many eligible members in a locality; thus they lacked the services a large prefectural club could provide.

The private welfare activities of kenjinkai were extensive. They tended, therefore, to preempt public relief services so that, as a result, few Japanese became public welfare clients. For example, the kenjinkai helped organize massive relief for the 10,000 Japanese made homeless by the San Francisco earthquake and fire of 1906. Because of this private assistance, virtually no Japanese applied to public authorities for disaster relief and rehabilitation.[5] In the middle of the Great Depression a Japanese spokesman in Los Angeles noted that "the number of destitute is increasing; and usually they are assisted by *kenjinkai*." Thanks to this assistance, hardly any Japanese were to be found on the rolls of public unemployment relief.[6] Of course, the language barrier and resulting ignorance of welfare rights played a part in curtailing the number of Japanese applicants for public welfare relief of various sorts. But these inhibitions might more quickly have disappeared had the kenjinkai not busied themselves in finding jobs for the unemployed and relieving the destitute.

### AVOIDING DISGRACE

Although stressed in public pronouncements, the welfare activities of the prefectural clubs were in practice restricted in scope by the

[4] John Modell, "The Japanese of Los Angeles," pp. 133–34.
[5] Russell Sage Foundation, *San Francisco Relief Survey* (New York, 1913), pp. 94–95; Herbert B. Johnson, *Discrimination Against Japanese in California* (Berkeley: Courier Publishing, 1907), p. 67.
[6] Fukuoka, "Mutual Life," p. 19; Modell, "Japanese of Los Angeles," pp. 161, 261.

social disgrace attendant upon accepting this relief. As a relief organization, the prefectural club stood at the apex of a pyramid of community agencies expected to aid needy Japanese. Those who obtained relief from the prefectural club did so only *in extremis* and testified thereby to a disgraceful lack of intimate social affiliations. The close family was conventionally expected to constitute the lowest level relief agency. Appeals for aid beyond this circle were then to be directed to extended relatives, friends, and so forth up the ladder of informal agencies, until finally the needy person lacking other resources might petition his prefectural club. "In actual practice the [indigent] family is cared for by the village or town, because it is considered a disgrace when a community cannot care for its own indigents."[7] The kenjinkai did not formally restrict their beneficence to Japanese who were participating members of their club, although they did, of course, draw the line at Japanese who were from another ken. But the direct relief of ken people in difficulty was, at best, an obligation grudgingly fulfilled by the kenjinkai. The following comments of the secretaries of some kenjinkai suggest the attitude of the prefectural organizations to indigent Japanese who had no other source of relief or assistance:

> [Indigents] were the ones who never joined any organizations, such as the Japanese Association, *kenjinkai*, trade association, or social club. They were not members of any religious organizations. They were transients who . . . spent money for their own pleasures. They never helped anybody when they were young and able; they were so selfish that they could not make any friends in their lives.

> It seems to be that [indigents] are the people who have the wrong attitudes toward life and society.

> Always [indigents] were people who despised the works of the association and laughed at those who are members.

> Yes, members [of the ken organization] help one another as far as

[7] Fukuoka, "Mutual Life," p. 15. See also Kitano, *Japanese Americans*, p. 73; Forrest E. La Violette, *Americans of Japanese Ancestry* (Toronto: Canadian Institute of International Affairs, 1946), p. 90.

they can. But it is strange enough that members never get in financial trouble.[8]

The striking feature of the prefectural clubs' attitude toward their own destitute was the condemnation of the poor for excessive individualism. This attitude contrasts starkly with middle class views of the poor in which the moral fault of the indigent is located in a lack of self-reliance.[9] Japanese kenjinkai, however, viewed extreme self-reliance and individualism as tokens of characterological depravity. Moreover, such individualism was conventionally taken to explain the predicament of the poor in an altogether logical and unemotional sense:

> Repeatedly the [prefectural] secretaries stressed the point that those who are assisted and cared for by *kenjinkai* are usually non-members who have no families, relatives, or friends. The absence of application for aid on the part of members is due to the fact that mutual aid is practiced in a direct, personal manner among members, before the need of a family is known to *kenjinkai*. ... Very naturally, cases brought to the attention of the *kenjinkai* are those in desperate condition, where there are no relatives or friends able to assist.[10]

Only those Japanese who lacked more intimate social ties made their way to the prefectural club in search of assistance. Joining and participating in community organizations were characteristics of those Japanese who never found it necessary to request aid from their prefectural club. Under these circumstances, the Japanese naturally interpreted the predicament of the indigent as tokens of a dissolute individualism and isolation from community life.

To be sure, the Japanese did not lightly undertake the support of the needy nor view without some disdain those who found it necessary to request charity. In this sense the kenjinkai encouraged individuals to be industrious, thrifty, and so forth, and so to make provision for hard times on their own. But, however grudgingly, applicants for relief were provisioned from the community storehouse rather than turned away to perish. Such relief was counted a moral

---

[8] Fukuoka, "Mutual Life," pp. 50–53.
[9] See Reinhard Bendix, *Work and Authority in Industry*, pp. 86–99.
[10] Fukuoka, "Mutual Life," pp. 51–52. See also Stuart Alfred Queen, *Social Work in the Light of History* (Philadelphia: J. B. Lippincott, 1922), pp. 275–76.

obligation. The mendicant poor were upbraided for cutting themselves off from the community and encouraged to develop the lower
level social connections which would relieve kenjin of the necessity
for supporting them. Prefecturalism thus played the most important
role in producing the Japanese-Americans' astounding prewar record
of virtually complete absence from public welfare rolls.[11]

### ECONOMIC IMPORTANCE OF PREFECTURAL TIES

The attitude of the Japanese toward the friendless destitute is
illuminated when the occupational and economic aspects of the
kenjinkai are examined. Regional loyalties embodied in the kenjinkai
carried over to the sphere of strictly economic relations. The prefectural clubs functioned as employment agencies for members. Members in need of work were able to secure an introduction to other
members in need of help through the intervention of the club's
secretary and social activities. The Japanese gave preference in hiring
to persons from the same prefecture, and Japanese employers were
expected to make hiring opportunities known to their kenjinkai.[12]
In the early days of Japanese settlement in America, especially before
the establishment of formal kenjinkai, Japanese boardinghouse keepers and hotel managers doubled as employment agents for Japanese
roomers. The hotels and boardinghouses attracted a clientele from
the ken of the owner-proprietor, and naturally the owner-proprietor
became the employment agent of kenjin residing with him. In this
manner ken affiliations soon became connected with the employment
prospects of a Japanese looking for work. Understanding this connection, many Japanese considered participation in prefectural
activities a wise policy.

Ken participation was further strengthened by the closure of
alternatives. In the general labor market the employment opportunities of Japanese were limited by discrimination to menial positions.
In the Japanese economy, employment opportunities were further

[11] Fukuoka, "Mutual Life," p. 86; Miyamoto, *Social Solidarity*, p. 58; Kitano,
*Japanese Americans*, p. 76; Kimura, "Locality Clubs," pp. 335–36; Leonard Bloom
and Ruth Riemer, *Removal and Return* (Berkeley and Los Angeles: University of
California Press, 1949), pp. 63–64.

[12] Modell, "Japanese of Los Angeles," pp. 133–34; Fukuoka, "Mutual Life," pp.
17, 51–53, 57; Miyamoto, *Social Solidarity*, pp. 74–75.

limited by the preference of other Japanese for members of their own kenjinkai. Ultimately, employment opportunities outside of domestic service were limited to those which employers from one's own prefecture were able to supply; and insofar as prefectural clubs provided a pipeline into the domestic service occupations, the kenjinkai were able virtually to monopolize the allocation of employment to Japanese.

Regional loyalties also affected areas of settlement in the United States. Thus, the Japanese in a given Pacific region tended to be from the same ken; for example, the San Francisco and East Bay Japanese were from the Hiroshima ken. People from the same ken also tended to concentrate in the same lines of work as well as in the same Pacific locale:

> The barbers in Seattle tended to be people from the Yamaguchi-*ken*, for Mr. I. came first and established himself in that line, and then helped his friends from Japan to get started. Then again, in the restaurant business, the majority . . . are Ehine-*ken*, for men like Mr. K. first got into this, and then aided his *ken* friends to follow in the same field. Homes like those of Mr. I. were places of congregation for young men who were eager to learn things . . . and in the course of their association learned such trades as their friends knew.[13]

The tendency of ken fellows to congregate in the same lines of trade was furthered by the prevailing paternalism in employment relations. An important aspect of this paternalism was the social obligation of the employer to enable a diligent employee to open a business of his own. Said a Japanese employer of this obligation: "There's a custom in Japan which you won't find in America: that a man who has worked for another for a long time will eventually be financed by his employer in starting a branch office of his own. In other words, it's natural that everyone should own his individual shop."[14] The bare sequence thus suggested was not, of course, a sequence limited only to Japanese. The notion of career movement

[13] Miyamoto, *Social Solidarity*, p. 75; also see Isamu Nodera, "A Survey of the Vocational Activities of the Japanese in the City of Los Angeles," p. 8.
[14] Miyamoto, *Social Solidarity*, p. 7. The "branch office" endowment was common among late Tokugawa merchants. See Takeo Yazaki, *Social Change and the City in Japan* (Tokyo: Japan Publications, 1968), pp. 214–15.

from wage employment to self-employment to employership is what Abraham Lincoln referred to as the "natural course of labor." In the American tradition the natural course of labor has provided a cornerstone of the ideology of entrepreneurial individualism. But Lincoln did not expect an employer to finance his apprentice. In his version, the financing of such an enterprise depended on the apprentice's thrift; moreover, the apprentice's new business opened as a competitor rather than "branch office" of his former boss. Of course, the Japanese custom is more comprehensible in light of the prefectural ties in which master and apprentice were involved. These reciprocal social obligations of a quasi-primary sort intervened between Japanese employer and employee, thereby weakening the purely contractual elements in their relationship.

The tendency of kenjin to prefer each other in hiring and to pile up in the same trades naturally produced problems of internal competition. Traditional guild organizations recommended themselves in this connection. Guild organization of their trades enabled Japanese to regulate internal competition by discussion and collective decision making, rather than by individualistic competition in a devil-take-the-hindmost scramble for survival. In every trade in which Japanese were extensively employed, they organized guilds. Naturally, the membership of the guild or trade association tended extensively to overlap with memberships in the kenjinkai, as well as with family and neighborhood groupings. Like the kenjinkai, the trade guilds combined benevolent, social, economic, and welfare functions. In this combination, the trade guilds went considerably beyond the normal range of activities of a Western trade association.

### JAPANESE TRADE GUILDS

The operation of the Japanese trade guilds is illustrated by the Kako Domei Kwai, the Japanese Shoemakers Guild. The organization and operation of the Kako Domei Kwai were typical of most urban Japanese trade guilds such as restaurants, boardinghouses and hotels, expressmen, dry cleaners, tailors, domestics, curio art goods, grocery stores, and so on. The Kako Domei Kwai was founded in 1893 by Japanese shoe repairmen who had been brought to San

Francisco by a Western capitalist, a Mr. Cheese. For a while the Japanese worked in Mr. Cheese's shoe factory on Ecker Street in San Francisco; but the Shoemakers' Union (white) of San Francisco, learning of their presence, forced Mr. Cheese to close his factory. The discharged Japanese shoe repairmen began to open their own shoe repairing establishments and formed the Kako Domei Kwai for their mutual benefit and protection. The Japanese repairmen did a good business, largely with a white clientele, despite the vigorous, sometimes violent opposition of the white Shoemakers' Union. After nine years of struggle, the white shoemakers recognized the permanency of the Japanese competition, and in 1904 struck a bargain with the Kako Domei Kwai concerning hours of labor, prices, and the business districts in which the Japanese would operate.

The internal organization of the Kako Domei Kwai followed the lines of traditional guild organization. The guild made every effort to control the market. According to the U.S. Immigration Committee, the Kako Domei Kwai

> not only fixes a scale of prices to be charged . . . but controls the location of shops and protects and furthers the interests of its members in various ways. In opening shops, no two may be located within 1,000 feet of each other. A member of the union operating a shop in a locality where no Japanese shop is in existence may be assisted by a loan of money from the organization. . . . The Union also maintains a supply house in San Francisco and several thousand dollars of the "business fund" accumulated from dues paid are invested in the stock of goods carried. . . . Finally, this organization controls apprenticeship to the trade, and maintains a system of fraternal benefits. . . . The advantages in competition derived from the organization are apparent.[15]

The fraternal benefits involved in the Japanese trade guilds were of many sorts. When a member of the guild was ill and unable to work, the trade guild requested other members to send their assistants to the shop of the sick man. Until the individual recovered, the as-

[15] United States Senate, Sixty-first Congress, 2d Session, *Immigrants in Industries*, pt. 25, *Japanese and Other Immigrant Races in the Pacific Coast and Rocky Mountain States*, vol. 1, *Japanese and East Indians*, p. 206. Also see Schichiro Matsui, "Economic Aspects of the Japanese Situation," pp. 66, 75.

sistants operated his store—normally for free. The assistants were
paid by their own masters, and all of the cash they took in on behalf
of the ill member was received by his family. When a member of
the guild died, the trade guild paid his survivors a lump sum of
money. When someone in a member's family died, the trade guild
paid the survivors a smaller sum as *koden*, or funeral money. At
the height of the Great Depression, a member of the Japanese Hotel
Association remarked that, "until a few years ago, the Association
had a special provision for . . . mutual aid to the members. But now
we do not have any. However, mutual aid is extended to members
of the Association individually, as the members know each other
very well."[16]

Reinforced by the overlapping solidarities of kenjinkai, family,
and neighborhood, the Japanese guilds provided the membership
with a critical organizational instrument for survival in business. A
preliminary task of Japanese trade guilds was the rebuff of white
competitors' efforts to expel them from the market. Particularly in
the early period of Japanese settlement, before a modus vivendi with
white tradesmen was achieved, the creation of Japanese business
establishments unavoidably entailed the initiation of competition
with white tradesmen already employed in the line. Threatened by
Japanese competition, white tradesmen responded with "Swat the
Jap" campaigns intended to stir up racial animosity against Japanese
business establishments and to enlist the race solidarity of the "white"
caste in the pecuniary interest of white tradesmen.[17] Such campaigns
took the form of boycotts, picketing, mob violence, arson, and threats
of reprisal directed against Japanese businesses, white patrons of
Japanese establishments, and white suppliers of these establishments.
Since organized labor was waging its own crusade against Japanese
immigration under the banner of the Asiatic Exclusion League,
white tradesmen had no difficulty in recruiting thugs for their "Amer-
icanism" campaigns of intimidation or in appealing to the racial
"idealism" of many poor whites.[18]

[16] Fukuoka, "Mutual Life," p. 30; Miyamoto, *Social Solidarity*, p. 98. See also
Queen, *Social Work*, p. 282.
[17] Gladys Hennig Waldron, "Anti-Foreign Movements in California, 1919–1929"
(Ph.D. diss., University of California, Berkeley, 1956), pp. 252–53, 265.
[18] Roger Daniels, *The Politics of Prejudice*, pp. 16–30, 97; Kainichi Kawasaki,

In San Francisco, grass roots campaigns against Japanese business and the reign of terror employed to implement them reached a peak between 1905 and 1908. Police rarely interfered. Similar campaigns went on in Los Angeles until the 1920s.[19] So long as such campaigns confined themselves to the marketplace, however, the Japanese were normally able to survive in business. The solidarity of the Japanese community and of the different trade guilds permitted the Japanese to carry on a successful defensive struggle in the market place. Faced with boycotts by white suppliers, the Japanese responded—as an organized group—in kind and took reprisals against the boycotters. "It was never impossible to find the weakest link in the line of boycotters and every effort to drive them [Japanese] out failed."[20] Thugs employed by the white merchants to terrorize Japanese businessmen were bought off through funds subscribed by the membership of the Japanese trade guilds. Sometimes the trade guilds employed private police to guard the premises of threatened Japanese against arsonists or strong-arm men. As for their white clientele, for every customer lost through the racial appeals of threatened white merchants, the Japanese were able to find another by providing better service and lower prices than their white competitors.

When, however, anti-Japanese campaigns moved into the political arena, the Japanese were largely unable to resist. Since foreign-born Japanese were aliens and ineligible for citizenship, the immigrant residents of California had not even the feeble voice of the minority vote to protect their interests. In both agriculture and city trade, political authorities, on the motion of various commercial interests, restricted Japanese competition. In the laundry trade, for example, the Anti-Jap Laundry League was formed in 1908 by white proprietors of steam laundries, the Laundry-Drivers Union, French laundry operators, and white laundry workers. The league conducted a two-pronged campaign against Japanese laundries. First, it attempted to reduce the business volume of the Japanese laundries by

"The Japanese Community of East San Pedro, Terminal Island, California" (M.A. thesis, University of Southern California, 1931), p. 164; United States Senate, Sixty-first Congress, *Immigrants in Industry*, p. 170.

[19] Johnson, *Discrimination Against Japanese*, p. 99; Carey McWilliams, *Prejudice* (Boston: Little Brown, 1944), p. 26; Waldron, "Anti-Foreign Movements," pp. 252ff.

[20] Miyamoto, *Social Solidarity*, p. 76.

boycott, personal solicitation of white patrons, and anti-Japanese billboard advertising. Second, it put pressure on San Francisco politicians to refuse city permits to Japanese laundries. In this political campaign, the league was partially successful in that city authorities denied Japanese applicants the permits necessary to conduct the new-fangled steam laundry. When in 1919 a Mr. Tsukamoto opened a steam laundry without a permit in defiance of the authorities, his laundry was closed by police. Mr. Tsukamoto's subsequent suit against the city of San Francisco in the Supreme Court of the United States was defeated.[21]

## JAPANESE AGRICULTURE

The most striking legal disabilities imposed on the Japanese were the various alien land laws enacted by the state of California in 1913 and thereafter. From the point of view of the white ranchers, the Japanese had been altogether too successful in agriculture. Primarily from farming backgrounds, the Japanese immigrants had naturally gravitated to agricultural pursuits in California. In the early period of Japanese immigration, growers welcomed the Japanese migrants who provided an inexpensive supply of harvest laborers, a task for which the resident Chinese population had grown too old because of legislated Chinese exclusion. However, the Japanese farm laborers began to work and lease land as contract, share, and tenant farmers, and ultimately began to purchase substantial amounts of land outright. In this progression, the Japanese were exceptionally advantaged by their acquaintance with traditional Japanese methods of intensive cultivation. The poor Issei farm laborers had little money and could rent or purchase little land; but from small plots of land they were able to generate extraordinarily large harvests because of their knowledge of methods of intensive cultivation.[22] They introduced new crops, notably rice, in the cultivation of which by dint of enormous effort they were able to make use of the most barren wastelands.

---

21 Matsui, "Economic Aspects," pp. 59ff.; United States Senate, Sixty-first Congress, *Immigrants in Industry*, pp. 189–90.
22 Jean Pajus, *The Real Japanese California* (Berkeley: James J. Gillick, 1937), p. 79; Daniels, *Politics of Prejudice*, p. 87.

Thus, the Japanese began to branch out of agricultural wage labor by purchasing small tracts of barren land at very low prices. Since they were able to cultivate this land more successfully than others had anticipated, they began to make money in agriculture.[23]

The issei shift from farm labor to independent and contract farming proved an embarrassment to large California agricultural concerns for two reasons. Of these two the direct competition of Japanese in the produce market was probably the less important. The Japanese system of intensive cultivation was successful only with particular crops, notably truck vegetables, berries, and flowers. To a considerable degree, white growers were uninterested in these specialties "because of the backbreaking labor involved."[24] Moreover, Japanese competition in agricultural products was limited to specific California markets, especially Los Angeles and San Francisco. Japanese agriculture was an insignificant competitor on the national market toward which California growers oriented their enterprise. However, the Japanese withdrawal from farm labor disconcerted California growers who relied on Japanese labor to harvest their crops. This refusal to serve as a permanent harvest labor force probably inflamed California growers more than did the direct competition of Japanese in the produce market.[25]

Through the Alien Land Law of 1913, California growers hoped to force the Japanese out of agricultural self-employment and into the position of agricultural laborers. The law drastically restricted the right of aliens ineligible for citizenship to own, rent, or lease agricultural land. However, the Japanese found loopholes in the law and were thereby able to progress in California agriculture until 1920. An important means of circumventing the law was to buy or lease land in the name of the native-born children of the issei farmers. As citizens, the nisei infants were exempt from the provisions of the

[23] Yamato Ichihashi, *Japanese in the United States,* pp. 178–206; T. Iyenaga and Kenoske Sato, *Japan and the California Problem* (New York: G. P. Putnam's Sons, 1921), p. 132.
[24] Bradford Smith, *Americans from Japan* (Philadelphia: J. B. Lippincott, 1948), p. 237.
[25] State Board of Control of California, *California and the Oriental,* p. 101; Daniels, *Politics of Prejudice,* p. 89.

law debarring landholding by aliens. In response to this successful evasion, California enacted a strengthened land law in 1920. This law was effectively administered and plugged up the loopholes previously permitting the Japanese to flourish in agriculture. As a result, Japanese agricultural holdings declined from 458,026 acres in 1920 to 330,053 in 1923 and 304,966 in 1925.[26] But, although the California growers were successful in restricting Japanese agriculture, they were not successful in forcing the Japanese population to serve as agricultural laborers. Banished from the soil, the Japanese moved to the cities. Although this tendency doubtless reflected the general rural-urban migration and its impersonal causes, the Japanese migration to the cities began in 1920—reflecting the precipitating effect of the stringent land law.[27]

In the early transition from agricultural labor to independent farming, the social organization of Japanese farm laborers played an important role. The Japanese boardinghouse keepers with their ken affiliations doubled as employment agents for their roomers. The boardinghouse keepers maintained connections with Japanese agricultural "bosses." The bosses recruited agricultural work crews and negotiated directly with the California farmers for the employment of their crews.[28] The system was quite popular with the growers, for it enabled them to secure labor through contact with appropriate bosses who took the entire responsibility of recruiting, transporting, and paying the crew. Rancher and farm laborer confronted one another only through the mediation of the boss. Unlike a labor contractor, a Japanese boss was an agent of his crew rather than a solo entrepreneur. In their contractual relationships with the growers, agricultural bosses were outspokenly mercenary on behalf of their crews. They negotiated with the employers concerning the wage rate and unhesitatingly allocated their crew to whichever rancher offered the men the best terms. The bosses were also quite prepared to take their crew out of any farmer's field the instant a competitor offered

---

[26] Ichihashi, *Japanese*, p. 196; Modell, "Japanese of Los Angeles," p. 35; Daniels, *Politics of Prejudice*, p. 88.

[27] Ichihashi, *Japanese*, p. 101; Nodera, "Survey of Vocational Activities," pp. 8–9.

[28] United States Senate, Sixty-first Congress, *Immigrants in Industry*, pp. 45–50, 62; Modell, "Japanese of Los Angeles," pp. 56–57.

a higher rate. Indeed, this propensity of the Japanese agricultural boss sometimes involved the violation of contractual agreements.[29]

The Japanese boss system in agricultural labor constituted an embryonic form of trade unionism. Insofar as the kenjinkai were able to monopolize the supply of Japanese agricultural labor, the Japanese boss was perforce dependent on the kenjinkai (through the boardinghouses) for his agricultural crew. Moreover, boss and crew typically shared a loyalty to a ken, dialect, religious sect, and circle of friends. Under these circumstances, relationships between boss and crew could not be entirely commercial. The boss was thus inhibited in the tendency to define himself as a profit-maximizing entrepreneur of agricultural labor and induced to take on the role of representative of his crew. The counterpart of the fraternal social ties uniting boss and crew was the strictly mercenary relationship between boss and employer. The contract labor system became "the central instrument" of the Japanese rise from agricultural day labor to independent farming.[30] Prefectural control of the labor supply and of the contractor enabled Japanese farm hands to extract maximally favorable terms from white ranchers and so expedited the development of widespread proprietary status.

In independent farming, the Japanese made similar use of thorough organization and cooperation. According to the California Board of Control, in 1920 there were nineteen local affiliates of the Japanese Agricultural Association of Southern California and thirty-six associations in northern and central California affiliated with the Japanese Agricultural Association and the California Farmers Cooperative Association.[31] Almost every Japanese farmer belonged to some Japanese agricultural organization. These associations were organized along the familiar lines of the trade guild, taking as their purpose the marketing of members' produce, control of prices and

[29] Matsui, "Economic Aspects," p. 72; Iyenaga and Sato, *Japan and the California Problem*, p. 127; Robert E. Park and Herbert A. Miller, *Old World Traits Transplanted* (New York: Harper and Brothers, 1921), pp. 177–78.
[30] Masakazu Iwata, "The Japanese Immigrants in California Agriculture," p. 28; Lloyd H. Fisher, *The Harvest Labor Market in California* (Cambridge: Harvard University Press, 1953), p. 25.
[31] State Board of Control, *California and the Oriental*, p. 104.

wages, regulation of labor disputes and of internal competition,
protection of farmers' interests, and guardianship of the social welfare
of members' families.[32]

The most striking feature of the pre-World War II Japanese
economy in California was the liaison between Japanese farmers
and urban Japanese wholesalers and retailers of farm produce. Japanese sellers specialized in crops that were largely monopolized by
Japanese growers. Since the bulk of Japanese trade with whites was
in agricultural products, the rural-urban liaison provided the critical
prop to the Japanese-American economy.[33] Marketing arrangements
were complex. In southern California, the Japanese farmers' associations of Guadalupe, San Luis Obispo, Pismo Beach, and
Lompoc, in conjunction with the Japanese Produce Merchants' Association of Los Angeles, formed the Japanese Cooperative Farm
Industry (JCFI) of Southern California in 1929. Jointly maintained
by the farmers and the merchants, this association controlled Japanese agriculture in Southern California. The Japanese Cooperative
Farm Industry took charge of produce distribution through Japanese-
owned outlets such as the Southern California Flower Market and
the City Market of Los Angeles.[34] The white-owned Wholesale
Terminal Market in Los Angeles posed a special problem for Japanese farmers. To deal with it they founded the Nippon-California
Farmers Association in 1909. This body represented the interests of
Japanese growers in negotiations with the market.[35]

The JCFI studied the produce market continuously in order to
determine the amount of produce which could be marketed while
maintaining the price. It also coordinated the activities of farmers
and merchants for their mutual benefit. A special fund reimbursed
farmers whose produce had been dumped by the JCFI in order to
maintain the price. The JCFI collected the daily proceeds from the
purchasers, forwarded them to the local Japanese farmers' as-

[32] Iwata, "Japanese Immigrants," p. 33; Fukuoka, "Mutual Life," p. 27.

[33] Bloom and Riemer, *Removal*, pp. 82–83; R. D. McKenzie, "The Oriental Finds
a Job," *Survey* 56 (May 1, 1926): 218; Davis McEntire, "An Economic and Social
Study of Population Movements in California, 1850–1944" (Ph.D. diss., Harvard
University, 1947), p. 292.

[34] Fukuoka, "Mutual Life," pp. 10, 28; Iwata, "Japanese Immigrants," p. 34.

[35] Nodera, "Survey of Vocational Activities," p. 108.

sociations which then issued checks to the individual farmers, so that farmers never confronted the market as individuals. Like other Japanese associations, the Cooperative Farm Industry held in reserve a welfare fund for the benefit of members. Of the income of the association, 40 percent went for operating costs and 60 percent for welfare and relief of needy members.[36]

Japanese cooperation in agriculture was, however, primarily informal. Japanese farmers spontaneously organized systems of mutual aid at the local level.[37] The Great Depression stimulated the JCFI to develop formal controls to supplement mutual aid on the local level. The Japanese experienced some strain in attempting to operate large secondary associations, because parochial and personalistic social connections constantly influenced operating patterns.[38] One way of circumventing this problem was to create larger structures by piling up primary grouplets. Most of the larger Japanese farms in California were amalgams of the holdings of several smaller families. The families operated the joint acreage as a sort of cooperative.[39]

The Japanese farmer involved in cooperative relationships with his Japanese neighbors could not operate his farm as a solo entrepreneur. Since others had connected their interest with his in meaningful ways, others had a legitimate interest in how an individual managed his enterprise. If a Japanese farmer were tempted to lease more land than he was able to manage, neighboring farmers would warn him against overextension. Should a farmer neglect his land, thereby jeopardizing those who had countersigned his notes, the neighborhood undertook a sterner warning. Where a farmer was in danger of economic collapse, Japanese neighbors would descend upon the farm and by mutual effort bring the land "up to proper condition as speedily as possible." A persistent individualism manifesting itself in an unwillingness to manage the farm as others thought it ought to be managed involved, in the extreme case, the

---

[36] Fukuoka, "Mutual Life," pp. 28, 37ff.; Matsui, "Economic Aspects," pp. 79–80.

[37] State Board of Control, *California and the Oriental*, p. 82; J. Merle Davis, "The Orientals," in *Immigrant Backgrounds*, ed. Henry Pratt Fairchild (New York: John Wiley, 1927), p. 189.

[38] Fukuoka, "Mutual Life," p. 70; Miyamoto, *Social Solidarity*, p. 78.

[39] National Labor Relations Board, "Los Angeles County Vegetable Growers Survey" (typewritten; Los Angeles: National Labor Relations Board, March 6, 1937), p. 5.

denial of cooperation—and subsequent banishment of the individualist from the Japanese economic structure.[40]

### JAPANESE FISHERMEN

Cooperative practices also prevailed among Japanese fishermen in California. Japanese fishermen tended to settle in communities populated by persons from their own ken. The important fishing community of Terminal Island, East San Pedro, for example, was settled originally by Japanese fishermen from the village of Taiji. These fishermen organized the Japanese Fishermen's Association of San Pedro in 1907. The association took charge of Japanese fishing activities—overseeing prices, working conditions, apprenticeship, welfare, and politicoeconomic representation of Japanese fishing interests. The association organized strikes against the canneries on behalf of higher prices for raw fish. The fishermen were convinced of the economic value of cooperation through the association:

> This association has . . . forced the price of fish up. When the price has fallen, the fall has not been to the low point that occurred before the rise began.
>
> .    .    .    .    .    .    .    .    .    .    .    .    .
>
> I have no hesitation in saying that wherever we find association principles ignored, a low rate of prices prevails, and the reverse is true where organization is perfected. The most approved remedy for low prices is cooperation.[41]

Shortly after its founding, the association erected the Fisherman Hall Community Center. This center busied itself with the extensive social, fraternal, and welfare activities of the trade guild.

### INDUSTRIAL PATERNALISM

In view of the racial discrimination experienced by Japanese in the general labor market, the characteristic paternalism of pre-World War II Japanese business is the more understandable. Since Japanese employees had little opportunity to secure employment in the general economy other than in menial positions, the Japanese-American economy was perforce their only alternative. In the Japanese economy, work was largely available only through the medi-

---

[40] State Board of Control, *California and the Oriental*, p. 82.
[41] Kawasaki, "Japanese Community," p. 132.

ation of kin and kenjin. To receive a job in the Japanese-American economy was to become the recipient of a benevolence bestowed upon one by virtue of social connections. Typically, the relevant social connections were those linking the issei so that nisei workers secured employment on the basis of their parents' social connections.

By virtue of the intrusion of fraternal ties into the economy, matters of wages and hours were largely removed from the direction of the market and hinged on normative conventions, custom, and social obligation. Under this control, the inhibition on the exploitation of Japanese workers by their employers was the very social obligation by which an employee had managed to secure a job in the first place. An unjust or exploitative employer could be curbed only through social pressures. Such pressures constituted the only legitimated defense of the Japanese worker. Traditionalism and paternalism in employment relations imposed on the employer the duty of fair treatment for his employees in return for the employees' loyalty and submission. Complaining, striking, and quitting—the defense of the Western worker against exploitation—were denied to the Japanese employee of a Japanese-owned firm.[42] The Americanized nisei experienced especial difficulty in conforming to the normative requirements of traditional Japanese paternalism:

> We had to put up with this sort of thing because jobs were so scarce and there were family obligations. My employer was a fellow church member and a friend of the family so he took advantage of me and honestly felt that he was my benefactor. The Japanese employers figured that the *Nisei* workers were part of a family system and that is why they took advantage. It may have been the system in Japan, but I could not take it.
>
> .  .  .  .  .  .  .  .  .  .  .  .  .  .
>
> [The issei employers] expected us to put in this overtime because it was supposed to be our duty to the store. Their idea was that it was the employee's responsibility to come to the aid of the company when it was busy. They certainly had funny ideas about a worker's duty to the company.[43]

[42] T. Shibutani, "Memorandum on a Comparative Study of the Resettlement Program in Chicago and St. Louis" (typewritten; Chicago: Evacuation and Resettlement Study, 1943). Also see La Violette, *Americans of Japanese Ancestry*, pp. 56–57, 91; Kitano, *Japanese Americans*, p. 20.

[43] Charles Kikuchi, "The Social Adjustment Process of the Japanese-American

The employers took the view that in hiring this or that individual they had bestowed a benevolence that obligated the favorite to the employer and justified very long hours, low pay, and hard work.[44] This aspect of the relationship was peculiarly American in that it stemmed, ultimately, from the shortage of work caused by Japanese exclusion from the general economy. But, of course, Japanese culture contributed to this result too.

Low pay, hard work, and long hours were the normal lot of the Japanese worker. But it is difficult to lay categorically the entire blame for such exploitation on the Japanese employer. After all, the small Japanese firms survived only on the basis of hard work and long hours. Certainly the nisei were very naive about the Japanese situation in California and heaped onto their employers frustrations which might more properly have been directed to the system of racial discrimination which barred them from all but menial positions in the general economy. Ultimately, this system was responsible for the economic plight of the Japanese worker. Then, too, the Americanization of the nisei caused them to perceive as exploitative economic relationships which were customary among the issei.[45]

---

Resettlers to Chicago During the Wartime Years" (M.A. thesis, Columbia University, 1947), p. 48; R. Nishimoto, "Japanese in Personal Service and Urban Trade" (typewritten, n.d.), p. 44. See also Leonard Broom and John I. Kitsuse, *The Managed Casualty* (Berkeley and Los Angeles: University of California Press, 1956), p. 10.

[44] La Violette, *Americans of Japanese Ancestry*, pp. 81–82.

[45] Jitsuichi Masuoka, "Changing Moral Bases of the Japanese Family in Hawaii," *Sociology and Social Research* 21 (November-December 1936): 163–66; Matsukichi Amano, "A Study of Employment Patterns and a Measure of Employee Attitudes in Japanese Firms at Los Angeles" (Ph.D. diss., University of California, Los Angeles, 1966), pp. 14–38. Cf. James C. Abegglen, *The Japanese Factory* (Glencoe, Ill.: Free Press, 1958), p. 99; Robert Evans, Jr., "Evolution of the Japanese System of Employer-Employee Relations, 1868–1945," *Business History Review* 44 (spring 1970): 110–125.

# Immigrant Brotherhood in Chinatown

# 5

Virtually all Chinese in the United States before World War II emigrated from one of seven districts in the South China province of Kwangtung, whose major port is Canton. In the United States the Cantonese immigrants early organized themselves into district associations, each of which recruited its membership from a particular Kwangtung district. For example, the largest of these district associations, the Ning Yeung Company, is composed of Sze Yap speaking Cantonese hailing from the Toi-shan district of Kwangtung province.[1] In 1942 there were seven district associations in San Francisco. Each association recruited its membership from particular Kwangtung localities. These seven district associations (or companies) were autonomous, but each was a member of the Chung Wah Kung Saw ("Meeting Hall of the Chinese People"), now officially known as the Chinese Consolidated Benevolent Association.[2] In the early period the officers of the city's Benevolent Association were elected by representatives of the various district associations. But surname associations and interest aggregations now have a voice in this election. The association has acted historically as the spokesman of the Chinese population, and the president of the association is popularly deemed the "mayor of Chinatown." The association itself is more widely known to the American public as the Chinese Six Companies. That name derives from an early period of Chinese-American history when the constituent district associations ("com-

---

[1] Gunther Barth, *Bitter Strength*, pp. 86–90; Stanford M. Lyman, "The Structure of Chinese Society in Nineteenth-Century America," p. 193; Virginia Heyer, "Patterns of Social Organization in New York City's Chinatown" pp. 44ff.; Wen-hui Chung Chen, "Changing Socio-Cultural Patterns of the Chinese Community in Los Angeles," p. 230.

[2] William Hoy, *The Chinese Six Companies*, pp. 14–15; Betty Lee Sung, *Mountain of Gold*, p. 136.

panies") were six in number. This structure asserted itself in all of the American cities in which Chinese dwelt in any number.

As a congress of deputies from the district organizations, the Six Companies created an organizational liaison among regional group- ings. Japanese *kenjinkai* lacked a similar congress in which they could be represented as districts. The Japanese Association of America, which served in the pre-World War II period as the political spokes- man for the Japanese population, was an entirely separate organ- ization. Membership in the Japanese Associations was voluntary and individual. The local Japanese associations elected the leader- ship of the organization. Insofar as Pacific localities tended to reflect regional origins, the local associations did tend to reflect the dom- inant kenjinkai of their neighborhoods; but any such overlap was entirely informal rather than structural, as among the Chinese.[3]

The Chinese Six Companies and constituent district associations were not voluntary organizations.[4] The officials of these institutions claimed that every Chinese in the United States was "automatically" a member of the Six Companies through his "automatic" member- ship in the district association representing him. Non-dues-paying self-defined nonmembers were nonetheless included on the member- ship rolls of the district associations and Six Companies. In actual fact, most Chinese were usually in arrears of dues to district as- sociation and Six Companies. Businessmen have been the only regular dues payers.[5] Yet even among non-dues-paying China-born persons, few would ever have denied that they remained in some sense members of their respective district association or of the Six Companies. The overstated claims of universality of membership and "compulsory" enrollment apparently did authentically represent a tacit legitimation of such claims by the vast majority of foreign-born Chinese.

[3] Michinari Fujita, "The Japanese Associations in America," *Sociology and Social Research* 13 (January-February 1929): 211; E. Manchester Boddy, *Japanese in America* (Los Angeles: by the author, 1921), pp. 167–71.

[4] Gor Yun Leong, *Chinatown Inside Out* (New York, 1936), p. 32; Lyman, "Structure," p. 204; Chen, "Chinese Community," p. 228.

[5] Chen, "Chinese Community," pp. 249–50; Heyer, "Patterns," pp. 69–70; Lyman, "Structure," pp. 205–11.

## CLAN AND DIALECT

Among the Chinese in America, surname associations reflected the persistence of the clan (*tsu*). Like the district associations, the family name associations included automatically every Chinese in the United States; however, the basis of inclusion was not regional origins but surname.[6] Thus, the Yee family association automatically included all Chinese of the surname Yee; the Wong association included those with the surname Wong. Single family associations were universally Toi-shanese because these immigrants were most numerous among the Chinese population, so that surname groups were appropriately large. Multiple family name associations were, for the most part, ad hoc combinations necessitated by the scanty representation of a clan among the immigrants and the consequent necessity of banding together with others to achieve an association of adequate size. Thus, for example, the Chee Tuck Sam Tuck family association included persons with the surnames Choi, Yeung, Eng, Chiang, and Tsao.[7] Members of surname associations addressed one another as "cousin" even when they were not so related in a Western sense. This salutation mirrored the fraternal social relations characteristic of the Cantonese sib.

Clan ties affected the pattern of settlement. The various Chinatown colonies around the United States each had one or more modal family groupings that dominated the colony's political, economic, and social life. A city's Chinatown came to be known by the clan or clans most prominent in it. In the large San Francisco enclave, for example, the surnames Chan, Lee, and Wong have predominated. The Yee clan dominated the Chinatowns of Detroit, Pittsburgh, and Cleveland. In Chicago Moi was the largest clan; and the Ong family was powerful in Phoenix. Gee was the strongest clan in Oakland. In Seattle the Chin family was dominant, while Jung and Leong shared dominance in Bakersfield.[8] The Chinese believed that the dominant

[6] San Francisco Chinese Chamber of Commerce, "San Francisco's Chinatown," p. 3.
[7] Heyer, "Patterns," p. 66; Ching Chao Wu, "Chinatowns: A Study of Symbiosis and Assimilation" (Ph.D. diss., University of Chicago, 1928), pp. 239–43; Lyman, "Structure," p. 173; Chen, "Chinese Community," p. 104.
[8] Chen, "Chinese Community," p. 105; Wu, "Chinatowns," p. 239; Leong, *China-*

clan in each city controlled business opportunities and protected its
"cousins' " interest against other clans. Naturally, aggressively pro-
tectionist policies on the part of dominant family groupings tended
to deter Chinese from minority clans from settling in an area. In
addition there was, of course, the simple propensity of persons to
settle where their friends had already located.

In three of the seven districts in Kwangtung from which Chinese
emigrated to the United States, the prevailing dialect was Sam Yap
("three districts' dialect"). In the other four districts, Sze Yap ("four
districts' dialect") was spoken. The broadest line of class differ-
entiation followed the Sam Yap–Sze Yap distinction. The Sze Yap
speakers have greatly outnumbered the Sam Yap speakers, but the
Sam Yap speakers were of loftier social origins than the Sze Yap
speakers whom they, moreover, regarded as culturally backward.
Sam Yap speakers have historically tended to predominate in the
larger, more profitable businesses and in the free professions. Sze
Yap speakers, on the other hand, tended to be laborers or to operate
smaller businesses such as one-man laundries. Relations between the
two dialectal groups were strained and sometimes hostile. In 1894
a dispute between the two flared into violent conflict. Sze Yap
speakers boycotted the businesses of Sam Yap merchants and beat
up those whom they caught violating their boycott. In reply, the Sam
Yap merchant's association, the Chew Yut, took aggressive counter-
measures against Sze Yap small business. To offset this pressure, the
Sze Yap formed a merchant's association of their own, the Hok
Shung. Both sides employed tong hatchetmen to terrorize their opponents. Ultimately, the intervention of the Chinese consul permitted
the opponents to agree to an armistice.[9]

### MUTUAL AID AND SOCIAL WELFARE

Both district and surname associations claimed a benevolent and
social purpose. Actually, they observed a rudimentary division of

---

*town,* pp. 35, 56; S. W. Kung, *Chinese in American Life* (Seattle: University of
Washington Press, 1962), p. 222.

[9] U.S. Industrial Commission, "Chinese and Japanese Labor in the Mountain and
Pacific States," p. 777; Helen Virginia Cather, "The History of San Francisco's
Chinatown," pp. 61–62, 71; Hart H. North, "Chinese Highbinder Societies in Cal-
ifornia," *California Historical Society Quarterly* 27 (March 1948): 23.

labor, albeit not without some overlapping of activity. Surname associations tended to emphasize benevolent and fraternal activities, whereas the district associations interested themselves in business matters. The early and permanent representation of district associations as constituent bodies of the Six Companies indicates their businesslike character. In part, this division of labor reflected only the larger constituency of the district associations and the consequently greater ease of administration through these units. In part, however, the commercial interests of the district associations mirrored the secondary nature of regional ties. Clan ties were family ties. Thus, clan members addressed one another in relationship terms but persons from the same region did not.

Before World War II, the surname associations performed many useful services for their memberships. They helped newcomers to find work and lodging, relieved the sick, buried the indigent dead, and helped widows and orphans to return to China. Although the scope of their family service has receded since 1940, the surname associations continue to be active in the welfare field. But even in their prime, the family name associations were not the principal agents of benevolence or mutual aid among the Chinese. The units actually performing these services were the village associations.[10] Regional and clan loyalties intersected at the level of the village. The village associations occupied an interstitial lowest-level position in the organizational tree of both family associations and district associations. In South China, kinship terms were extended to unrelated villagers, for example, to villagers not sharing the same surname. However, frequently surname and village coincided so that villagers tended to be of the same clan. Beyond the village level, of course, the two organizing principles went their separate ways so that persons from the same district were less frequently of the same clan. At the village level where the principles of family name and location coincided, reciprocated loyalties were naturally most intense.

Normally, only those indigent came to the attention of family or district association who lacked integration in some lower order village community. Since few Chinese lacked such ties, few Chinese

[10] Chinese Chamber of Commerce, "San Francisco's Chinatown," p. 3; Heyer, "Patterns," p. 84; Lyman, "Structure," pp. 304–08.

applied to family or district associations for assistance. Moreover, upon petition for relief, family associations were likely first of all to inquire into an applicant's community background in order to determine which lower order circle ought to care for him. Anxious to avoid the disgrace of being found publicly remiss in caring for its own indigent, each such community had a concrete motive to make independent provision for the welfare of all those in its circle. In this manner the social pressure of the larger community reinforced the moral integration of the constituent subcommunities. Of course, a man with no clansmen or fellow villagers near was in a perilous position. Traditional Chinese recognized no benevolent obligations to non-kin.[11]

In New York City some village associations included as many as 800 or 900 persons. Most village associations maintained a one-room headquarters, usually in an apartment house. Known as the *fong*, groupings of this order usually included from 10 to 100 members. Fongs affiliated with either district or family name organizations.

> The *fongs* are Sunday groupings and they are to a large extent recreation groupings. In them elder men most often take responsibility for the younger men, and in them the able bodied look after those who are too old to work. In these aspects they are very much like extended families. Indeed, they are, in many cases, no more than an extension of the male population of the village *tsu*.[12]

Fong and tsu provided the organizational nuclei for the operation of the *hui* financial system. The fongs took the responsibility for aiding member students to finance and complete their education and for helping members to establish themselves in business. "Loans are . . . made but it is more frequent for money to be given outright."[13] Fong members felt a moral obligation to secure employment for a recently arrived member of their circle. Such employment was ordinarily located either in their own business or in that of some one of their friends. Those unemployed or unable to work more frequently se-

11 Mély Giok-Lan Tan, "Social Mobility and Assimilation: The Chinese in the United States," p. 208; Stuart H. Cattell, "Health, Welfare, and Social Organization in Chinatown, New York," p. 66.
12 Heyer, "Patterns," pp. 62–63. See also Sung, *Gold Mountain*, pp. 134–35; Cattell, "Health," pp. 36–37.
13 Heyer, "Patterns," p. 60.

cured aid from fong members than from distant "cousins" or from their district association. Chinese rarely appeared on the rolls of publicly sponsored indoor or outdoor relief.[14]

Between 1900 and 1940, in only two instances did the Chinese obtain assistance from tax funds. Following the San Francisco fire and earthquake of April 1906, when Chinatown was "entirely burned out," the Chinese did receive some public aid. In proportion to their numbers, however, the Chinese received only one-thirtieth of the free soup and rehabilitation accorded other San Franciscans. Moreover, such emergency assistance as the Chinese received was thrust on them "as only a few Chinese applied voluntarily for relief." In the main, assistance to Chinese rendered homeless and destitute by the disaster was entirely provided by the Chinese themselves. The Six Companies, district associations, and family associations collected funds from Chinese in the United States and organized their own relief for the refugees.[15]

The second occasion on which the Chinese secured aid from public authorities was the Great Depression. The extent of this aid is difficult to ascertain with precision; but conservative estimates based on official statistics indicate that the percentage of Chinese receiving federal unemployment relief in 1933 was generally much lower than the figures for Negroes and whites, though not as low as those for Japanese (Table 7). These low figures are the more remarkable in view of the poverty of the Chinese relative to more advantaged whites. The Chinese resort to public assistance was originally mediated through the Six Companies. "With the exception of a few cases in the main registry, no Chinese single men applied for [federal] relief until February, 1933, when a Chinese Single Men's Registry was established in the Building of the Chinese Consolidated Benevolent As-

---

[14] See U.S. Department of the Interior, Census Office, *Eleventh Census: 1890*, pt. 1, *Report on Crime, Pauperism, and Benevolence in the United States* (Washington, D.C.: U.S. Government Printing Office, 1896), p. 269; U.S. Bureau of the Census, *Paupers in Almshouses, 1910* (Washington, D.C.: U.S. Government Printing Office, 1915), p. 22; Rev. O. Gibson, *The Chinese in America* (Cincinnati: Hitchcock and Walden, 1877), pp. 364–65; J. Merle Davis, "The Orientals," in *Immigrant Backgrounds*, ed. Henry Pratt Fairchild (New York, 1927), p. 184; *New York Times*, June 21, 1936, sec. 2, p. 1, col. 7.

[15] Russell Sage Foundation, *San Francisco Relief Survey* (New York, 1913), p. 75.

TABLE 7

*Persons Receiving Federal Emergency Unemployment Relief as Percentage of All Residents by Race or Nationality for Selected Cities, October 1933*

|  | Negro | White | Chinese | Japanese |
|---|---|---|---|---|
| Chicago | 38.4 | 10.1 | 4.3[a] | [b] |
| Los Angeles | 33.3[a] | 8.8[a] | 3.6[a] | 0.3[a] |
| New York | 23.9 | 9.2 | 1.2[a] | 0.1[a] |
| Philadelphia | 34.4 | 8.2 | 1.8[a] | [b] |
| San Francisco | 21.9[a] | 11.0[a] | 13.3[a] | 0.0[a] |

SOURCE: Federal Emergency Relief Administration, *Unemployment Relief Census: October, 1933. United States Summary*, Report no. 1 (Washington, D.C.: U.S. Government Printing Office, 1943), Table 9–A, p. 78.

[a] Estimated figures. For basis of estimation, see Appendix, p. 191.
[b] Total resident population less than 1,000.

sociation." The Six Companies' registry issued meal tickets to the unemployed and also provided shelter for the homeless. In undertaking this exceptional relief activity at a time of mass unemployment and great distress, the San Francisco Six Companies applied directly to public authorities on behalf of destitute members. The role of the Federal Emergency Relief Administration (FERA) was at first limited to footing the relief bill. Disbursement of FERA funds was in the hands of the Six Companies until February 1935, when its shelter was closed "as the policy of the FERA encouraged individual case work rather than congregated care in the shelter."[16]

Even during the Depression, the Chinese did not abandon traditional benevolence. In the fongs, family associations, and trade guilds, traditional mutual aid prevailed. Some family associations kept a barrel of rice in the foyer from which a "cousin" might remove without charge as much as he needed to feed himself or his family. The borrower was, however, expected to return the rice or the purchase price thereof whenever he found himself in more fortunate circumstances.[17] The family associations did not experience a problem of "relief chiselers" who took more rice than they needed, sold free association rice, or failed to return what they had received. The associations did not closely administer the dispensation of the rice,

[16] California State Emergency Relief Administration, "Survey of the Social Work Needs of the Chinese Population of San Francisco, California," p. 40.
[17] Richard Kock Dare, "The Economic and Social Adjustment of the San Francisco Chinese for the Past Fifty Years" (M. A. thesis, University of California, Berkeley, 1959), p. 13.

nor did they find it necessary to investigate the authenticity of the need of persons desirous of securing aid. Indeed, the system was noteworthy in that efforts were made to permit the needy to secure victuals unobtrusively, without a humiliating display of dependency. The family associations' uncautious approach to the dispensation of food reflected the social ties which knit together the "cousins." This relationship imposed on the more fortunate cousins the duty of relieving their unfortunate relatives and on the less fortunate cousins the obligation to deal correctly with the benevolent relief afforded them by their fellows.

Moreover, Chinese custom imposed on employers the duty of lending assistance to needy relatives. So long as the employer remained faithful to his paternalistic tradition, kin and friends in need had a preemptive claim on his assistance. In return for charitable and timely aid, the indigent were to owe their benefactor lavish praise and faithful service. For example, in the home of his father, a prosperous San Francisco merchant, Pardee Lowe recounts that "Many a kinsman coming for talk stayed not only overnight but for weeks—even in some cases years. Our neighborhood drygoods store was a perpetual Chinese work-relief project. It was to these relatives mainly that we were 'children of virtue.' "[18] In hard times, it was meritoriously customary for Chinese employers to take on *extra* help in their businesses, rather than to fire surplus hands. This custom contrasts dramatically with capitalistic theory and practice, and nicely indicates the manner in which the clannish social relationships of employer and employee influenced the conduct of Chinese business.[19]

### INSTITUTIONAL RULES

In their practical day-to-day operation, the Chinese district and surname associations did not provoke a lively interest among the Chinatown population. Active membership participation was not even encouraged. Active participation came under the aegis of fong and family circle, which were also the principal welfare institutions.

[18] Pardee Lowe, *Father and Glorious Descendant* (Boston: Little Brown, 1943), pp. 66–67.
[19] Carl Glick, *Shake Hands with the Dragon* (New York: Whittlesey House, 1941), p. 241.

The daily activities of the territorial and surname associations were commercial and regulatory.

These associations administered rules of business registration, goodwill (*p'o tai*), and location. Members were expected to register their businesses with the associations to which they belonged. Sales of businesses or of business goodwill (*p'o tai*) had also to be conducted on the premises of the institution before Chinese witnesses. For these services, the institutions charged modest fees.[20] If they wanted institutional recognition and protection, member proprietors were obliged to adhere to these forms and to pay the requisite fees. Since the territorial and surname associations adjudicated disputes and enforced the commercial law in Chinatowns, businessmen were anxious to enjoy their recognition. Businessmen who complied only with American law did not thereby come to possess a title to property recognized by Chinatown associations.

Of course, Chinatown associations had no redress in American courts against members who chose to violate their rules. An Irish policeman ignored the governmental authority these associations claimed for themselves in Chinatowns. Social pressure, boycott, and ostracism were the only sanctions available. Threats of revealing illegal entry into the United States could also be made whenever an aggrieved association was in possession of this information about a rule violator. Normally, these sanctions were adequate for the enforcement of commercial rules generally understood and accepted by the China-born population. On occasion, however, exceptional recalcitrance occurred. In the early days, tong hatchetmen provided an ultimate sanction for Chinese amenable to no other.

In thus administering and enforcing the rules, Chinatown associations intervened actively in commerce. This intervention distinguished them from the Japanese kenjinkai which did not formally intervene in the conduct of member-owned businesses. Such intervention was, among the Japanese, entirely under the aegis of the various trade guilds. Insofar as Japanese trade guilds were full of kenjin, prefectural affiliations came to play an important role in Japanese commercial life. But the Chinese territorial and even

---

[20] Mary Roberts Coolidge, *Chinese Immigration*, pp. 123–25; Leong, *Chinatown*, pp. 36–37; Heyer, "Patterns," pp. 131–32.

surname associations formally intervened in the conduct of member-owned businesses, even though their role was regulatory. Hence, Chinese business was subject not only to the tongs and to the trade guilds, but also to the regulations imposed by family associations, district associations, and the Six Companies. In sum, Chinese business was subject to a good deal more institutional regulation than was Japanese business, and the link between Old World social status and New World occupation was even more pronounced among the Chinese than among the Japanese.

## CHINESE TRADE GUILDS

In every line of work in which Chinese were extensively engaged, they organized trade guilds. The most important trade guilds were those of the laundrymen, cigar makers, restauranteurs, clothing and underwear manufacturers, and domestic servants.[21] As occupational associations, the trade guilds were ostensibly open to all Chinese engaged in a particular line of work. However, the Chinese trade guilds developed local memberships drawn principally from a particular surname or district association. Thus, in San Francisco, the Sam Yup Company controlled wholesale merchandising, tailoring, and the manufacture of overalls and shirts. The Yan Wo Company dominated the laundry business. Hotel work came to be a virtual monopoly of the Tom family. In the fruit and candy store business, the Dear family reigned. In some cases, the emergent trade guild became a formal (rather than informal) adjunct to the district association; for example, Hakka cooks were organized into a trade guild as a subdivision of their district association, the Tsung Tsin Company. Among the Chinese fruit farmers in the Sacramento Valley of California, all of the tenant farmers were members of the Yeung Wo Company.[22]

The Chinese trade guilds enforced the rules of location, registra-

[21] Rev. Ira M. Condit, *The Chinaman as We See Him*, pp. 68–69; Rev. A. W. Loomis, "The Chinese Six Companies," *Overland Monthly* 1 (September 1868): 226.

[22] Chinese Chamber of Commerce, "San Francisco's Chinatown," pp. 2–3; Cather, "History," p. 24; Lyman, "Structure," p. 322. Also see Milton L. Barnett, "Kinship as a Factor Affecting Cantonese Economic Adaptation in the United States," pp. 40–48. Cf. Francis L. K. Hsu and J. H. Hu, "Guild and Kinship Among the Butchers in West Town," *American Sociological Review* 10 (June 1945): 357–64.

tion, and compensation as did the district associations, family associations, and to some extent the Six Companies. For example, the rules of the old laundrymen's guild specified that there must be at least ten doorways between Chinese laundries. The trade guilds also regulated wages, working conditions, terms of apprenticeship, competition, and prices. In this effort they exerted more active influence on the daily conduct of Chinese business than did the other Chinese associations. The guild house served as a social center and an employment office for members. Board and lodgings were also available. Rules of the laundrymens' guild permitted only those to open laundries who had gone through an apprenticeship, paid their fees, and joined the guild. "If a non-guild employer starts a washhouse, the guilds will underbid him and run him out, but their constitution forbids them to underbid each other." According to H. H. Bancroft, the laundrymens' guild sometimes hired tong assassins to kill nonguild laundry operators.[23] This extreme punishment followed the Chinese pattern; in Old World cities the trade guilds also claimed enormous authority and murdered any who violated their rules.[24]

Chinese trade guilds were not trade unions. Both employers and employees were characteristically enrolled in the guild of their trade. The interest of the trade as such was supposed to determine the policy of the trade guild. That the Chinese trade guilds were able more or less persistently to suppress the employer-employee distinction and to assert the interest of the trade as such is attributable in great part to their patterns of recruitment. Recruitment tended to follow lines of dialect, regional origins, and clan and so to guarantee that masters and men would share some salient identity crosscutting class lines. In view of the clan, regional, and dialectal homogeneity of the trade guilds, their tendency to define the interest of the trade as the interest of the membership is the more understandable.[25] In

[23] Coolidge, *Chinese Immigration*, pp. 406–07; Hubert Howe Bancroft, *History of California*, 7 vols. (San Francisco: History Company, 1890), 7:347. See also Alexander McLeod, *Pigtails and Gold Dust* (Caldwell, Idaho: Caxton, 1947), p. 118.

[24] Kenneth Scott Latourette, *The Chinese: Their History and Culture*, 3rd ed. (New York: Macmillan, 1946), p. 576; Max Weber, *The Religion of China*, pp. 14–20.

[25] Barnett, "Kinship," p. 46. Cf. John Stewart Burgess, *The Guilds of Peking*

the laundry trade, for example, Cheng distinguished only two forms of apprenticeship: apprenticeship based on kinship and apprenticeship based on regional ties or personal friendship. Of these two forms, apprenticeship based only on friendship or regional ties was the more contractual. Although both the San Francisco and New York City laundry guilds had formal regulations concerning the terms and conditions of apprenticeship, Cheng nonetheless observed that apprenticeships based only on regional affiliation or friendship might be "badly exploited by the master." Fortunately, almost "every Chinese laundryman has family connections" so that exploitation of apprentices was, in Cheng's opinion, less common than it would otherwise have been.[26]

Since the Cantonese have traditionally preferred partnerships to solo proprietorships, their firms used relatively little hired help. Instead, the workers were partners and, therefore, co-owners of the firm. Partners were almost invariably clan "cousins." Moreover, when hired labor was required, the partners gave preference to fellow clansmen. "One would choose to buy from a brother's store, patronize the restaurants operated by members of the same family, employ persons with the same family name—such has been the moral obligation and the accepted mode of behavior."[27] This spirit of clannish fraternity gave a distinctly cooperative character to traditional Chinese-owned firms, and so tended to reduce employer-employee tensions. Traditional Chinese have, in fact, disapproved of Western patterns of industrial relations in which a solo entrepreneur orders around hired hands who are not also his kin. They have felt that this pattern invites labor trouble and internal dissension.

The laundry trade has been a mainstay of the Chinese economy in the United States since 1853. After World War I, Chinese hand

---

(New York: Columbia University Press, 1928), pp. 19, 211–12; Gideon Sjoberg, *The Preindustrial City* (Glencoe, Ill.: Free Press, 1960), p. 191.

26 David Te-chao Cheng, "Acculturation of the Chinese in the United States: A Philadelphia Study" (Ph.D. diss., University of Pennsylvania, 1946), p. 112. Also see Louis J. Beck, *New York's Chinatown* (New York: Bohemia, 1898), pp. 57–62; Paul C. P. Siu, "The Chinese Laundryman: A Study of Social Isolation" (Ph.D. diss., University of Chicago, 1953), p. 92.

27 Chen, "Chinese Community," p. 255. See also Siu, "Chinese Laundryman," pp. 92–102.

laundrymen began to experience intense business competition from mechanized steam laundries.[28] The white laundryman proved unable to compete with the steam laundry. His independent business gave way to a laundry–dry cleaning chain store. "The American steam laundry business hurt the Chinese laundrymen by encroaching on their markets, and it was entirely possible for a few large steam laundries in the hands of Chinese to do the same."[29] However, the Chinese Hand Laundry Alliance prevented this development. Under watchful regulation, a few Chinese-operated steam laundries were set up, and the hand laundrymen farmed out a portion of their wash to the steam laundries. The laundrymen continued to act as distributors and to perform finer laundry operations themselves. Mechanized laundries permitted the Chinese proprietors to reduce their hours of work and still to earn an "adequate" return. In this manner the guild organization of the laundry trade intervened to control mechanization of the trade. Proletarianization of these small entrepreneurs was checked, at least for some decades, by their extraordinary capacity to organize collective resistence.

### TONGS, TONG WARS, AND MERCHANTS

The U.S. Industrial Commission listed sixteen highbinder tongs in the United States in 1900, but a contemporary journalist claimed that there were in that year thirty tongs in San Francisco alone.[30] The two largest fighting tongs were the Hip Sing and the On Leong. Highbinder tongs were trade guilds of Chinese gangsters. As such, the tongs controlled gambling, opium, prostitution, extortion, and violence. Just as one could not open a laundry or restaurant without the approval of the relevant trade guild, so one could not traffic in prostitution, gambling, or opium without the consent and protection of a highbinder tong.

According to Mr. William Hoy, a spokesman for the San Francisco

[28] Siu, "Chinese Laundryman," p. 48. See also Barnett, "Kinship," p. 41; Chen, "Chinese Community," p. 338–39; Cather, "History," p. 10; Eliot Grinnell Mears, *Resident Orientals on the American Pacific Coast* (Chicago: University of Chicago Press, 1928), pp. 303–04.

[29] Heyer, "Patterns," p. 134–35.

[30] U.S. Industrial Commission, "Chinese and Japanese," p. 762; John E. Bennett, "The Chinese Tong Wars in San Francisco," *Harper's Weekly* 44 (August 11, 1900): 746–47.

Benevolent Association, the gangster tongs were originally formed to represent Chinese from smaller minority surnames who were few in number and felt themselves to be exploited by the dominant clans.[31] When it is recalled that clan membership was a virtual prerequisite for permission to take a job or open a business in the tightly controlled, institutionally dominated Chinatown economy, the plight of these minority Chinese becomes evident. Since the clans and district associations controlled admission to the various guilds, ineligible Chinese were virtually excluded from the economy. The same exclusion befell disgraced Chinese who were banished from their clan. According to Lyman, the founders of the Kwong Duck, Hip Sing, and Suey Sing tongs alleged that the "cause of their disaffiliation from clan or *kongsi* was unfair and arbitrary justice dispensed by the latter in matters of business or property." Two infamous tong men, Hong Ah Kay and Gaut Sing, are said to have been driven to their criminal trade because of dispossession by clan arbitrators.[32]

Unlike other Chinese associations, gangster tongs were open to all Chinese on the basis of "merit." Indeed, underworld gangs did not tolerate dual allegiances so that service as a hatchetman involved a clean break with ascribed loyalties to clan, district, and village. Initiation into a tong emphasized the hatchetman's inexorable commitment to the organization. For the veteran tong "soldier," expulsion from the tong was tantamount to a sentence of death. If the tong itself did not kill an offending member, the relatives of his murdered victims could freely avenge themselves on an expelled hatchetman no longer under the military protection of the tong.[33]

The fighting tongs clearly specified the rights and duties of recruited hatchetmen at the time of initiation. Contractual specification was necessary because recruits were unrelated so that ascribed moral obligations did not apply. In return for the risks of their occupation, tong soldiers received numerous welfare guarantees from their employers. In 1899 an American missionary turned over to the U.S.

---

[31] Hoy, *Six Companies*, p. 8; Chen, "Chinese Community," p. 270.
[32] Lyman, "Structure," p. 312.
[33] Winifred Raushenbush, "The Great Wall of Chinatown," *Survey* 56 (May 1, 1926): 156.

Industrial Commission a letter of appointment sent by the Chee Kung
Tong to a mercenary fighter. The letter specified the contractual quid
pro quo in the hatchetman's profession:

> To Lum Hip, *salaried soldier*:
> This tong appoints salaried soldiers to be ready to protect ourselves
> and assist others. . . .
> All, therefore, who undertake the military service of this tong must
> obey orders and without orders you must not dare to act. . . . You
> shall always work to the interest of the tong and never make your
> office a means of private revenge. . . .
> If in the discharge of your duties you are slain we will undertake to
> pay $500 sympathy money to your friends. . . .
> If you are wounded, a doctor will be engaged to heal your wounds,
> and if you are laid up for any length of time, you shall receive $10
> per month. If you are maimed and incapacitated for service, you shall
> receive the sum of $250 and a subscription shall be opened to defray
> the expenses of your passage [to China].
> This document is given as proof as an oral promise may not be
> credited. It is further stipulated that you in common with your com-
> rades shall exert yourself to kill or wound anyone at the direction of
> this tong. If in so doing you are arrested and have to endure the miseries
> of imprisonment, this society undertakes to send $100 every year to
> your family during the term of your incarceration.[34]

The rival tongs controlled conflict among themselves by staking
out territories over which they claimed exclusive control of illegal
activities. Thus, in New York City, the On Leong Tong monopolized
criminal activities on Mott Street in Chinatown, while the Hip Sings
claimed Doyer Street and part of Pell Street. "The whole city, where
Chinese restaurants and laundries exist, is also divided up into territories."[35] Violation of territorial sovereignty by a rival tong provided
a casus belli. Although disagreements between tongs were typically
settled without resort to violence, the tong war provided an ultimate
arbitrator in cases in which neither side was willing to compromise.
In nineteenth-century tong wars, fighters hacked at one another with

[34] United States Industrial Commission, "Chinese and Japanese," p. 771. See
also Stanford M. Lyman, *The Asian in the West*, pp. 33–56.
[35] Glick, *Shake Hands*, p. 262.

small axes and earned thereby the designation "hatchetmen." The warriors retained this title even after they discarded that weapon in favor of revolvers and machine guns.

The role of merchants in the tongs is difficult to assess. On some accounts, tong hatchetmen forced unwilling Chinese merchants to pay membership dues as a form of protection. Those who declined to pay were dragged from their stores, beaten or killed, and their equipment was smashed.[36] Dues-paying merchants received the protection of the hatchetmen. The protection which the tongs sold to merchants was protection from rival tongs as well as from the seller. Unprotected merchants were easy targets for any gang of tong hoodlums.

On the other hand, the tongs sometimes took a hand in resolving commercial disputes among districts or clans. According to a recent account, "rivalry between the tongs developed because of competition for business or for location among some Chinese merchants."[37] The role of tong violence in settling commercial disputes is apparent in the bitter On Leong–Hip Sing struggle at the turn of the century. Gunned down by Hip Sings in 1897, the legendary Little Pete had headed the On Leong war effort on behalf of Sam Yap commercial interests.[38]

So long as the Chinatown population was divided into ascriptively bounded, mutually hostile coteries, each jealously defending its interests, tong warfare offered the only solution to their business rivalries. The first step toward controlling this problem was the formation in 1910 of a unified Chinese Chamber of Commerce from a fusion of Chew Yut and Hok Shung. This fusion increased institutional control of the business rivalries that had precipitated the disastrous tong war of 1894. The second step was the formation of the Chinese Peace Society in 1913. The Peace Society provided a mediation service for embittered disputes which would, in the old

[36] Heyer, "Patterns," p. 95. Also see Lowe, *Father*, p. 85; C. N. Reynolds, "The Chinese Tongs," *American Journal of Sociology* 40 (March 1935): 221.

[37] George De Vos et al., "The Chinese Family in San Francisco: A Preliminary Survey" (mimeographed, 2 vols.; School of Social Welfare, University of California, Berkeley, 1966), 1:51. See also Rose Hum Lee, "The Hua-ch'iao in the United States of America," in *Colloquium on Overseas Chinese*, ed. Morton H. Fried (New York: Institute of Pacific Relations, 1958), pp. 38–39.

[38] Cather, "History," p. 64; Richard H. Dillon, *The Hatchet Men* (New York: Coward-McCann, 1962), p. 291.

days, have been referred to tong struggle for decision.[39] But only insofar as a superarching moral community has actually emerged have the Chinatowns overcome their need for private warriors.

### COMPARISON OF CHINESE AND JAPANESE

Among both Chinese and Japanese immigrants, kinship and regional origins were the strongest social ties. These ties had moral significance. Ties of blood and land were purely ascriptive in that they pinned every immigrant's social status on involuntary social associations in the Old World. A person had not chosen to be born in a particular place into a particular family; no one could change these facts. Nonetheless, these facts placed an immigrant in the Chinese or Japanese social order in North American cities.

Organized kinship and regional subgroups considered themselves morally obligated to look out for the social welfare of other people of their sort. To this end they carried on mutual aid among themselves, and so were able to exist without much assistance from public welfare authorities. The same ascriptively defined, mutually supportive moral subcommunities also directed the economic activities of members. Their cooperative trade guilds made it easier for members to own and operate small business enterprises. Hence, among both Chinese and Japanese, high rates of business proprietorship and low rates of welfare dependency were related in that both rates reflected the activities of mutually supportive, ascriptively bounded moral communities. Entrepreneurial individualism was not the cause.

On the other hand, purely ascribed social statuses were more prevalent, important, and rigid among the Chinese then among the Japanese. Both Chinese and Japanese had regional associations, extended families, and nepotistic trade guilds. But only the Chinese had clans and tongs; and only the Japanese heeded their consulate. Moreover, for reasons which reach far back into the past, the Japanese had developed neighborliness a good deal further than had the Chinese immigrants.[40]

That the Japanese did not elaborate the centralized institutional

[39] Hoy, *Six Companies*, p. 22.
[40] See Lyman, "Structure," p. 87–153; idem, *Asian in the West*, pp. 57–64.

controls which governed the Chinese nor employ armed thugs to settle internecine quarrels is, in the last analysis, a reflection of Japanese neighborliness and nationalism. These qualities cut across the impenetrable barriers otherwise created by ascriptive ties to subgroups. Thus, potential hostilities were obviated because rivals were equipped to define themselves into a national or neighborhood community and because their consulate wanted them to do so. Among the Chinese, in contrast, neighborhood and nation counted for little against ascribed connections of family, clan, village, and dialect. Within these ascribed communities, Chinese were able to cooperate actively; and so long as boundaries were strictly maintained, coexistence was possible. However, the Chinese were less able than the Japanese to convert propinquity into moral community. As a result, linguistic, family, and regional communities among the Chinese could establish at best an armed truce.

To this blunt statement of the argument, certain qualifications are required. In the urban Chinatowns, proprietors could hardly fail to fall into destructive internal competition without institutional safeguards against such a development. First of all, their businesses were very close to one another; and second, the total volume of pedestrian trade was observably finite. Among the agricultural Japanese, on the other hand, problems of internal competition posed no such problem. The farms were not physically heaped together; nor were the separate farmers in competition for a finite amount of trade. The Japanese produced truck vegetables for urban consumers whose total appetites far exceeded what the Japanese could hope to produce, if not to sell. Hence, for the Japanese, the main opponent was an impersonal market for truck vegetables rather than Japanese competitors. The principle threat was the powerful white ranching interest which resented Japanese agriculture. To meet this challenge, aggressive cooperation for mutual security was necessary. The premium was on successful production rather than on staking out protected monopolies. These considerations also apply to Japanese urban trades, the bulk of which were concerned with marketing Japanese-grown produce. Here again, the threatening competition was that of non-Japanese producers rather than of Japanese rivals for a limited

market. Japanese residential areas hardly developed a tourist trade
at all, but had they done so institutionalized defense against internal
competition would clearly have served a useful purpose.

These fortuitous differences in settlement and in occupation account in large measure for the singular development of tong violence
among the Chinese and for the lack of it among the Japanese. The
tongs reflected the extraordinary difficulties of internal competition
in the Chinatown enclaves. Hatchetmen policed Chinese merchants
who might otherwise have been tempted to overstep the circum-
scribed boundaries within which they were permitted to exercise a
controlled monopoly. Moreover, the Chinatown enclaves heaped
together in close proximity representatives of different dialectal,
regional, and family groupings whose relations were highly competitive and always liable to explode into violence. Residentially
scattered, urban and rural Japanese were able to congregate by
loyalties without stepping on one another's toes.

Finally, as Lyman has correctly emphasized, the Chinese urban
population was disproportionately composed of single males. The
Japanese recourse to "picture brides" tended quite early to reduce
the preponderance of males among them, but the Chinese did not
make use of a similar device. Rootless urban males had an understandable interest in vice; tongs responded to this interest. The ties
of clan and district were not counterbalanced by nuclear family
ties as they were among the Japanese. By the time the Japanese began
to migrate to cities, their peak period of male preponderance had
passed. These demographic characteristics of the two populations
tend to account for the much greater scope of organizational domination among the Chinese as well as for Chinese crime in the early
period.[41]

---

[41] *Ibid.*, pp. 27–32. On the other hand, relative to other immigrants, and pointedly
to blacks, both the Chinese and Japanese populations were lop-sidedly male throughout the pre-1940 decades. The imbalanced sex ratio permitted resident Orientals
to form proportionately few husband-wife families. Evidently, the want of these
nuclear families did not impede the development of ethnic businesses; nor did the
missing nuclear families produce high rates of welfare dependency among sojourning bachelors.

AMERICAN LOGIC.

THIS MAN is not responsible for THIS MAN even if they do belong to the same race.

THIS MAN is responsible for all that THIS MAN does because they belong to the same race.

Figure 1. "American Logic." (Photo from *The Crisis* [New York], March 1913.)

Figure 2. To accommodate the clamor of his followers for personal appearances, Divine had constantly to travel from Heaven to Heaven. To ease this burden, he sent Faithful Mary to California as his plenipotentiary in 1937. With an adoring following of her own, Faithful Mary soon attempted to break away from the Kingdom, and denounced Divine to the newspapers. Although Faithful Mary's revolt was unsuccessful, Divine never again experimented with delegations of his charismatic authority. His private aircraft was, therefore, indispensable for Divine's personal administration of his small business empire. (Photo from John Hoshor, *God in a Rolls Royce,* New York, 1936, p. 245.)

Figure 3. On June 4, 1932, Suffolk County judge Lewis Smith sentenced Father Divine to one year's imprisonment and a $500 fine after convicting him of being a public nuisance. Three days later judge Smith dropped dead of a heart attack. "I hated to do it," said Father Divine in his jail cell. Shortly thereafter, an appellate court reversed his conviction and ordered his release from jail. Father's followers interpreted this train of events as manifestations of Divine's supernatural powers. Here, Mother Divine and a band of disciples greet Father on the occasion of his release from jail. (Photo from John Hoshor, *God in a Rolls Royce,* New York, 1936, p. 73.)

Figure 4. Home offices of the Liberty Life Insurance Company in Chicago, 1922. In the rear office sits Frank L. Gillespie, founder and first president of the company. Now the Supreme Life, this firm has become the third largest Negro-owned life insurance company in the United States, with assets of $33 million and $208 million of life insurance in force in 1965. This success is a testimony to the conservative style of management and actuarially sound policies which the company has always pursued. (Photo from Robert C. Puth, "Supreme Life: The History of a Negro Life Insurance Company, 1919-1962," *Business History Review* 43 [spring 1969]: 15. Reproduced by courtesy of the publishers.)

# The Value of Life Insurance To Colored People

Is a text from which a little sermon could well be preached in every colored church in America.

There is scarcely a family whose members do not have some sort of Policy in some sort of Company or Society or Order. These are usually for just enough to give a decent burial. The funeral expenses take practically all the proceeds and there is nothing left to meet the obligations which face the widow after she returns from the funeral. The problem of rent, food, clothes, books and school expenses for the children are not theories. When the grocer's boy brings the package he wants the money; and when the landlord calls he wants the rent.

**The man who carried $50 to $200 in a weekly benefit society or a secret society on the assessment plan earned enough and could easily have paid the premium on $1,000 to $5,000 in an old line legal reserve life insurance company whose rates are fixed and subject to no assessment, if he only had known.**

He could have made impossible the long hours of bending over a needle or the cook stove or the wash tub that came to his widow, if he had carried the necessary amount of life insurance. He could have assured his beautiful daughter the education she desired, the amusements she wanted, the clothes she craved—and which she got, somehow. He could have kept his boy in school and he would have grown up a credit to the memory of his father, a respected citizen of his community, and a successor to his father's business, instead of the wanderer or menial or ne'er-do-well. He could have changed the destiny of every member of his family! He had it in his power to make them bless his memory or bewail his shortsightedness! What a tremendous responsibility!

Are you, reading this, preparing for the future of your family or are you leaving them to shift for themselves after you are gone? What will become of your son? Will he leave school and go to work prematurely? Will your daughter give up her training upon which she has just entered? Must your wife go out and hunt work to support herself and the younger children? Will you leave money enough to pay the balance due on the home you have been purchasing? Or will your wife lose the place?

**You can secure to those you love future independence, you can protect your obligations, you can save your business if, while you are alive, sound and well—and that is NOW—you secure the necessary amount of life insurance.**

You can secure this life insurance in a strong, well managed life insurance company which has met every requirement demanded of it, owned, organized and operated by our people, the only one of its kind in the world, at rates within your reach if you act to-day. No matter where you live we can Protect you. Tear off this coupon and mail it to-day to

**Please send me particulars about insurance.**

**Amount $**.....

**Sex** ............

**Age** ...............

**Weight**..................

**Occupation** ...............

**Name** ......................

**Address** ........................

(C. Mar. 1915)

## STANDARD LIFE INSURANCE CO.

**200 Auburn Avenue, ATLANTA, GEORGIA**

**Capital Fully Paid - - $100,000.00**

**Over One Million and a Quarter Insurance in Force**

**Issues Policies from $250.00 to $5,000.00**

**HEMAN E. PERRY, President**
**HARRY H. PACE, Secretary**

Figure 5. Life insurance advertisement in *The Crisis* [New York], March 1915, p. 252.

# Here's the Money Maker for Colored People

**I WILL HELP YOU** earn more money than you are now making. You know what more money would mean to you. 53,000 men and women in all parts of the country can **testify to my ability to help you.**

I am the founder of the **INTERNATIONAL LIBERTY UNION OF THE WORLD**, the greatest secret Industrial Benevolent and Protective order for the toiling millions of men and women the world has ever known. Through this order I am devoting my life and energy, assisted by 53,000 members, to provide **immediate work, higher wages, family protection, self-education, co-operative buying and selling, mutual uplift and cash benefits** to all who will join with me in this **"I-L-U FAMILY"** and **FOLLOW MY LEAD TO BETTER CONDITIONS.**

If you are looking for pleasant work that will pay you well and in which you can use **all or only spare hours,** you must write me immediately for full particulars of this remarkable offer, enclosing ten cents for a three months subscription to our official magazine, **THE UNION JOURNAL,** which with the letters and circular matter I will send you, will convince you that I am able to help you. **Write me today.**

## W. C. Critchlow, Pres. I-L-U

287 **I-L-U Building**        **Dayton, Ohio, U. S. A.**

Figure 6. This advertisement appeared regularly in Chicago's leading black newspaper, the *Defender,* during the spring of 1910. Critchlow's "money maker" turned out to be selling insurance on commission for the ILU. Perhaps Critchlow himself was a well-intentioned reformer; nevertheless, his methods of recruiting salesmen doubtless turned up many gypsters and scoundrels. On paper, Critchlow's fraternal order offered cheaper insurance prices than did more reliable agencies. Hence, Critchlow's tottering order and his casually recruited salesmen were able to get hold of the life savings of many gullible bargain hunters.

Figure 7. Chinese children in San Francisco, circa 1910. In general, only the wealthiest Chinese could afford to support wives and children in the United States. The richness of these children's attire bespeaks the opulence of their parents who dressed them in the Chinese fashion expecting, as they did, to return one day to China. Parents who permitted their children to grow to maturity in the United States were often disgusted by the lazy, selfish attitudes the young people learned here. (Photo courtesy of the Bancroft Library, University of California, Berkeley.)

Figure 8. Provision store in San Francisco, circa 1885. "Thousand-year-old" eggs
and exotic vegetables attest to the unusual consumer demands of the sojourning
Chinese. The produce carries no price tags as customers bargained with the owner
for each item. Under these circumstances, being related to the owner was advantageous in securing fresh produce at a low or, at least, a reasonable price. (Photo
from the Department of Special Collections, General Library, UCLA.)

Figure 9. Although Chinese-owned supermarkets have won some support, especially among native-born Chinese, Chinatown residents still prefer to shop at specialty stores. The separate butcher shops, groceries, and fish markets preserve a valued friendliness in merchant-customer interactions. Therefore, on shopping days, the streets of San Francisco's Chinatown are crowded with pedestrian shoppers lugging their purchases from one small store to another. (Photo by Ted Barnes.)

Figure 10. In contrast to Chinatown produce stores of 1885 (Figure 8), price tags abound in this 1971 photograph. Even so, being related to the proprietors ordinarily entitles a shopper to special bargains and quality. (Photo by Ted Barnes.)

Figure 11. Grant Street at Leavenworth in San Francisco's Chinatown as it looked in 1922. (Photo from the Ira B. Cross Collection, courtesy of the Bancroft Library, University of California, Berkeley.)

Figure 12. The same intersection (see Figure 11 above) as it looked in 1971. The wax museum, cocktail lounge, and Japanese-made carp suggest a substantial increase in tourist traffic since 1922—and a decline in Chinatown's Old World charm. American banks did not locate in Chinatown in 1922, but virtually every major California bank had branches there in 1971. Also, a comparison of the two photos gives the probably correct impression that population density and traffic problems increased markedly in the intervening forty years. (Photo by Ted Barnes.)

Figure 13. Oath-bound highbinders dressed like ordinary Chinese laborers, but they concealed weapons in the capacious sleeves of the loose-fitting outer garment. Protected by graft from the American police, highbinders served as enforcers for Chinatown institutions, gamblers, and protection racketeers. However, bloody turn-of-the-century tong wars provoked so much public indignation that American police were forced to intervene. Here a San Francisco illustrated newspaper depicts a bullet-riddled Chinese expiring under a fatalistic wall motto while his assassin holds a smoking revolver. (Photo courtesy of the Bancroft Library, University of California, Berkeley.)

Figure 14. Gambling and prostitution were the principal entertainments of the womanless Chinese sojourners. Some were opium addicts. In popular legend, the cellars of Chinatown were connected by tunnel with secret dens in which unspeakably sordid crimes were daily occurrences. The "Street of the Gamblers" was San Francisco Chinatown's notorious vice district. Arnold Genthe's photograph was taken in 1896. The sinister, vice-ridden popular image of the Chinese has since given way to one which emphasizes their sobriety and industriousness. (Photo courtesy of the Department of Special Collections, General Library, UCLA.)

Figure 15. Public posters and displays have been and remain a typically Chinese way of disseminating information. This group of men are reading newspapers displayed in a publisher's window in 1971; in the far left-hand side of Figure 14, men are reading wall posters in 1896. (Photo by Ted Barnes.)

Figure 16. Like other Americans, Chinese have been disgusted and horrified by the U.S. military rampages in Indochina. However, unlike other Americans, the "wisest" Chinese have been afraid to voice their opinions lest this expression become a pretext for mass incarceration of citizens of Chinese descent. Memories of the Japanese internment still haunt Asian-Americans. Since their elders refused to speak out, some Chinatown youths turned to demonstrations and wall slogans to express their rage. (Photo by Ted Barnes.)

Figure 17. Offices of Japanese labor contractors in Fresno, circa 1915. Ranchers applied at the Japanese information bureau for gangs of farm hands, such as those toiling in the field in Figure 18. The ranchers paid a per capita sum to the labor contractors, who made the actual disbursements to the Japanese-speaking workers. The building on the left housed both the Tulare County Japanese Association and evening classes in English under the auspices of the Presbyterian Church. (Photo from the Ira Cross Collection, courtesy of the Bancroft Library, University of California, Berkeley.)

Figure 18. Japanese farm hands in Tulare County, circa 1915. Until the mid-1920s when motor vehicles became general, Japanese hands transported themselves to the appointed fields by means of bicycles. Each gang of farm laborers usually consisted of men from the same village or prefecture in southern Honshu. (Photo from the Ira Cross Collection, courtesy of the Bancroft Library, University of California, Berkeley.)

Figure 19. Kamikawa brothers building in Fresno, California, circa 1915. In addition to the hotel, general store, and bicycle repair shop pictured here, the Kamikawa brothers also operated a bank between 1908 and 1912. When voluntarily liquidated, the bank had combined assets of $40,000, of which 10 percent was in the premises, vault, and fixtures. Since the brothers were highly influential in the local Japanese community, being related to them was advantageous for any Japanese seeking work in the Fresno area. (Photo from the Ira Cross Collection, courtesy of the Bancroft Library, University of California, Berkeley.)

Figure 20. The Sumitomo Bank building towers over the Los Angeles Little Tokyo district in this December 1970 photograph. The San Pedro Street bank is one of eight branch banks operated in California by the Sumitomo Bank of California, a division of the Sumitomo Bank, Ltd., of Osaka, Japan. The Sumitomo Bank is taking an active role in carrying forward plans for the commercial redevelopment of the surrounding neighborhood. But spokesmen indicated that the bank's participation in local commerce began to develop only during the decade of the 1960s. Theretofore, they add, the Sumitomo served only as a conduit for monetary transfers between Japan and the United States. (Photo by the author.)

# Urban League
# and Business League

# 6

Negro migration to the industrial centers of the North has historically proceeded on direct northerly axes. From the southeast, Negro migration streamed northward to mid-Atlantic and New England cities, especially Philadelphia, New York, and Boston. From the Mississippi delta, migrants followed the river northward to Chicago and Detroit. Since 1940, a third line of Negro migration from Louisiana, Oklahoma, and Texas has established growing black colonies in Los Angeles, San Francisco, and Oakland (Table 8).[1] That blacks from the same regions of the South tended to settle in the same urban places in the North was in part simply a reflection of geographical proximity. However, the patterned migration also reflected social ties linking earlier migrants and stay-at-homes. Through the mails, stay-at-homes learned from the pioneers about conditions and opportunities in the northern cities in which the pioneers had taken up residence. When the people back home became ready to migrate, they naturally headed for the cities about which they had information and in which they had friends or relatives.

These streams of migration made it possible for southern-born blacks in the North to cluster together on the basis of regional ties as did Chinese and Japanese immigrants, but few blacks chose to do so. For example, some Chicago blacks formed locality clubs such as the Vicksburg Club, the Natchez Club, the Louisiana Club, and the Arkansas Club. These clubs had recreational, benevolent, and occupational purposes; however, only a tiny fraction of eligible persons ever took any interest in club activities.[2] In this respect,

[1] Lyonel C. Florant, "Negro Internal Migration," *American Sociological Review* 7 (December 1942): 784; *Report of the National Advisory Commission on Civil Disorders*, p. 117. Also see J. Max Bond, "The Negro in Los Angeles," pp. 184–85.
[2] St. Clair Drake, "Churches and Voluntary Associations in the Chicago Negro

TABLE 8

*Negro Population and Percentage Urban for the United States and*
*Geographical Divisions, 1910, 1920, and 1930*

|  | 1910 | 1920 | 1930 |
|---|---|---|---|
| *United States* | | | |
| Population | 9,827,763 | 10,463,131 | 11,891,143 |
| Percentage Urban | 27.3 | 34.0 | 43.7 |
| *The North* | | | |
| Population | 1,027,674 | 1,472,309 | 2,409,219 |
| Percentage Urban | 76.9 | 84.9 | 88.3 |
| *The South* | | | |
| Population | 8,704,427 | 8,912,231 | 9,361,577 |
| Percentage Urban | 21.3 | 25.3 | 31.7 |
| *The West* | | | |
| Population | 50,662 | 78,591 | 120,347 |
| Percentage Urban | 78.6 | 74.0 | 82.5 |

SOURCE: U.S. Department of Commerce, Bureau of the Census, *Negroes in the United States, 1920–1932* (Washington, D.C.: U.S. Government Printing Office, 1935), Table 8, p. 53.

southern-born black migrants did not differ from interstate white migrants among whom state or city of origin has never provided an important locus of participation or loyalty. However, southern-born Negroes did differ dramatically in this respect from the Chinese, Japanese, and even the West Indian Negroes among whom regional origins were critical nuclei of social organization.

International migration is a more drastic form of uprooting than is interstate migration. The obvious difference is particularly pronounced within the United States where, despite some regional variations, elementary cultural forms are relatively homogeneous throughout the nation. Interstate migration is, moreover, taken relatively lightly by Americans—even when compared with citizens of other industrialized nations. This attitude reflects more than the cultural and geographical ease of mobility; it also reflects acceptance of social and geographical mobility as a way of life. In view of this American tradition, it is not surprising that neither black nor white interstate migrants have felt it necessary to erect organizational monuments to their state of origin.

However, less obvious differences also distinguished the regional attitudes of Negroes and other nonwhite migrants. Interstate Negro

Community," pp. 152–53; Vattel Elbert Daniel, "Ritual and Stratification in Chicago Negro Churches," *American Sociological Review* 7 (June 1942): 353.

migrants to the urban North brought with them—or soon developed
—quite different attitudes toward their southern past than did Oriental immigrants to their antecedents. Whereas Chinese and Japanese
immigrants harkened back nostalgically to peasant traditions of
Kwangtung or southern Honshu, interstate Negro migrants experienced ambivalence about life in the South. Social protest was always
an important motive inducing blacks to leave the South.[3] Japanese
and Chinese immigrants, on the other hand, came to the United
States only in search of economic opportunity. Social protest did not
figure in the reasons which induced them to leave home. Migration
as protest involves a rejection of a way of life, whereas the mundane
search for economic opportunity need not. The absence of the protest
motive among the Oriental immigrants and its prominence among
black migrants indicates the groups' respective opinions of the world
they had left behind.

Confronted with color discrimination, Chinese and Japanese could
invidiously compare their social situation in the United States with
that which they had experienced in the Orient. Discrimination and
minority status were unique features of sojourner life in America.
Relative to these disabilities, conditions were easier in Asia. Hence,
Orientals had this reason for preferring the Orient and harkening
back to the Old World. On the other hand, Negro migrants experienced the urban North as an improvement over the South in respect
to both social and economic conditions: "I'd rather be a lamp post
on Lenox Avenue than the governor of Georgia." Naturally this
sensible preference ought not to be taken to suggest that the black
migrant in the urban North experienced his lot there as perfectly
satisfactory or that he was not frequently disappointed in even his
more modest expectations. The point is only that in northern cities
Orientals experienced their social situation as relatively depriving,
whereas southern-born blacks experienced much the same objective
conditions as relatively ameliorated. This attitudinal difference, in
turn, affected the propensity of migrants to organize new social
structures on the basis of regional nostalgia.

[3] Carter G. Woodson, *A Century of Negro Migration* (Washington, D.C., 1918),
p. 168; Chicago Commission on Race Relations, *The Negro in Chicago*, pp. 84–86;
Gunnar Myrdal, *An American Dilemma*, 1:195; LeRoi Jones, *Blues People* (New
York: William Morrow, 1963), pp. 95–96, 105.

Chinese and Japanese immigrants viewed themselves as representatives of non-Western but nonetheless worthy cultural traditions. This attitude naturally suggested region of origin as a fulcrum for individual and collective identity. Ties to Chinese and Japanese culture, specifically to the language, customs, religion, and mores of provinces or villages of origin, provided an obvious and meaningful standard around which Oriental immigrants could organize their social life in the New World.

In contrast, southern-born blacks lacked a highly evaluated past which would stimulate the establishment of organizations based on regional loyalties.[4] Insofar as Africa might have been regarded as a region of origin, southern-born blacks experienced a special difficulty in that they were not self-consciously aware of themselves as retaining or exemplifying elements of any of the West African cultures.[5] Moreover, even had blacks been aware of themselves as representatives of West Africa, they would withal have remained unable to create organizations parallel to the *kenjinkai* or district associations. These associations were based on provincial rather than national loyalties. They did not represent "Japanese" or "Chinese" but only Japanese from this or that specific prefecture, or Chinese from one or another of the seven Kwangtung districts. To have achieved a parallel level of organization, American-born blacks would have needed to be aware of themselves as Ibo, Nupe, Yoruba, and so on, rather than simply as "Africans."[6]

In fact, even insofar as some blacks were aware of themselves as

[4] Ray Stannard Baker, *Following the Color Line* (New York: Doubleday Page, 1908), p. 216.

[5] In the famous debate, Herskovits has argued that in fact American Negroes did maintain many African cultural characteristics. He has disputed the Park-Frazier thesis that slavery deprived North American blacks of all vestiges of West African culture. This argument has recently received support from Keil, who has shown that aural-oral patterns of African origin are expressed in black Americans' religious and musical forms. Yet no one has shown that black Americans were self-consciously aware of any West African cultural survivals. Naively carrying on African traditions and being self-consciously aware of carrying them on are two different matters. Only self-conscious awareness involves conscious identification and the organization of social life on the basis of cultural ties. Cf. Melville J. Herskovits, *The Myth of the Negro Past;* E. Franklin Frazier, *The Negro Church in America;* Charles Keil, *Urban Blues* (Chicago, 1967).

[6] See Harold R. Isaacs, *The New World of Negro Americans* (New York, 1963), p. 97.

West Africans, such awareness was typically nonconvertible into personal identity and social organization. Adopting the perspective of unenlightened whites, lower class Negroes especially tended to regard Africa as a region of steaming jungles, naked savages, blood-thirsty cannibals, and idolatrous religious beliefs.[7] This image was hardly conducive to personal identification with Africa or to social organization on the basis of African origins. Pregnant with so many unfortunate consequences for American blacks, this view was a reflection of the Negro's cultural assimilation through long involvement in the civilization of the whites.

Negro life in the South offered no basis for subordering the migrant communities in the North along regional lines as the Oriental communities were ordered. Southern life was too homogeneous to permit meaningful distinctions among blacks from different states or counties, even had the black migrants desired to institutionalize their southern heritage.[8] For example, Georgia-born blacks could not be easily distinguished on cultural grounds from Alabama-born blacks. Religion, diet, dialect, and the like were virtually identical. In this respect, black migrants did not differ from southern-born white migrants who also lacked cultural distinctiveness, so that whites from one southern state or county were culturally indistinguishable from whites from some other southern state or county.[9]

Chinese and Japanese arrived as sojourners who desired to return to the Old World as soon as they had grown rich in the New World. Foreign-born Orientals were denied U.S. citizenship. A permanent, residential commitment to the United States was not achieved among the Orientals until the immigration act of 1924. Unlike Oriental sojourners, Southern-born blacks were U.S. citizens by birth. They arrived in the urban North committed to permanent residence there. They did not intend to save their money so that they might return to the South to enjoy in retirement the cultural amenities of their Old Kentucky or Sewanee River homes. The blacks ambivalence toward regional heritage contrasts with the Orientals' retention of the tie

[7] *Ibid.*, pp. 105–322; Barnard Magubane, "The American Negro's Conception of Africa" (Ph.D. diss., University of California, Los Angeles, 1967).

[8] Cf. Clyde Vernon Kiser, *Sea Island to City*, pp. 210–13.

[9] Lewis M. Killian, "Southern White Laborers in Chicago's West Side" (Ph.D. diss., University of Chicago, 1949), p. 178.

and suggests the groups' divergent attitudes toward their regional origins. Moreover, intending to return, Chinese and Japanese so-journers had a practical motive for maintaining a tie with their province or village of origin. Urban Negroes lacked this motive.

Negroes long resident in the North, especially those of the middle class, regarded the newcomers with the urbanite's contempt of the country bumpkin. To this contempt was added a vigorous condem-nation of the newcomers' unruliness, promiscuity, and ignorance.[10] Quite different was the reception accorded to new arrivals by Chinese and Japanese. Through clan, *fong*, and *kenjinkai*, the newcomers had claims upon the assistance of their predecessors. Jobs, lodging, and help were supplied the arrivals by those who recognized a mean-ingful relation to them through region of origin. Thus, the appearance of new immigrants was an occasion for reasserting social and cultural ties to a place of origin, rather than, as among Northern blacks, an occasion for drawing a heavy line between city folk and country folk. Quite apart from the practical ramifications of this differential help-fulness, the pioneers' attitude toward the newcomers is suggestive of the very different estimations of their regional heritage which were characteristic of Orientals and of northern blacks.[11]

In view of these extremely different attitudes toward regional heritage, it is clear that Negro social organization in the urban North could not duplicate that of the Orientals among whom regional ties were cornerstones of social organization. Since regional as-sociations barely existed, they could hardly serve as building blocks of Negro business as they served the Orientals. Nor could familial organizations or kinship ties structure the Negro community's pro-vision for autonomous social welfare as they structured that of the Chinese and Japanese. If the Negro migrant was to develop a business structure, he had perforce to follow a different path than the one employed by Orientals. If the black communities of the urban North were to develop autonomous provisions for social welfare, such provisions had perforce to differ from those of the Chinese and Japanese.

[10] Woodson, *Century*, p. 187; Gilbert Osofsky, *Harlem: The Making of a Ghetto* (New York, 1963), pp. 5–6, 43–44; Jones, *Blues People*, p. 106; Allan H. Spear, *Black Chicago*, p. 168.
[11] Cf. E. Franklin Frazier, *Black Bourgeoisie*, pp. 112–129.

In general, urban Negro communities had to depend on voluntary organizations as the foundation of their social structure, because Old World ties of region, tribe, and extended kinship had been torn up by slavery and had not been subsequently regenerated on a new basis. Thus, in laying a foundation for business development or for autonomous social welfare provision, urban Negro communities had willy-nilly to employ voluntary organization. Overlooking for the moment the role of churches and fraternal orders, two other voluntary organizations were of special significance. The National Urban League devoted itself to the social welfare of urban blacks; the National Business League oversaw the development of Negro-owned business. These two voluntary organizations functioned as counterparts of the Oriental regional associations, extended families, and clans; but unlike any of the Chinese or Japanese groupings, both the Business League and the Urban League were voluntary associations the members of which did not share migrant solidarity. Moreover, the people whom these two voluntary associations served were not subordered into ascriptively bounded moral communities as were Chinese and Japanese. Both the Business League and the Urban League were chronically unable to create moral solidarity on a voluntary basis.

THE NATIONAL URBAN LEAGUE

Established in 1911, the National Urban League soon opened branches in the major cities of the North. "It is a matter of general knowledge that the Urban League had its origin in the problems incidental to the urbanward migration of Negroes."[12] The newcomers obviously required assistance in acclimating themselves in the big cities. Urban League chapters supplied them with important social services such as housing and employment assistance, health information, child care, community organization, and vocational guidance. In addition, the Urban League waged an uphill struggle with unfriendly city administrations on behalf of improved social

[12] Charles S. Johnson, ". . . And the Pursuit of Happiness," in National Urban League, *Fortieth Anniversary Yearbook* (New York: National Urban League, 1951), p. 16; also see Chicago Commission on Race Relations, *Negro in Chicago*, p. 146; John T. Emlen, "Philadelphia Armstrong Association," *Southern Workman* 53 (September 1924): 412–13; Myrdal, *American Dilemma*, 2:837.

services in ghetto areas and equal opportunity policies in public employment. The efforts of the Urban League opened new employment opportunities to blacks in both manual and nonmanual occupations.[13]

In rendering these valuable social services, the Urban League chapters functioned as counterparts to the regional associations of the Chinese and Japanese.[14] Yet the Urban League was structurally quite different from Oriental organizations. League chapters were interracial in composition. The league "made no attempt to enlist a large public following." Cultivation of grass roots in the ghetto was limited to the employment of "public relations" for the improvement of the organization's "public image."[15] For financial support, the league relied on white philanthropists. Authority in the league passed downward from an elite of wealthy, educated persons of both races to a clientele of uprooted blacks whose behavior was to be "uplifted." This structure mirrored the cultural isolation of the Urban League from its lower class clientele and also suggested a certain aloofness on the part of league supporters toward those in need of uplift.[16]

The structural and cultural isolation of the Urban League from its clientele was further accentuated by the spirit of social work professionalism which animated its activities. Indeed, the league was a pioneer in the application of scientific methods to problems of social welfare. In confronting lower class blacks, league social workers unavoidably operated in a structured, bureaucratic context. The relationship of league workers and needy blacks was accordingly one of "case workers" and "clients."[17] Case workers did not have a moral obligation to particular people.

[13] Myrdal, *American Dilemma*, 2:838; Arvarh E. Strickland, *History of the Chicago Urban League*, pp. 45, 89–90; Spear, *Black Chicago*, pp. 169–74; Drake, "Churches and Voluntary Associations," pp. 230–31.

[14] Strickland, *History*, p. 40.

[15] *Ibid.*, p. 123; Chicago Commission on Race Relations, *Negro in Chicago*, pp. 146–47; L. Hollingsworth Wood, "The Urban League Movement," *Journal of Negro History* 9 (April 1924): 119–20; James Q. Wilson, *Negro Politics*, p. 298.

[16] Strickland, *History*, p. 123; Myrdal, *American Dilemma*, 2:703; Frazier, *Black Bourgeoisie*, p. 289; Drake, "Churches and Voluntary Associations," p. 228. Also see J. Max Bond, "The Negro in Los Angeles," pp. 243–49.

[17] Spear, *Black Chicago*, pp. 171, 173. Cf. Richard Cloward and Richard Elman, "Advocacy in the Ghetto," *Trans-Action* 4 (December 1966): 32.

League clients were not league members. Membership was reserved to those upper class Negroes and white philanthropists who
supported the organization, but did not employ its welfare services on
their own behalf. The league's clients were poor blacks, typically
those in trouble and, accordingly, those of the very poorest social
stratum. These persons had only fleeting relations with the league.
That is, when in trouble, a client fell back upon the social services
provided by the league. But as soon as his difficulty was settled, a
client's connection with the organization was terminated—at least
until such time as he might again require the league's intervention.
Clients did not develop social ties with other clients. This pattern
of involvement prohibited the development of the Urban League
into a community as opposed to a community-servicing organization.
At any moment, participation in league activities was reserved to
upper class administrators and transient, poor blacks. No permanent,
middle class bloc intervened between the extremes of social status
otherwise represented in the league.

Like the Urban League, the regional associations of the Orientals
were available to persons in extreme difficulties, although they did not
carry on mundane relief or social welfare activities. The regional
associations were also aristocratic in structure in that the official
positions were monopolized by the wealthier businessmen. But positions of responsibility in the Oriental associations included no non-
Chinese or non-Japanese. The associations supported themselves
from the contributions of the membership without assistance from
philanthropists. Especially in the early period, the administrators of
the regional associations were not highly educated in a formal sense,
even in their own cultural traditions. They especially lacked western
higher educational qualifications. The regional associations rarely
employed trained, western-educated social workers.

Accordingly, the attitude of these regional associations toward the
lower strata of the Chinese and Japanese populations was not one of
"uplift." A higher status Oriental official might consider himself
able to participate in higher (Oriental) cultural symbols to a more
sophisticated degree than the indigent recipient of organizational
benevolence, but he did not conceive of indigent lower class persons

as in need of cultural uplift. In this respect he differed from educated Urban League case workers who were not simply more educated in a cultural tradition than their clients, but were rather estranged from the folk understandings which the migrants brought with them from the South. Hence, officials of the regional associations were not culturally isolated from the rank-and-file membership of their institutions as were the Urban League case workers from their clients.

Welfare activities conducted under the aegis of the regional association were moralistic rather than professional. The relationship of helper and helped was not that of case worker and client. Those Japanese and Chinese in need of assistance had a valid moral claim on other persons from the same village or province and, hence, on the regional association. This claim involved reciprocated obligations; assistance was not owed to all Chinese or Japanese, but only to those from the same village or province. This moral obligation emphasized the cultural ties linking recipients of benevolence and those who bestowed it. The act of bestowing benevolence tended to integrate recipient and donor into a moral community by reasserting the cultural ties which bound the parties together. In contrast, the bestowal of benevolence by league case workers tended to emphasize the social and cultural gap between case workers and the clinical objects of their professional expertise. It did not create a moral bond.

Membership in the regional associations was not restricted to an elite. All Chinese and all Japanese from a given region were in some sense members of the regional association. The connection with regional ties was not, therefore, a transitory one to be severed as soon as an individual was on his feet. Nor was involvement in the activities of the immigrant associations limited to persons of extremes of social status: the very wealthy and the very poor. Since these ties crosscut social class lines, they also involved Chinese and Japanese of middling social status. For such persons, membership in clan, fong, or kenjinkai was simply an important form of social participation and a locus of personal identity. On the other hand, because the Urban League was a purposive welfare organization rather than a brotherhood of migrants, the league was unable to enlist the mundane participation of black people of the middle class and stable working class. This lack of participation by blacks who were neither upper class nor indigent naturally affected the climate of the league, rendering it much starker and more bureaucratic than the Oriental regional associations.

Of course, the kenjinkai, district associations, and clans did not engage in mundane welfare work as did the Urban League. They intervened only in extraordinary cases of hardship in which no lower level source of aid was available. Since most daily problems were handled informally by such lower level agencies (friends, fellow villagers, relatives), the immigrant associations had rarely to take formal cognizance of specific cases. As welfare organizations, the single most important function of regional and family name associations was to bring pressure on subcommunities to care for their own needy members. Regional and clan particularism interfered with the development of more impersonal welfare practices.[18] The Urban League was unable to bring public pressure on ascriptive subcommunities to take care of their own members because there were no mutually supporting subcommunities of blood and land among urban blacks. As a result, the league itself had virtually exclusive responsibility for the welfare of lower class blacks. This responsibility was too heavy a burden for the slender resources of the league to support without assistance.

To function most effectively, indeed, to survive on its slender budget, the Urban League needed to reduce the burden of social work by inducing potential clients (migrant blacks) to take, wherever possible, preventive measures against their own destitution. For example, the league needed to induce lower class blacks to adopt practices of thrift, industry, and other bourgeois personal virtues in order to minimize their probability of someday needing help. Similarly, the league chapters needed to encourage the formation among potential clients of mutually supportive groupings capable of absorbing some of the burden of relief work. Therefore, they hired community workers to "go into the churches attended by migrants and instruct the communicants in thrift, pride, personal hygiene, deport-

[18] Forrest E. La Violette, *Americans of Japanese Ancestry* (Toronto, 1946), p. 90.

ment, and other civic virtues."[19] But hired speakers only went into places frequented by migrants; they were not themselves associated with such places in a membership capacity. Since, moreover, the relationship of clients to the Urban League was impersonal and since clients did not form permanent social ties with one another, they obtained only immediate relief from their contact with the league. They did not acquire those habits of personal industry and mutual aid which would have tended to prevent their relapse into destitution. These difficulties were not the "fault" of the league. They do, however, distinguish that organization from immigrant brotherhoods which were able to rely on powerful social controls to enforce everyday conduct conducive to the prevention of personal destitution and to conduct mutual aid.

Although there were no locality clubs to perform welfare services for poor migrants, there were, of course, more voluntary associations interested in welfare activities than simply the Urban League. Churches, settlement houses, and fraternal orders performed important welfare services at the grass roots level.[20] The welfare vacuum among migrants did not affect those who were members of voluntary associations which did offer such helpful services. Only those blacks who were not members of such voluntary associations truly lacked all access to social assistance other than that provided by the Urban League or public agencies. However, among that segment of the population most at risk in respect to destitution and welfare emergency—the poorest class of blacks—rates of participation in voluntary associations were also lowest. Hence, that class of urban blacks most at risk in respect to various forms of destitution was also the class most lacking voluntary association memberships intervening between individuals and the league. The mass of unorganized, black, and impoverished humanity dependent on the slender resources of the league for private social assistance was very large indeed. Rates

[19] Strickland, *History*, p. 45; Fred S. Hall, ed., *Social Work Yearbook, 1935* (New York: Russell Sage Foundation, 1935), p. 294; D. Wellington Berry, "Uplift Work Among Nashville Negroes," *Southern Workman* 42 (August 1913): 438–45.

[20] Strickland, *History*, p. 35; C. W. Areson and H. W. Hopkirk, "Child Welfare Programs of Churches and Fraternal Orders," *Annals* 121, no. 210, (September 1925): 85–95; Hall, ed., *Social Work*, pp. 294–96.

of welfare dependency in the urban North were accordingly very high among lower class blacks.[21]

In contrast, the brotherhoods of the Chinese and Japanese included virtually every immigrant simply because the relevant ties were ascriptive rather than voluntary. As a result, very few Orientals lacked membership in groups capable of rendering welfare services. The availability of these services reduced popular dependency on public welfare agencies. Ascriptive suborganization of the Oriental populations permitted regional and family associations to oversee the whole community while limiting their active intervention to those few cases of indigence for which no lower level groups could be assigned responsibility. Ascriptive ties were simply more comprehensive than voluntary ones. The difference affected particularly those lower status persons most at risk in respect to indigence.

The social services provided by some voluntary groups (churches, settlement houses, fraternal orders) tended to "enhance the reputation" of the sponsoring organizations among poor blacks. These voluntary organizations gained membership because of the social services they rendered.[22] These voluntary groupings did not welcome the competition of the Urban League in this field or its efforts to call on public authorities for supplementary aid. By offering welfare services, the league undercut their own membership appeal. Such competitive rivalries did not occur within the Oriental welfare system since the different units, being based on ascriptive ties, were not in competition for the allegiance of a voluntary membership. Hence, whereas the district and family associations attempted to shame lower order communities into living up to their traditional responsibilities, the small, black voluntary associations resented what they viewed as the competition of the league.

The Urban League's permanent welfare objectives focused on inducing government agencies to expand existing operations and to

[21] Alfred E. Smith, "The Negro and Relief," *Monthly Report of the Federal Emergency Relief Administration* (March 1–30, 1936), pp. 11–13; Richard Sterner, *The Negro's Share* (New York: Harper and Brothers, 1943), pp. 214, 221; Myrdal, *American Dilemma*, 1:353–63; *Fortune* 20 (July 1939): 78. See also Bond, "Negro," p. 272.
[22] Strickland, *History*, p. 35; Spear, *Black Chicago*, p. 171.

undertake new responsibilities in areas previously unserviced by any public agency.[23] Its success was characteristically evaluated in terms of its achievement of this objective. The expansion of public welfare facilities relieved the organization of immense burdens which it was unable to bear without assistance. For example, expanded facilities in public employment agencies reduced the pressure on league chapters to serve as private employment agencies, and so released scarce facilities for other welfare work.[24] In view of the shortage of resources available, the league's relentless interest in sharing with public agencies the burdens of welfare work among Negroes made excellent sense. The league found New Deal liberalism quite congenial.

On the other hand, prefectural clubs, district associations, and especially the Six Companies strove more or less consistently for monopolization of welfare services among their populations and jealously attempted to interpose themselves between public welfare agencies and their own populations. These tactics buttressed the continuing authority of traditional elites, even though they tended thereby to deprive poor migrants of welfare services they might otherwise have received. The conservative, even reactionary, posture of the Oriental associations reflected the desire of local elites to retain traditional controls and privileges in their own bailiwick.

### THE NATIONAL NEGRO BUSINESS LEAGUE

Founded in 1900 by Booker T. Washington, the National Negro Business League has been the leading organization representing the interest of Negro business. The league grew quite rapidly in the early years. In 1914/15, Monroe Work reported 295 chartered locals, of which 51 were located in northern states. As of 1948, however, there were only 123 local business leagues and Negro chambers of commerce; of these, 17 were located in northern states.[25] However, these figures, suggestive of the national importance of the Business League,

[23] Hall, ed., *Social Work*, p. 619; Drake, "Churches and Voluntary Associations," pp. 241–43.
[24] Lester B. Granger, "The Road Ahead," in National Urban League, *Fortieth Anniversary Yearbook*, p. 26.
[25] Monroe N. Work, ed., *Negro Yearbook, 1914–15* (Tuskgegee, Ala.: Negro Yearbook Publishing Company, 1915), pp. 304–08; Florence Murray, ed., *The Negro Handbook* (New York: Malliet, 1949), pp. 205–09. Cf. William A. Aery, "Business Makes Men—Especially if the Men Are Negroes," *Survey* 34 (1915): 550.

cannot gainsay the organization's failure to achieve its founder's objective. Washington intended the league to "encourage more and more of our people to enter business." Growth of the Business League he viewed as a means toward that objective; but, although the league grew and extended its influence to the "remotest corners of the land through the organization of local leagues of businessmen," this growth did not increase the proportion of Negroes in business as Washington had desired.

Although Andrew Carnegie and other white industrialists were heavy financial backers of the Business League in its first decade, the Business League has not subsequently been financially dependent on white philanthropists. Also, unlike the Urban League, the Business League has not included white people on its board of directors. On the other hand, membership in the league was open only to business-men. Although quite a conventional restriction, this policy excluded from membership all but an occupational elite of Negroes. Hence, the league was in no sense an organization of community partici-pation. Instead, league chapters tended to become coteries of the more successful Negro businessmen banded together on the basis of shared material interests.[26] In ethos the organization was officially bourgeois; the profit motive occupied a supreme niche in its pantheon of public values. Here again the league departed from the custom of the immigrant Chinese and Japanese, for none of the Oriental or-ganizations were bourgeois in the sense of institutionalizing the rational-instrumental striving for profit as the supreme social value.[27] Instead of mutual aid, the Business League touted self-interested individualism. Instead of traditional values, they emphasized the secular profit motive. Instead of immigrant brotherhood, there was the structural isolation of the successful. Ironically, these archtypi-cally entrepreneurial characteristics persistently interfered with the organization's capacity to stimulate Negro-owned business, its raison

[26] Earl Ofari, *The Myth of Black Capitalism*, p. 33; Spear, *Black Chicago*, p. 73; Vishnu V. Oak, *The Negro's Advance in General Business* (Yellow Springs, Ohio: Antioch Press, 1949), p. 118. See also C. C. Spaulding, "Is the Negro Meeting the Test in Business?" *Journal of Negro History* 18 (January 1933): 66–70.

[27] Cf. Frazier, *Black Bourgeoisie*, esp. pp. 125–26; Clarence E. Glick et al., "Changing Ideas of Success and of Roads to Success as Seen by Immigrant and Local Chinese and Japanese Businessmen in Honolulu," *Social Process in Hawaii* 15 (1951): 56–70.

d'être. As a result, an undercurrent of racialism ("buy black") competed with the official bourgeois ("buy cheap") ideology.

RECRUITMENT AND TRAINING

The growth of Negro-owned business clearly required a continuous
expansion of its base of recruitment so that new recruits to business
occupations would more than reproduce the number of businessmen
existing at some earlier moment. The failure of the Negro business
sector to grow is in a simple and direct sense attributable to the
Business League's inability to recruit new people. Occupational inheritance is notoriously characteristic of proprietary occupations;
hence, the expansion of a business sector requires that occupational
inheritance be supplemented by the recruitment of persons whose
parents had not themselves been proprietors.

Closely related to the question of numerical recruitment is the
problem of training new recruits. In a stable small business sector
marked by occupational inheritance, the training of new recruits is
conducted informally in the family. Those who will inherit the business learn the requisite skills in the course of unpaid family labor as
juveniles. This means of transmitting skills and information inter-
generationally is inadequate when the objective is not merely the
reproduction of a business population but its absolute and propor-
tional increase. Under these circumstances, appropriate instruction
must reach persons who are not involved in an existing network
of informal education. Such induction breaks the informal cycle
of hereditary transmission and extends skills to segments of the
population which did not previously possess them.

The induction and training of new persons becomes especially
crucial when for any reason an occupation does not naturally reproduce itself. In the case of small business, for example, a proportion of the children of small proprietors become proprietors
themselves. But another proportion do not. Most of those who choose
not to take over father's small business will do so because their own
path to upward social mobility lies in the white-collar occupations
and professions. For such persons, critical occupational skills are
acquired at school rather than at home. But since the children of
the proprietors lose interest in small business, the small business

sector cannot even reproduce itself if the only recruits it secures are drawn from the children of the proprietors themselves. To reproduce itself, much less to grow, the small business sector requires the means to induct lower class youth uninvolved in the informal process of hereditary transmission. Only lower class youth are likely to view proprietorship as a vehicle of social ascent. Middle class youth, even the offspring of the proprietors themselves, are likely to feel that they can "do better" than small business.[28] Hence, the success of the Business League's attempt to expand Negro business depended crucially on its ability to recruit and train lower class blacks.

This sine qua non of business development, the Business League was chronically unable to attain. Since the league chapters were structurally isolated voluntary associations of the wealthy, they were unable to reach lower class black youth. The social worlds of the young slum-dwelling black and the prosperous businessman could not interpenetrate. As a result, the Business League was unable to introduce lower class youth to blacks already employed in business; information about business careers could not circulate through the population; and lacking information, black youth was not in a position to select business as a vocation. Moreover, since the chapters institutionalized no community participation, the ascribed social status of youth outside the structure of hereditary recruitment and training could not be overcome. No provision was made for institutional settings in which sponsorship of lower class youth could occur. In the extreme case, a young lower class black with business interests might display in his daily conduct the recommended Algeresque qualities yet be unable to secure the sponsorship of established businessmen because he lacked an institutional milieu in which his conduct could attract public attention. Had the league chapters been organizations of community participation, merit and sponsorship would have been in much closer relationship. The league's bourgeois ethos provided no reason for profit-maximizing businessmen to take an economically irrational interest in the welfare of some poor black youth.

[28] See Joseph A. Pierce, *Negro Business and Business Education*, pp. 268–69; Oak, *Negro's Adventure*, pp. 81–82; George Edmund Haynes, *The Negro at Work in New York City* (New York, 1912), p. 114.

Enrolling cross sections of the population, territorial and surname associations and extended families were regularly able to bring young men of the lower class into contact with self-employed "cousins" or kenjin. These contacts introduced Oriental youth to the world of business and diffused knowledge about proprietary occupations to lower social strata. Since territorial clubs were intimately related to the trade guilds, contacts in such clubs normally involved contacts in trade guilds. Moreover, when a young immigrant took a job in a business owned by kenjin, his employers were supposed to feel a moral obligation to sponsor him later in a business of his own or to admit him to partnership. Therefore, specific middle class people had a moral obligation to help specific working class people become middle class businessmen.

### CONSUMER CREDIT

White merchants in black areas were obvious rivals of the Negro Business League. To increase the number of Negro-owned businesses, the league chapters needed only to expel the white proprietors from black neighborhoods and then to replace the expelled whites with blacks. Since white merchants dominated ghetto trade, expelling them offered enormous potential for increasing the size of the Negro retail sector. For example, the New York *Age* reported that Negroes owned 40 percent of businesses in Harlem in 1925, but this 40 percent turned over only 4 percent of local retail sales. On Chicago's South Side, Negroes operated about 50 percent of businesses in 1938; this 50 percent, however, received only 10 percent of the consumer dollars spent in the area.[29]

Naturally, black businessmen wanted to take this lucrative trade away from white merchants and to obtain a monopoly of ghetto commerce for themselves. To this end, they attempted to popularize the idea that the black customer proud of his race would purchase goods and services only from black vendors. Along with this appeal to racial pride went the elaboration of the "double duty dollar" theory. This mercantilist economic doctrine purports to show that

[29] New York *Age*, March 28, 1925, p. 1; St. Clair Drake and Horace R. Clayton, *Black Metropolis*, 2:438. Also see Kiser, *Sea Island*, p. 29; Myrdal, *American Dilemma*, 1:308.

Negroes who spend money at Negro-owned businesses help themselves through a circulation effect. The idea is that black merchants spend their income in black neighborhoods, thereby creating new demand for products and service in the ghetto and generating new jobs for ghetto residents. On the other hand, the white merchant's income follows him to his lily-white neighborhood where it creates additional demand for products and services and new jobs for whites only. Thus, white merchants were accused of "bleeding" the ghetto of its wealth. These racialist economic ideas are voguish today in some black circles, but the National Business League has been their historic though unofficial exponent.[30]

However, the Business League proved unable to supplant the white merchants. Despite decades of antiwhite appeals, boycotts, and slogans, whites owned 85 percent of businesses in central Harlem in 1967. The racial balance of ownership was equally lopsided in other urban ghettos in that year and had obviously not improved in half a century.[31] Moreover, a Business League survey of seven cities found that Negro proprietorships in 1968 were still disproportionately centered in service trades, especially barbering, beauty culture, and dry cleaning. Whites continued to dominate the lucrative core areas of ghetto retailing. Grocery and liquor retailing remained firmly in the hands of white merchants; appliances, furniture, and clothing stores in black ghettos were almost invariably white owned.[32]

In a standard explanation of this persistent situation, black merchants are alleged to have experienced exceptional difficulty in attempting to break into the core retail areas of the ghetto because the black entrants have been unable to grant consumer credit on as extensive terms as those available at stores operated by white, partic-

[30] Harold L. Sheppard, "The Negro Merchant: A Study of Negro Anti-Semitism," *American Journal of Sociology* 53 (September 1947): 96–99; Abram L. Harris, *The Negro as Capitalist*, pp. 182–83; Myrdal, *American Dilemma*, 2:815; Drake and Cayton, *Black Metropolis*, 2:430–33. See also Stokely Carmichael and Charles Y. Hamilton, *Black Power* (New York: Vintage, 1967), pp. 172–73; Raymond S. Franklin, "The Political Economy of Black Power," *Social Problems* 16 (winter 1969): 286–301.

[31] Theodore L. Cross, *Black Capitalism* (New York: Atheneum, 1969), p. 100; Alex Poinsett, "The Economics of Liberation," *Ebony* 24 (August 1969): 150, 152; Eugene P. Foley, "The Negro Businessman," p. 108.

[32] Andrew F. Brimmer and Henry S. Terrell, "The Economic Potential of Black Capitalism," pp. 10–11, 25.

ularly Jewish, competitors. But since black consumers are poor, they especially need credit to "finance" most purchases.[33] When out of work because of illness or unemployment, they have absolutely required consumer credit to carry them over the hard times. Hence, the black merchants' chronic inability to render installment financing or consumer credit is alleged to have driven black trade into the hands of stronger white competitors who were able to grant the credit their customers demanded.[34]

This standard explanation has, however, failed to consider the highly unsatisfactory relations between white creditors and black debtors which have emerged from this process. The credit situation in particular has been responsible for a bitter exacerbation of relations between proprietors and customers. Blacks have often felt themselves grossly overcharged for inferior goods sold by unscrupulous "Jew" merchants who take advantage of their need for credit to jack up prices far beyond those prevailing on a cash-sale basis. Needing credit, the black consumer has been dependent on the usurious terms offered by "friendly," "no-money-down" white merchants. Naturally, awareness of this dependency and of the price paid for it has bred bitter resentment at the vicious cycle of poverty–credit–high prices which the black consumer experiences.[35] White merchants in the ghetto have claimed that their carrying charges are necessarily high because, in order to survive in business, they must extend credit on liberal terms to attract trade, but these liberal terms permit a high rate of default.[36] Defaults drive prices and carrying charges up even further, since the cost of each default must be added to the costs borne by nondefaulting customers. As prices rise, impoverished blacks require more and more credit in order to "finance"

[33] David Caplovitz, *The Poor Pay More* (Glencoe, Ill.: Free Press, 1963), pp. 53–54; *Report of the National Advisory Commission*, p. 139; Louis L. Knowles and Kenneth Prewitt, eds., *Institutional Racism in America* (Englewood Cliffs, N.J.: Prentice-Hall, 1969), p. 25.

[34] Myrdal, *American Dilemma*, 1:308; Drake and Cayton, *Black Metropolis*, 2:443.

[35] *Report of the National Advisory Commission*, pp. 139–40; Carmichael and Hamilton, *Black Power*, pp. 20–21; Caplovitz, *Poor*, pp. 15ff.; Harris, *Negro as Capitalist*, p. 183. See also *The Autobiography of Malcolm X* (New York: Grove Press, 1964), p. 193.

[36] Richard Berk, "Doing Business in the Ghetto," p. 127; Cross, *Black Capitalism*, pp. 33–36.

purchases, and they become less and less able to bear the cost of completing the scheduled payments. The vicious spiral proceeds with prices, interest rate, demand for credit, and defaults chasing each other heavenward. Periodic repossessions and garnishments reminded blacks that white merchants had the support of the police in collecting, but blacks have not felt that the police offered them any protection from gouging merchants and loan sharks.

Resentful of higher prices and inferior quality, black consumers had a concrete motive for shoplifting away some of the merchants' exploitative profits. Pilfering and stealing have accordingly been frequent in black areas. Costs resulting from extensive shoplifting were offset by price increases and by cheating consumers with inferior quality merchandise, false weights, and so on: "It has become a dog-eat-dog world, with the merchants and the customers having nothing in common except a mutual necessity. The customer steals; and the merchant cheats."[37] Naturally, higher prices and merchant cheating further aggravated black resentment, thereby strengthening the motive for retributive shoplifting. On the other hand, rampant shoplifting intensified the ghetto merchant's fear of and disgust with his clientele and provided a motive for additional price increases and escalated cheating.

In the Harlem riots of 1935 and, more recently, the nationwide disturbances following the Watts uprising of 1965, embittered relations between merchants and customers culminated in the burning and looting of ghetto businesses. Most of the burned-out owners were white. But "Negro-owned" or "Soul Brother" placards in display windows have not guaranteed the protection of businesses owned by blacks.[38] For stores in riot zones, the first line of defense against looters and arsonists was a feeling among rioters that the owners were not exploitative in their practices. Notwithstanding an element of chance, stores with exceptionally unsavory local reputations were singled out for retribution by the mobs. The second line of defense against looting and arson was the timely appearance on the scene of the store owner and local friends, all armed with baseball bats and

[37] Robert Conot, *Rivers of Blood, Years of Darkness* (New York, 1967), p. 80.
[38] *Report of the National Advisory Commission*, pp. 19–61. Cf. "The Harlem Riot," *Opportunity* 13 (April 1935); Claude McKay, "Harlem Runs Wild," *Nation* 140 (April 3, 1935): 383.

giving the appearance of intending to use them on any persons who ventured to attack the store. In either case, the unscathed survival or blazing destruction of a ghetto business depended to a great degree on an owner's community relations.[39]

Since no whites operated retail businesses in Chinatowns or Little Tokyos, the problem of racially provoked merchant-community hostilities could never arise in those enclaves. The absence of local white merchants also deprived Chinese and Japanese of convenient opportunities to burn down white-owned businesses. Moreover, when trading with whites, Orientals made a point of doing an exclusively cash business. Their ability to do so reflected the ready availability of intragroup credit resources. One could borrow from clansmen or fellow villagers what one needed to pay cash to a white merchant. As a result, white merchants and Oriental customers never became involved in the embittered cycle of credit and high prices which set the stage for looting and burning in black areas.

On the other hand, in trade among themselves, both the Chinese and the Japanese were extremely liberal in extending credit. Liberal and informal credit policies worked smoothly in the Chinatowns and Japantowns because of institutionalized social trust. Oriental people generally traded with clansmen or fellow villagers. In the Japanese case, credit laxity on the part of merchants did create some difficulties because erosion of the traditional family system in the course of acculturation had undercut consumer responsibility without undercutting a merchant's traditional responsibility to meet the needs of a family despite its lack of money.[40] By 1939, Japanese merchants were attempting, without much success, to introduce installment buying contracts in trade with Japanese customers. Such innovations mirrored the breakdown of the moral solidarity characteristic of the immigrant generation. That equivalent difficulties did not tax the Chinese is probably attributable to the greater resiliency of traditional

---

[39] Berk, "Doing Business," pp. 130–131; Walter J. Raine, "The Ghetto Merchant Survey," in *The Los Angeles Riots*, ed. Nathan Cohen (New York: Praeger, 1970); pp. 609–610; Tom Hayden, *Rebellion in Newark* (New York: Random House, 1967), p. 30, 33.

[40] Shotaro Frank Miyamoto, *Social Solidarity Among the Japanese in Seattle*, pp. 81–82; Harry H. L. Kitano, *Japanese Americans*, p. 75.

social ties among them, as well as to the aggressive role of the Six Companies in enforcing traditional business relations.

The Japanese in Hawaii adapted the tanomoshi to installment purchase.[41] Small proprietors, such as carpenters, tailors, and watch vendors or repairers, would organize a tanomoshi among their Japanese clientele as a means of drumming up trade and enabling their customers to "finance" a purchase. In a "suit tanomoshi" a tailor might enlist seven Japanese customers who would agree to pay $5 a month against a $35 suit. At the first meeting of the tanomoshi, the seven customers would jointly create a pool of $35 which would be awarded by interest bidding to one of their number. The winner paid for his suit with his tanomoshi pot. And so it would go until each of the seven had his suit financed through the tanomoshi. This method was a true means of installment purchase because each of the seven men, save only the very last, received his suit before he had completed all payments. The last man paid less than the earlier takers because of interest payments to the tanomoshi.

Naturally the capacity of Japanese tradesmen to organize such associations among their clientele depended on the tradesmen's social connections. The tanomoshi worked only when the tradesmen knew and trusted their customers, and when customers knew and trusted the tradesman and one another. So long as customers patronized kenjin and fellow villagers, mutual trust was reliably present. Mutual trust permitted consumers to enjoy the advantages of installment purchase without interest charges, and it gave to a Japanese tradesman an important commercial advantage over non-Japanese rivals. The Japanese tradesman was able to offer his customers the advantage of installment purchase without interest payment, whereas a non-Japanese rival had to add carrying charges to the cash price. Hence, other things being equal, the Japanese tradesman charged less for his product and time payment service (tanomoshi) than did his non-Japanese rival.

Obviously white merchants in black neighborhoods could rarely

---

[41] Ruth N. Masuda, "The Japanese Tanomoshi," *Social Process in Hawaii* 3 (May 1937): 16–19; John F. Embree, *Acculturation Among the Japanese of Kona, Hawaii* (Menasha, Wis., 1941), p. 91.

establish with their customers the same trusting relationships that characterized the relationships of Oriental merchants and immigrant customers. The color line intervened. In this respect, Negro merchants had a local advantage; by stressing the moral obligations of race pride in commerce, the Negro merchants tried to turn this advantage to profitable account.

However, the Negro merchants' endless appeals to racial pride did not actually create the sort of moral solidarity against which money could be safely lent. Mutual trust of the classic moral in-group would have permitted black merchants to extend credit on more liberal terms to black customers than could white competitors, to reduce the interest rate in installment purchasing, and generally to offer all customer services more cheaply than whites.[42] Under these circumstances, the poor blacks' need for credit would virtually have compelled them to buy only from black merchants. As it was, the poor blacks' need for credit had the opposite effect—tending to drive them into white-owned stores.

Had the Business League been based on ties of blood and land, then black customers would have in fact shifted their buying, especially their credit buying, to stores operated by persons of their extended family, tribe, or locality. Such a pattern would, in turn, have introduced an ascriptively derived moral community into commercial relations. Naturally this community would have facilitated internally lax credit relationships based on social trust and would have created thereby the usual advantage of the in-group merchant. But, since urban blacks were not subordered into kinship, tribal, or locality groups, the Business League could not appeal to such ties and had to make due with appeals to "race" solidarity.

### BUSINESS COOPERATION

Among the Chinese and Japanese, kinship and locality ties carried over into the community's division of labor. As a result, kenjin, or "cousins," tended to pile up in the same occupations. Since the same

[42] Max Weber, *Ancient Judaism*, esp. pp. 343–55; idem, *The Sociology of Religion* (Boston: Beacon Press, 1963), esp. pp. 250–251. Also see Benjamin Nelson, *The Idea of Usury* (Princeton: Princeton University Press, 1949).

sort of ties were so weak among urban Negroes, these particular loyalties could not structure that community's division of labor. Hence, the black business population which arose was composed of unrelated competitors. These persons cooperated only on the basis of shared interests, unlike the Orientals among whom both material interests and immigrant loyalties buttressed economic cooperation.

This difference deleteriously affected the success of the Business League and the trade associations which were derivatives of it. In 1930 there were thirteen Negro trade associations representing Negroes in insurance, banking, tailoring, beauty culture, construction, farming, and undertaking. These were trade associations rather than trade guilds. Typically, these voluntary associations were able to recruit only a small fraction of the Negro practitioners of the trade in a local area.[43] Because these associations were not immigrant brotherhoods, they lacked informal social sanctions so extensive as those of the Oriental trade guilds. This lack deleteriously affected their ability to recruit membership, to conduct mutual aid, and to organize guild-style cooperation concerning wages, prices, and so forth.

In 1929 Albon Holsey organized the Colored Merchants Association (CMA) under the auspices of the Business League. Holsey's organization "aimed to reduce the operating costs of the Negro retail merchant through cooperative buying, the standardization of goods and equipment, and group advertising."[44] In cities with ten or more retail stores operated by Negroes, the individual proprietors were to band together to form a "voluntary chain." Conditions of membership in the chain included the purchase of at least 8 percent of wares from a single local wholesaler named by the New York office who agreed to pass on discounts to the small Negro owners. Moreover, the members of the voluntary chains were to emphasize the CMA brand products and to coordinate advertising campaigns and specials. In October 1929 there were twenty-five CMA member stores operating

---

[43] Pierce, *Negro Business*, p. 210; J. B. Blayton, "Are Negroes Now in Business, Business Men?" *Journal of Negro History* 18 (January 1933): 61–62; Joseph R. Houchins, "Negro Chambers of Commerce," p. 3; Drake, "Churches and Voluntary Associations," p. 212.

[44] Harris, *Negro as Capitalist*, p. 178.

in Harlem; by May of 1930, this number had increased to seventy-five stores in Harlem and the Bronx.[45]

Minimal though these infringements on solo entrepreneurship were, the CMA proved unable to recruit enough Negro grocers and to secure adequate cooperation from those who did join. Concerning the causes of his organization's failure, Holsey wrote:

> The success of all voluntary chains depends upon the members working together. For example, we held a meeting every week of the member grocers in New York City to decide on "specials" for the following week. . . . Some members would not attend these meetings, although we had an experienced grocery merchandising man to help. Then we had the unpleasant and unhappy experience of having certain member-grocers undersell or oversell the selected "specials," thus causing the Harlem public to feel that we didn't know what we were doing.
>
> Many of the wholesale grocers fought the C.M.A. movement openly and bitterly, and the lack of loyalty on the part of several of our member-grocers played right into the hands of the wholesalers who set out to destroy the Movement.[46]

Holsey's organization would have had vastly improved chances of success had it been able to call on regional or tribal loyalties among the membership. The foot-dragging noncooperation of many members and the lack of internal unity in the face of hostile wholesalers and white rivals weakened the movement. Both precipitants of failure could have been eliminated or vastly decreased in scope had the CMA possessed means of sanctioning Negro retailers when "out of role" in leisure hours. To succeed, the CMA needed more internal discipline than its voluntary associational structure could readily provide.

[45] Pierce, *Negro Business*, pp. 210–11; Roi Ottley, *New World A-Coming* (New York, 1943), p. 120; H. M. Foster, "Negro Chain Stores," *Nation* 132 (March 11, 1931): 272; "Color Enters Big Business," *Outlook and Independent* 155 (May 28, 1930): 139.

[46] Oak, *Negro's Adventure*, pp. 64–65.

# Church, Sect, and Father Divine

# 7

The church was the only black organization tolerated under the slave regime, and it emerged from the Civil War as the most important autonomous social institution of the freedmen. It has historically been the primary social institution able to enlist the voluntary participation of broad masses of black people. In the urban North, the Baptist and Methodist churches especially lost some of the stature they enjoyed in the South. On the one hand, these traditional Negro denominations were deserted by upper class Negroes in favor of "white denominations" (Table 9). On the other hand, lower class black migrants deserted the larger established churches in favor of "holiness" or "pentacostal" storefronts.[1] The general secularism of urban life in the North also tended to reduce the religious fervor and participation of blacks of all social strata. Although these tendencies deleteriously affected the social organization of black communities in the urban North, the church in general retained even there its preeminence as a grass-roots institution. According to W. E. B. Du Bois, roughly 32 percent of Negroes in Philadelphia's black wards were church members in 1896/97. A 1901 survey revealed that 50 percent of blacks in a lower class Chicago precinct were church members. Clyde Kiser reported that 42 percent of Harlemites were church members in 1930.[2]

Of course, like other voluntary associations, churches recruited

[1] Benjamin E. Mays and Joseph W. Nicholson, *The Negro's Church*, p. 98; Vattel Elbert Daniel, "Ritual and Stratification in Chicago Negro Churches," *American Sociological Review* 7 (June 1942): 358–61; E. Franklin Frazier, *Black Bourgeoisie*, p. 128; Allan H. Spear, *Black Chicago*, pp. 93–94. Also see Mary Ellen Ogden, "The Chicago Negro Community: A Statistical Description," (mimeographed; Chicago: Works Projects Administration, 1939), pp. 116ff.
[2] W. E. B. Du Bois, *The Philadelphia Negro* (Philadelphia, 1899), pp. 221–24; Spear, *Black Chicago*, p. 93; Clyde Vernon Kiser, *Sea Island to City*, pp. 52, 222. Also see James Q. Wilson, *Negro Politics*, pp. 127–28.

TABLE 9

*Religious Affiliations of Negroes Listed in
Who's Who of the Colored Race,
1915, by Region of Residence*

| | Percentage Distribution | | |
| | North[a] | South[a] | Number |
|---|---|---|---|
| *Religious Affiliation* | | | |
| No religion mentioned | 20.8 | 12.3 | 199 |
| "White" denomination[b] | 27.1 | 20.9 | 297 |
| Negro denomination[b] | 52.0 | 66.7 | 774 |
| Total | 99.9 | 99.9 | |
| Number | 498 | 772 | 1270 |

SOURCE: F. L. Mather, ed., *Who's Who of the Colored Race* (Chicago, 1915). Tabulation includes only native-born persons resident in the United States.

[a] The South was defined as the Confederate states plus Oklahoma and Washington, D.C. All other places were classified as in the North.

[b] "White" denominations included: Presbyterian, Protestant Episcopal, Roman Catholic, Congregationalist, Quaker, Unitarian-Universalist, Disciples of Christ. All other denominations were classified as Negro denominations.

their membership principally from middle and upper income groups. Low income people and relief recipients rarely joined. Many poor nonjoiners complained that "dicty" church members looked down upon their shabby clothing and Southern grammar. On the other hand, if low income people belonged to any club or association, they were most likely to belong to a church. In general, church was the only voluntary association capable of enlisting any active participation among slum-dwelling blacks from the South. Moreover, many poor blacks who did not attend church or pay any regular support nonetheless considered themselves church members in some sense.[3] The influence of the church among black folk was greater than church attendance figures would suggest.

In the worst slum districts the only churches were converted storefronts. Often the congregants of a storefront church had migrated together from the South. Sometimes their rural pastor led their migration; and sometimes the congregants sent for the pastor when they had earned enough money to rent a storefront.[4] The partiality

[3] St. Clair Drake, "Churches and Voluntary Associations in the Chicago Negro Community," pp. 207, 282.

[4] *Ibid.*, pp. 149–50; LeRoi Jones, *Blues People* (New York, 1963), p. 125. Southern whites in Chicago also set up storefront churches to serve congregants from particular southern counties. The white southerners often brought their pastor with

of migrants for storefronts thus derived, in significant measure, from the opportunities storefront participation afforded for fraternization with people one had known in the South. The regional tie also tends to underscore the virtually exclusive ability of these pentacostal churches to enlist the voluntary participation of migrant blacks.

The fraternal orders were second only to the church in respect to the capacity to enlist active participation of a large number of blacks. Indeed, many fraternal orders developed from the churches. Fraternal orders differed in respect to the religiosity of their ritual. Some orders rubbed the religious veneer quite thin; in others, generally those with Biblical names, the influence of fundamentalist theology pervaded the entire order. Middle and upper class Negroes preferred the less religious orders; lower class blacks gravitated to orders which were religiously expressive in ethos.[5] In 1922 the most prominent orders in Chicago were the Odd Fellows, Prince Hall Masons, Ancient Order of Forresters, the Good Samaritans, Seven Wise Men, Knights of Honor, Mosaic Templars of America, the True Reformers, and the Order of St. Luke.[6] Like the churches, the fraternal orders suffered a decline of stature in the urban North. According to Frazier, secularism and the competition of other forms of social participation generally "caused the older fraternal orders to lose much of their appeal." The decline of fraternalism in the North was especially pronounced among the religiously expressive lower class orders and among the citified youth. Only the more secular and somewhat "sporty" Elks managed to profit from the migration.[7] The various fraternal orders catered to different social strata, and each gained social prestige on the basis of the socioeconomic level of its members. Poor blacks less frequently joined fraternal orders—or they were snobbishly excluded. Hence, most fraternal members were of middling socioeconomic status. Nevertheless, except for the churches, no other organizations in the urban North were able to recruit the

---

them when they traveled north. See Lewis M. Killian, "Southern White Laborers in Chicago's West Side" (Ph.D. diss., University of Chicago, 1949), pp. 82, 150–54.

[5] Du Bois, *Philadelphia Negro*, p. 224; James Weldon Johnson, *Black Manhattan*, p. 169; E. Franklin Frazier, *The Negro in the United States*, p. 302.

[6] Chicago Commission on Race Relations, *The Negro in Chicago*, p. 141. Also see Drake, "Churches," pp. 71–77.

[7] Frazier, *Negro in the United States*, p. 378.

voluntary participation of a larger proportion of blacks than were the fraternal orders.[8]

Both church and fraternal order tended to institutionalize a moral community. These organizations were, first of all, moralistic in that they stressed ethical conduct on the part of the membership. Membership in a church congregation or in a fraternal order formally involved public commitment to a set of moral or ethical ideals. Other members shared these ideals. In this manner, church and fraternal orders produced moral community.

Church and fraternal order also encouraged active membership participation and a public way of life. Active participation usually involved a fusion of institutional and extra-institutional roles, so that members were in one another's company when away from the institution as well as when actively participating in institutional activities. For example, lodge brothers or sisters maintained cordial social relations with one another even on nights when they did not come together as a body to engage in formal lodge activities. Thus, the lodges and the churches tended to buttress the moral communities which they institutionalized with a public way of life. This way of life naturally increased the visibility of extra-institutional behavior which was played out before audiences composed of fellow members. These circumstances were conducive to the juxtaposition of public and ceremonial affirmations of moral belief with the actual conduct exhibited by an individual in his everyday life. When public affirmation and practical conduct diverged too manifestly, lodge brothers or church members were present to remind an individual of his ceremonial utterances and to encourage him to bring his practical conduct into conformity with his professed ideals. In this manner, the public way of life characteristic of actively participating members of fraternal orders and churches resulted in peer group scrutiny of daily conduct and increased the social pressure on an individual to conform to the standards of his membership group.

[8] Du Bois estimated that 17 to 25 percent of blacks in Philadelphia belonged to some fraternal or fraternal beneficial organization in 1896–97 (*Philadelphia Negro*, p. 185). See also James Johnson, "Fraternal Societies Aid Race Progress," *Crisis* 45 (July 1938): 235; Charles W. Ferguson, *Fifty Million Brothers* (New York: Farrar & Rinehart, 1937), pp. 184ff; Inabel Burns Lindsay, "The Participation of Negroes in the Establishment of Welfare Services" (Ph.D. diss., University of Pittsburgh, 1952), p. 144.

In sum, the churches and fraternal orders tended to institutionalize expressive moral communities based on membership participation and a public way of life. In these particulars the churches and orders differed markedly from the Urban League and the Business League. The formal and instrumental associations institutionalized neither widespread membership participation, nor moral community, nor a public way of life. These orders and churches were similar to the regional and kinship associations of the Orientals which also rested on moral community, membership participation, and a public way of life. Certainly these two sets of institutions were much closer to one another than was either to the Business League or Urban League.

### VOLUNTARY ASSOCIATIONS AND MORAL COMMUNITY

Yet despite their similarities to Oriental regional associations, churches and fraternal orders were typically unable to attain the intensity of internal social solidarity that was characteristic of *fong* and *kenjinkai*. The difficulties of the black associations in this respect reflected the general problems of voluntary associations operating on a culturally undifferentiated mass.[9] Both church and fraternal order were expressive voluntary associations; membership in either was open to anyone willing to make an appropriate confession of belief and able to pass whatever conditions of membership that were imposed. As voluntary associations, the churches and fraternal orders had to create solidarity among a voluntary membership which was ascriptively unrelated. No ascribed social barriers automatically and spontaneously structured the social participation of migrant blacks. Hence, in order to create mutually supportive moral community among the membership, churches and fraternal orders needed to impose a social structure on an otherwise undifferentiated mass lacking primary ties to one another. They had, in short, to create reciprocated social obligations among persons who did not otherwise recognize them.

The capacity of the churches and fraternal orders to create and

---

[9] Cf. Edwin S. Harwood, "Urbanism as a Way of Negro Life," in *Life Styles in the Black Ghetto*, ed. William McCord et al. (New York: W. W. Norton, 1969), p. 26; C. Wayne Gordon and Nicholas Babchuck, "A Typology of Voluntary Organizations," *American Sociological Review* 24 (February 1959): 22–29.

sustain intense internal solidarity depended on their ability to impose an ethical discipline upon the membership.[10] The more rigorous the ethical discipline, the more intense would be the internal solidarity of the moral community. In general, the imposition of ethical discipline required the churches and fraternities to achieve a total rather than segmental control over members' motives, beliefs, associations, and conduct.[11] This total level of control voluntary associations are notoriously unable to achieve without Draconian measures.

Imposing an ethical discipline required, first of all, the social isolation of the voluntary membership in the community. Social isolation was a prerequisite of intense internal solidarity for three principal reasons. First, the strength of the ethical discipline depended on the fusion of members' institutional and extra-institutional roles. If the members led a public life in one another's company, then the members would police each other's behavior in enforcing congruence between practical conduct and professed ideals. This informal enforcement would thereby tend to harness individuals to the ethical discipline of the institution. Second, isolation and peer scrutiny buttressed the mutual confidence of the members in one another. A public way of life did not permit skeletons in the closet, part-time sinning, or undetected lapses from the path of virtue. Hence, the membership could be morally certain of one another's ethical reliability. Third, social isolation underwrote the continued devotion of members to the ideals and beliefs of their membership group by insulating them from skeptics and nonmembers. Without such social isolation, the membership would come into close contact with worldly persons who might precipitate doubts, defections, lapses from virtue, and personal unreliability.

The practical test of the intensity of the moral community established by a church or fraternal order ultimately came down to whether its ethical discipline was manifested among lodge brothers or congregants in an outward and visible style of life distinguishing them from nonmembers. Such a deviant style of life would isolate the membership from worldly blacks, throw them into one another's extra-

[10] The question of "occupational community" as treated in the sociology of work is relevant here. See Seymour M. Lipset, Martin Trow, and James S. Coleman, *Union Democracy* (Glencoe, Ill.: Free Press, 1956), pp. 106–40.
[11] Bryan R. Wilson, "An Analysis of Sect Development," p. 4.

institutional company, expose them to peer group scrutiny and normative control, create a basis for social trust, induce group consciousness, inflame their zeal, and generally stimulate internal solidarity to an intense degree. In short, practical change of life and adoption of a deviant perspective in the black community needed to become a criterion of membership in church or fraternal order if these voluntary associations were to create intense internal solidarity. But such criteria had to be imposed on recruits who were otherwise indistinguishable from nonmember blacks.

In contrast the regional associations of the Orientals were not strictly voluntary associations. Membership in prefectural association, district association, fong, or clan depended on ascribed characteristics. Only those Japanese and Chinese were eligible for membership who had been born in the appropriate place or bore a specific surname. Moreover, unlike the Negro communities, the Chinese and Japanese communities were not culturally homogeneous. Only the constituent subgroups were culturally homogeneous. Hence, the regional associations and clans did not need to impose any discipline to create internal solidarity; this solidarity emerged spontaneously. For example, Cantonese from Toi-shan spontaneously spent their waking hours in one another's company. In part this pattern reflected a preference for one another's company; but it also reflected the unwillingness of non-Toi-shanese to associate with Toi-shanese (and vice versa) and the subsequent necessity for Toi-shanese to band together. Fused roles subjected Orientals to the normative scrutiny of their membership group. Mutual trust and group isolation similarly emerged without heroic effort or sacrifice on anyone's part. Group consciousness required no deliberate cultivation. Cultural distinctiveness was the basis of regional association in the first place. All of these spontaneous characteristics of the regional groupings tended to create and perpetuate intense internal solidarity. These mechanisms reinforced the spontaneous solidarity the immigrants brought with them from the Orient.

Since the population base of the Negro churches and fraternal orders was culturally undifferentiated, imposition of an ethical discipline in the service of social solidarity depended importantly on selectivity in recruitment. Only those could be welcomed to full membership who were willing to adopt a group's life style. Admission of recruits unwilling to effect drastic changes in their personal life would naturally have undercut the development of ethical discipline and social solidarity. In the case of the churches, these requirements of intensive solidarity involved the transformation of church into sect. Strictly speaking, churches are structurally incapable of enforcing the kind of discipline necessary for intensive internal solidarity. Only a sect can accomplish this objective, because (by definition) the sect alone exposes its recruits to lengthy scrutiny, testing, and the risk of rejection.[12]

In the cultivation of internal solidarity, religious organizations emphasizing heterodox religious opinions have an advantage over those espousing orthodox theological ideas. Public assent to a respectable religious theory does not radically isolate a new recruit from the world or immerse him in an isolated social circle of the faithful. Easy social intercourse between exponents of differing but equally respectable religious opinions tends to undercut the enforced isolation of the faithful, to introduce role separation, to reduce member commitment, and to promote critical thinking. Hence, such easy social intercourse is undesirable from the point of view of sect solidarity. Stigma attaching to public adherence to deviant beliefs tends, on the other hand, to isolate fanatics in a separate deviant circle of the faithful. No one else wants to associate with them. This isolation from the "world" is, in turn, conducive to role fusion, group consciousness, and a general lack of critical thinking about the theology of the group. For this reason, weirdly deviant opinions on theological matters more successfully induce membership solidarity than do conventional religious opinions.

Heterodox opinions have another advantage in respect to the

---

[12] "Indeed, a church is a corporation which organizes grace and administers religious gifts of grace. . . . A sect, however, is a voluntary association of only those who, according to the principle, are religiously and morally qualified." H. H. Gerth and C. W. Mills, eds., *From Max Weber* (New York: Oxford University, 1958), pp. 305–06. See also Ernst Troeltsch, *The Social Teaching of the Christian Churches*, 2 vols. (1931; reprint ed., New York: Harper and Brothers, Harper Torchbooks, 1960), 2: 993; H. Richard Niebuhr, *The Social Sources of Denominationalism*, (New York: Henry Holt, 1929), pp. 17–18; Benton Johnson, "A Critical Appraisal of the Church-Sect Typology," *American Sociological Review* 22 (February 1957): 88–92.

cultivation of membership solidarity. The more improbable a sect's religious theory, the finer the strainer through which recruits must pass in order to attain full membership. Having passed the initiatory period of intense scrutiny, converts thereafter face a continuous choice between convenient apostasy and social martyrdom. Those who choose social martyrdom thereby isolate themselves from the "world" and expose themselves to social control by the circle of the faithful. The period of intense scrutiny and the mandatory embracement of some improbable heterodoxy eliminates many weaker proselytes who might otherwise have defected after being awarded the "prize" of full membership.

Churches and fraternal orders might attempt to impose severe ethical disciplines upon their recruits and members; but they could not force people to join, to remain in the fold once they had joined, or to live the approved public life. Churches and fraternities were voluntary organizations; people might affiliate or disaffiliate as they pleased. The stricter the ethical demands made on members and the more deviant the required beliefs, the fewer people would elect to join a church or fraternal order.[13] In determining what behavioral and intellectual sacrifices to demand of members, churches and fraternal orders had willy-nilly to choose between a large amorphous membership and a small fanatical one. If these voluntary organizations required no change in members' life styles, were moderate in their intellectual, emotional, and ethical requirements, hued closely to orthodox ideas, and did not test the recruits too severely, then the churches and fraternal orders might recruit large followings. If, on the other hand, they made immoderate demands on members whom, moreover, they put to severe preliminary tests for authenticity of belief and depth of conviction, then few people would choose

[13] When their specific appeals for a "new order of life" correspond to mass unrest and when sect leadership is charismatic, sects may temporarily recruit new members because of rather than despite their disciplined life style and peculiar doctrine. But proliferating sects-in-general unavoidably tend to encounter a business-as-usual attitude on the part of potential proselytes to whom heterodoxy and discipline are per se unwelcome. See Herbert Blumer, "Social Movements," in *An Outline of the Principles of Sociology*, ed. Robert E. Park (New York: Barnes & Noble, 1939), ch. 22; Ward H. Goodenough, *Cooperation in Change* (New York: Russell Sage, 1963), pp. 287–303. Also see John Lofland and Rodney Stark, "Becoming a World Saver: A Theory of Conversion to a Deviant Perspective," *American Sociological Review* 30 (December 1965): 862–75.

to join the organization and many who chose to join would be rejected as unfit. Such organizations could not normally anticipate the development of a large following.

The sectarian transformation of churches and fraternal orders was persistently inhibited by vigorous competition among ministers, churches, and fraternal orders for membership.[14] Intense, sustained, interorganizational competition for members tended to force a watering down of the economic, social, and moral demands which such institutions could make on recruits and, consequently, tended to reduce institutional capacity to generate high levels of internal solidarity among those who were, for the moment, enrolled in the organization. Of course this sort of competition was not limited to blacks. As Max Weber observed of white churches: "It is, of course, an established fact that this [ethical] selection has often been very strongly counteracted, precisely in America, through the proselyting of souls by competing sects, which, in part, was strongly determined by the material interests of the preachers."[15] What Weber observed of Americans in general was true with a vengeance of Negroes, among whom the entire pressure for social mobility was channeled into churches and religious orders. Equivalent pressures did not build up among whites, who had other avenues of social mobility available to them because of their socially advantageous skin color.

The church was the primary avenue of social mobility available to lower class blacks.[16] This avenue was, moreover, open on a purely entrepreneurial basis to all contestants. Especially among lower class blacks, the religious belief prevailed that ministers required no formal theological preparation for their vocation, only a "call" from God. This call was a purely individual experience: "The 'call' was supposed to have come through some religious experience which indicated that God had chosen him as a spiritual leader."[17] However,

[14] J. J. Watson, "Churches and Religious Conditions," p. 127. Cf. Peter L. Berger, *The Sacred Canopy*, pp. 138–39.

[15] Gerth and Mills, eds., *From Max Weber*, p. 306.

[16] Frazier, *Negro Church*, pp. 43–44; Carter G. Woodson, *The History of The Negro Church*, 2d ed. (Washington, D.C.: Associated Publishers, 1921), pp. 278, 301; Gunnar Myrdal, *An American Dilemma*, 2:875.

[17] Mays and Nicholson, *Negro's Church*, pp. 10–11; Frazier, *Negro Church*, p. 17.

the practical distinction between true and false vocations depended on the capacity of a preacher to attract a paying clientele. The size of the ministerial population was limited only by what the traffic would bear. Since the ministry was the virtually exclusive avenue of social mobility open to lower class blacks and since the occupation required no educational certification, many impoverished blacks felt the call to preach. Those who were able to provide their congregants with an enjoyable religious experience earned thereby a license to continue, while those who proved unable to compete in the religious marketplace were induced to return to manual labor.

Despite the efforts of the respectable denominations, duly ordained ministers were persistently unable to monopolize the administration of grace. In the rural South, itinerate preachers called to their vo-cation continued to attract substantial followings solely on the basis of their individual charisma, direct revelations, and, occasionally, miracles. In urban settlements, established preachers occupying the pulpits of respectable, ivy-covered edifices struggled vainly to sup-press the competition of "jackleg" revivalists operating in storefronts. In Chicago, for example, 700 preachers competed for 500 black pulpits, 75 percent of which were located in storefronts.[18] Many storefront revivalists were sincere though ignorant, but a few were black Elmer Gantries, "parasitical fakers even scoundrels who count themselves successful when they have under the guise of religion got enough hard-working women together to insure them an easy liv-ing."[19] The hallmark of all revivalists was a shouting, screaming emotional harangue which climaxed their religious orations. Duly ordained pastors condemned this style of delivery in private, but competitive pressures emanating from the storefronts forced many to imitate it.[20]

[18] St. Clair Drake and Horace R. Cayton, *Black Metropolis*, 2: 629; Earl Ofari, *The Myth of Black Capitalism*, pp. 50–51; Woodson, *History*, pp. 250ff.; Frazier, *Negro in the United States*, pp. 352–55; Guy B. Johnson, "Some Factors in the Development of Negro Social Institutions in the United States," *American Journal of Sociology* 40 (November 1934): 329–37.

[19] Johnson, *Black Manhattan*, p. 164. Also see Watson, "Churches," p. 123; Edward Byron Reuter, *The Mulatto in the United States* (Boston: Richard G. Badger, 1918), p. 274.

[20] Wilson, *Negro Politics*, pp. 127–28; Charles Keil, *Urban Blues* (Chicago,

CHURCH, SECT, AND FATHER DIVINE

The free expansion of the ministerial population, the proliferation of churches, and the competition of churches for congregants induced the clergy to take a permissive attitude toward the responsibilities of church membership. The doors of the churches were open to the repentent, and the doctrinal or ethical demands of the churches were few. Services were normally terminated by public invitations to join the congregation.[21] The primary obligation of congregational membership was financial support of the church. Doctrinal fanaticism or insistence on strict ethical conduct tended to disappear when ministers appealed for the financial support of a hotly contested clientele.

Clergymen had to compete with fraternal orders as well as with one another. The preachers were especially hostile to the fraternal orders and rained denunciation from their pulpits.[22] Fraternal spokesmen rebutted ministerial criticism on the grounds that the orders made ethical demands on their members whereas the churches were lax in this regard. The church could not develop practical benevolence because it lacked a "systematic plan . . . enforced upon its members by discipline." Fraternal spokesmen vaingloriously claimed to "reprove the apathy" of the churches.[23] But these hopeful claims notwithstanding, fraternalism was actually unable to develop fanatic moral community among lodge brothers. As voluntary organizations, the fraternals lacked a ready-made membership base. The various lodges were in competition for the allegiance of a shifting mass. Like the ministry, the field of fraternal work offered opportunities for social mobility to lower class blacks. These opportunities induced many persons to organize secret societies. "Almost any man who did not care to work hard and had learned the

1966), p. 8; Howard W. Odum, *Social and Mental Traits of the Negro* (New York: Columbia University Press, 1910), pp. 73–74; Watson, "Churches," p. 121; E. T. Krueger, "Negro Religious Expression," *American Journal of Sociology* 38 (July 1932): 22–31.
  [21] Mays and Nicholson, *Negro's Church*, p. 152; Watson, "Churches," pp. 124–25; Woodson, *History*, p. 252; Drake, "Churches and Voluntary Associations," p. 190.
  [22] Drake, "Churches and Voluntary Associations," p. 210. Also see Odum, *Traits*, p. 132.
  [23] Charles H. Brooks, *A History and Manual of the Grand United Order of Odd Fellows in America* (Philadelphia, 1893), p. 200.

general principles of secret society organization could create a comfortable berth for himself by starting a society."[24] The population of fraternal orders was limited only by the willingness of blacks to pay membership dues. As quickly as fraternal orders collapsed, new ones arose to replace them. Churchmen were unable to suppress the competition of fraternal orders.

Interfraternal competition was exacerbated by prevailing patterns of multiple membership. Typically, lodge brothers and sisters held simultaneous membership in competing fraternal orders. "Most of the colored men belong to more than one secret order, and many belong to as many as four or five at the same time."[25] Although fraternal spokesmen claimed that overlapping memberships did not interfere with "living up to obligations," the practice distinctly tended to inhibit internal solidarity. Overlapping memberships institutionalized easy social intercourse with exponents of rival philosophies, broke down the social isolation of an order's membership, and stimulated critical thought. Exposure to competing fraternal truths encouraged lodge brothers to doubt the truth of any. Dissatisfied, skeptical, or errant members were able easily to affiliate with a rival fraternity rather than bend to local demands for normative or intellectual conformity. Each lodge's hold on its membership was tenuous, and any taxing requirement of belief or life conduct could be expected to deplete the membership ranks drastically. The fraternal orders were not, therefore, in a position to repose unlimited trust in lodge members. For example, despite their name, the Brothers and Sisters of Love and Charity required members applying for sick relief benefits to submit a doctor's certificate as proof of illness.

Although competition for membership and overlapping memberships systematically impeded the creation of fanatic social solidarity in the churches and fraternal orders, neither competition nor overlapping membership troubled fong, clan, or kenjinkai. Since the critical social ties in these Oriental organizations were ascribed, each association possessed a ready-made membership bloc over which it had exclusive authority. These blocs were not in competition for the

[24] W. J. Trent, Jr., "Development of Negro Life Insurance Enterprises," p. 20.
[25] Fannie Barrier Williams, "Social Bonds in the 'Black Belt' of Chicago," *Charities* 15 (October 7, 1905): 42. See also Odum, *Traits*, p. 109.

membership allegiance of a shifting mass. For example, Toi-shanese could belong only to the Ning Yeung Company. Hence, the Ning Yeung Company was not in competition with any other Chinese company for the loyalties of those hailing from Toi-shan. Overlapping membership could never occur since no person could gain admittance to a regional organization other than the one representing his own region of birth. Membership in the Ning Yeung Company was, moreover, compulsory for every Toi-shanese. The alternative to membership was social isolation.

Since regional and clan organizations did not compete for membership, Oriental elites did not compete for leadership as did ministers and fraternal moguls. Oligarchical and authoritarian rule were the natural result. Oligarchs did not welcome the internal competition of self-made rivals; but unlike Negro elites, Oriental oligarchs were in a position to suppress internal competition because disgruntled rivals could not readily withdraw and form a new organization. The ultimate weapon against oligarchy in the Negro fraternals—mass quitting—could not so readily occur in the ascriptively defined, traditionally legitimated regional association or clan. Venality and racketeering were commonplace in the Chinese district associations and Six Companies, but those who cashed in on their position were not simultaneously propelling themselves up the socioeconomic hierarchy.

Regional and kinship groupings naturally tended to achieve a total rather than segmental control over their membership. Consequently, the regional ties of Orientals resulted in the formation of social groupings which were, in their internal social structure, very similar to religious sects. But for selectivity, all of the mechanisms producing internal solidarity in religious sects were reproduced in Oriental regional associations. Immune to competition, the regional and clan associations had this extremely important additional advantage over voluntary sects. In this manner, Orientals naturally came by intense social solidarity which they just as naturally and easily maintained, whereas churches and fraternals could attain less intense levels of internal solidarity only through the most Draconian measures.

Ascriptively based social ties embraced the entire Chinese and

Japanese population. Hence, all Chinese and all Japanese were automatically enrolled in solidary moral communities. In contrast, only those Negroes were involved in church and fraternal order who chose to join. Interorganizational competition for membership tended, moreover, to reduce each organization's internal solidarity. Thus, even that minority of blacks who chose to participate in church or fraternal order were usually enrolled in organizations notably less solidary than those that encompassed all Orientals. In only a very few extreme and disreputable cases were Negroes able to create on a voluntary basis organizations as solidary in their internal structure as the typical Oriental groupings.

### FATHER DIVINE'S PEACE MISSION MOVEMENT

Sparked by the mass unemployment and miseries of the Great Depression, there occurred a burgeoning of mystic, sectarian holiness cults in the black neighborhoods: "Under the economic stress, hundreds of cultists— fakers and charlatans of every brand—swept into the Negro communities, set up shop, and began to flourish in a big way."[26] Such small, tightly knit and solidary bands of religious enthusiasts had always existed on the fringes of ghetto life. But the Depression stimulated such widespread interest in these cults that they temporarily advanced from the fringes to center stage. The most prominent of these sects were the Mt. Sinai Holy Church of America, the United House of Prayer for All People (Bishop Grace), the Church of God (Black Jews), the Moorish Science Temple of America, and the Father Divine Peace Mission Movement.[27] Of these sects, the latter achieved the most spectacular growth during the 1930s. At the height of the Depression, Father Divine was the single most powerful man in black America. By 1935 he claimed two million (mostly black) followers, although Roi Ottley conceded only half a million.[28] Estimates of Divine's worldwide following ran as high as twenty million in 1936.

Father Divine achieved this pinnacle of mass acclaim only after

[26] Roi Ottley, *New World A-Coming* (New York, 1943), p. 86.

[27] Arthur Huff Fauset, *Black Gods of the Metropolis* (Philadelphia: University of Pennsylvania Press, 1944), pp. 9–10.

[28] Ottley, *New World*, p. 92. Also see John Hoshor, *God in a Rolls Royce* (New York: Hillman-Curl, 1936), p. 139.

long years of humble, unrecognized toiling in the vineyard. Born George Baker, Father Divine began his theological career as one of the numberless company of black evangelists "called" to serve God in Georgia. As such, his spectacular career followed the classical route of social ascent through the evangelical ministry. George Baker might have lived out his days in the obscurity of the Georgia backwoods had not local rednecks taken exception to his preaching. Rough handling induced him to travel north where he then passed a theological apprenticeship first under the storefront tutelage of one Father Jehovia in Baltimore and later under the Rev. St. Bishop the Vine on 133rd Street in Harlem.[29] From these instructors he absorbed a theological doctrine which proclaimed "every man a God" or God dwelling in every man.

Although Father Jehovia's conception of God dwelling within every man was never entirely abandoned, Father Divine's mature ministry moved steadily away from this early influence. God was increasingly withdrawn from the membership of the church and from humanity in general and located in the person of George Baker himself. The metamorphosis of George Baker was measured. After completing his apprenticeship with St. Bishop the Vine, he adopted the title Major J. Devine. Somewhat later, the *e* gave way to *i* and he became Major J. Divine. Finally, under the stimulus of his followers' adulation and his own ambition, he permitted himself to be known simply as Father Divine. The theology of this advanced stage of development was simple: "Father Divine is God."[30] As God Himself, Father Divine naturally bulked larger in contrast with his congregants than Baker did as simply a talented spokesman of God. Formally, his disciples retained "that of God" in themselves, but their small portions of divinity receded in practical importance as they were confronted with the authentic pristine divinity.

Father Divine moved from Harlem to Sayville, Long Island, in October 1919 with a band of twelve disciples.[31] There he established his first "Heaven" in which Major Divine acted as God while his "Angels" circulated about him. In Sayville, Father Divine secured a

[29] Hoshor, *God*, p. 32.
[30] Robert Allerton Parker, *The Incredible Messiah* (Boston: Little Brown, 1937), pp. 78–107; Hoshor, *God*, p. 36.
[31] Hoshor, *God*, p. 36.

license to operate an employment agency. His Angels hired themselves out by day, especially in domestic service. The Angels soon acquired a reputation for exceptional diligence, honesty, and reliability. They were in demand as domestic workers. The Angels contributed all of their earnings to the Heaven and received in return free room, board, clothing, and allowances. Complete communism prevailed in Father Divine's Heaven in Sayville. Divine provided a free employment service for all who cared to benefit from it. Through the employment service, the small sect introduced itself to other Negroes in domestic service and secured new converts. But the rate of growth was slow in the early years; according to John Hoshor, the Sayville Heaven numbered in 1924 only thirty to forty souls.[32]

In early 1930, however, the Peace Mission Movement went into high gear with the arrival of a busload of Pentacostal blacks from Harlem. Father Divine and his small band of disciples treated the arrivals to a banquet of fried chicken, mashed potatoes, ice cream, and coffee. The visitors were welcome to eat as much as they could; there was no charge. Asked where he obtained the financial wherewithal to treat his numerous guests to a free banquet, Divine intimated that his heavenly powers enabled him to provide. This miracle redounded to his credit. As economic conditions worsened, the news circulated among unemployed, starving Harlemites that Father Divine's Sayville Heaven provided free chicken dinners. Thousands of Harlemites visited the Sayville Heaven, enjoyed the sumptuous free repast, and listened to Father Divine's preaching. Those who came were invited to join Divine's angelic flock, to take up residence in Heaven, and to enjoy abundant happiness and eternal life on earth. This was an inviting proposition, especially to unemployed, starving people. The rub was, however, that in return for these measureless benefits recruits had to promise celibacy and chastity because Father Divine tolerated no sex in Heaven.[33] Moreover, full members had to live in a Heaven and turn over all of their earnings to the Kingdom, and every recruit had to subscribe to the proposition that "Father Divine is God." As a public token of their faith, recruits had

---

[32] *Ibid.*, pp. 32–40. Hadley Cantril, *The Psychology of Social Movements* (New York: John Wiley, 1941), p. 127; Claude McKay, *Harlem: Negro Metropolis* (New York, 1940), p. 331.

[33] Hoshor, *God*, pp. 46–47; Ottley, *New World*, p. 89.

also to abandon their worldly name and adopt a "Kingdom name" by which they would thereafter be known. Kingdom names were unmistakable: Faithful Mary, Happiness Sunshine, Gospel Glory, Wonderful Peace, and the like. Regular attendance at worship services was also expected.

These requirements were harsh; Father Divine drove a hard bargain. Nonetheless, under the beneficent influence of the Depression, the Peace Mission Movement attracted many blacks willing to meet this price. Terms that had seemed unacceptably stiff to most blacks in 1924 seemed in 1931 a good deal more reasonable.[34] Subordinate Heavens were constructed to house the burgeoning population of Angels, all of whom worked and contributed their entire income to the Kingdom. The main Heaven was moved from Sayville to Harlem in 1932 after Father Divine's miraculous release from jail on a charge of public nuisance.

The growth of membership in the Peace Mission Movement during the Depression outstripped Father Divine's capacity to place his converts in domestic employment. Self-employment provided a practical remedy for Divine's supply problem:

> Father ordered followers to form groups large and small and to set up businesses of all kinds, as "Divine Peace Mission Movement Cooperatives." They were to function under a set of rigid regulations imposed by Father. The most important of these was that, while followers gave all their money and all their services to establishment of communalism, they were to take out no profits from their investments but only enough money to supply them with the barest necessities.[35]

In starting a business, local Divinites pooled their funds and their labor. "Divine Peace Mission Movement Cooperatives" spread into every field of small endeavor. Between 1933 and 1937, Father Divine became Harlem's leading landlord. His followers leased three apartment houses, nine private homes, and three meeting halls with upstairs dormitories. Followers also operated several grocery stores, ten barber shops, ten dry-cleaning establishments, and twenty to thirty huckster wagons featuring vegetables, fruit, and fish at "evan-

[34] Cantril, *Psychology*, p. 139.
[35] Sara Harris, *Father Divine: Holy Husband*, p. 55.

gelical" prices. A coal business shuttled trucks between Harlem and Pennsylvania coal fields. In addition, Divine's followers acquired similar interests in Newark, Jersey City, Bridgeport, and Baltimore. Laundries and restaurants were, however, the most numerous of the Divine enterprises. Father's twenty-five restaurants in Harlem made a significant contribution to the relief of misery in the Depression. His restaurants sold thousands of wholesome ten-cent meals to the unemployed; in addition, his restaurants dished up 2,500 free meals a day in Harlem alone. Divine's lieutenant, Faithful Mary, headed a Peace kitchen in Newark, New Jersey, which fed 96,000 starving people in one Depression year.[36]

After the Depression, Divine's business expansion continued, although membership decreased. By 1953 Angels operated hundreds of cooperative "Peace" garages, laundries, meat markets, grocery stores, barber shops, construction and painting firms, tailor shops, furriers, restaurants, hotels, boardinghouses, and photographic studios in major cities from New York to Los Angeles. Critics of Father Divine condemned his "chain-store religion." Father Divine himself, on the other hand, took an affirmative view of his small-business empire which he dubbed "God, Incorporated."[37]

Since this widespread network of small businesses was operated and owned by Negro followers of Father Divine, the conditions of their special success are relevant to understanding why Negroes in general did not make much headway in small business. According to Austin Norris, an attorney close to Divine's business practices:

Father Divine's success can be explained with one simple word— cooperation. The Peace Movement is doubtless the most successful example of cooperation in the world today. It is organized as a combine of small cooperatives, groups of men and women banded together to purchase real estate or to buy businesses. It is organized on principles of honesty and justice . . . and is effectively held together by the love and trust all members feel toward [Father Divine]. Most important, all the cooperators have no interest in the profit motive. They really

[36] *Ibid.*, p. 56; Ottley, *New World*, p. 92; McKay, *Harlem*, pp. 38, 91–92; Hoshor, *God*, p. 144.
[37] Harris, *Father Divine*, pp. 11, 213; Marcus Bach, *Strange Sects and Curious Cults* (New York: Dodd, Mead, 1961), pp. 126–32.

don't wish to make money for themselves. They are in business for . . .
advancement of the cause of their God.[38]

The followers of Father Divine distinguished themselves from ordinary black people by their fanatical religious convictions. Social
connections emanating from this religious bond naturally provided
the Divinites with special bonds of economic confraternity: "Although the individual ["Peace"] businesses operate independently
of one another, they are mutually friendly and help each other out
whenever they can. The mutual help is inspired by two facts, first
that there are many followers who hold some interest in several businesses, and, more important, that they feel thoroughly united by
their universal loyalty to 'Father's principles.' "[39]

Unlike more respectable denominations in Harlem, the Peace
Mission Movement blessed its adherents with worldly opportunities.
Believers were preferred for employment in Peace Mission businesses. Hence, the sectarian religious faith became reflected in division of labor. Those who confessed a belief in Father Divine could
secure employment in one of his enterprises; and naturally, the
prospect of such employment was a significant inducement to confession of faith in Father Divine.

On balance, this policy proved successful. Followers of Father
were generally better workers than nonadherents. In some part, this
situation resulted from the kinds of demands that Father Divine made
of his followers. Although a confession of faith was basic, a mere
confession was not enough unless it were linked with an outward
and visible change of life which "proved" the genuineness of the
conversion. His movement had its roots in nonconformity and he
commanded his followers to work hard and prosper: "My mind is
that everyone of you should be practical, profitable, and good for
something . . . and produce more and earn more than what you
could in the mortal world."[40] The rationale of Divine's movement
was abundant prosperity for all. This was the message he preached
over free chicken dinners to the starving unemployed of Harlem.
Securing this prosperity, especially in the midst of the Great De-

[38] Harris, *Father Divine*, p. 210.
[39] *Ibid.*, p. 213. Also see Parker, *Incredible Messiah*, pp. 228–29.
[40] Parker, *Incredible Messiah*, pp. 228–29.

pression, required each and every adherent to work diligently at Father's business. As a popular Peace Movement hymn proclaimed:

> If you say you love Him,
> Get a job and go to work.[41]

Those who did not work hard or prosper evidenced a lack of real faith; those who really did love Father Divine naturally worked hard. Hard work and prosperity were simply outward and visible manifestations of the faith. Salvation was not to be attained in an afterlife; salvation for Divinites involved prosperity on earth—now.

In order to become an Angel, the reborn were commanded by Father Divine to "cancel insurance policies, and to withdraw from fraternal organizations."[42] The cash surrender value of the canceled policies was turned over to the Peace Mission Movement. Divine argued that the maintenance of private insurance policies implied a lack of faith in his provision. The consequences of this policy were, naturally, to weaken the capacity of individuals to withdraw from the movement and to strengthen Father Divine's power over them. Welfare provision was taken over exclusively by Father Divine, upon whom the individual member needed perforce to place exclusive reliance. He also commanded his followers to resign at once from public relief programs: "I desire you to know that a true believer and follower of Mine would not seek help from the Welfares [sic], for such is unevangelical, contrary to this Christ teaching . . . contrary to My Will and command, for My Way and principle is to cause each and every one to be independent that they might be Abundantly Blessed, Practical, and Profitable."[43] Having withdrawn all followers from public welfare rolls, Father Divine faced the problem of provisioning them in the Depression doldrums. He insisted that his followers ought to be eligible for WPA jobs even though none of them were recipients of public aid; however, the law excluded them on this ground and Divine was unable to effect a favorable change

41 McKay, *Harlem*, p. 66.
42 Parker, *Incredible Messiah*, p. 62. See also Hoshor, *God*, pp. 263–65.
43 Ottley, *New World*, pp. 97–98. Father Divine also commanded his Angels to obtain education. Angels were overrepresented in Harlem's evening adult schools (*New York Times*, December 8, 1935), pt. 2, p. 9, col. 1.

in the law. Small businesses provided the main solution to his problem of provisioning the heavenly host.

Transitory though it was, Father Divine's success raises two obvious questions. First, why was he able to organize the development of widespread Negro-owned business in the very teeth of the Great Depression, whereas blacks in general were unable to achieve a similar success under far more felicitous economic conditions? Second, why was he able to eliminate welfare dependency among his Angels, whereas blacks in general were espcially dependent on and overrepresented in public assistance during the Great Depression? Obviously, family stability made no contribution.

The Peace Mission Movement institutionalized a mutually supportive moral community which was based on active participation and a public way of life. In these respects, the Peace Mission resembled the Oriental regional and kin groupings. The Peace Mission Movement was able to reproduce among a minority of blacks much the same sort of cooperative social relations which were characteristic of entire Oriental communities. Oriental communities were based on ascriptive ties of family, clan, and regional origin. Because of their peculiar social history, Negroes could not reproduce such ascriptive communities. The Peace Mission Movement created a voluntary rather than an ascribed moral community. Withal, the Peace Mission Movement's internal solidarity facilitated small-business operations and mutual aid insurance among member blacks just as the internal solidarity of fong, clan, and kenjinkai facilitated them among all Orientals. The secret of Father Divine's miracles was his special ability to induce sect members to cooperate. This cooperation and trust distinguished Divine's Angels from worldly blacks and accounts for the unique achievements of Kingdom adherents.

Naturally, the prosperity of Divine's cult depended on the continued belief of the Angels in Father's divinity. Without this belief, there could have been no God, Incorporated. Maintaining this implausible belief was, however, immensely difficult, because Father Divine had to contend with the propaganda of vocal enemies among whom "envious clerics of his own race" were prominent.[44] Much as they disliked one another, respectable ministers, storefront holy rol-

44 Sutherland Denlinger, "Heaven Is in Harlem," *Forum* 95 (April 1936): 215.

lers, and rival cultists shared a greater hatred of Father Divine, whose proselytes were recruited from their own dwindling congregations. Sufi Abdul Hamid, "Daddy" Grace, and Bishop Lawson spearheaded the anti-Divine crusade. These and others of Divine's legion of enemies ridiculed his claim to Godhood and set traps to ensnare him in scenes of carnal indulgence with female adherents. They spread rumors about sexual deviation in the Kingdom and encouraged disgruntled Angels to turn informer. Hamid vowed to drive "that fake Divine" out of Harlem and died mysteriously in the attempt. "Daddy" Grace purchased a Divine Heaven and peremptorily evicted Father and his angelic host after having summoned the press to witness this ouster of God from his Heaven. The national press awarded spectacular coverage to a confrontation between Father Divine and Prophet Jones in an obvious attempt to discredit both.[45] Although the tactics of Divine's unrelenting enemies varied, their common theme was always a vocal denial of Father's divinity, the central ideological prop upon which his Kingdom rested. When Father Divine died in 1965, his Angels finally ceased to believe that he was God; so they quarreled over the property and dissolved the Kingdom.

To maintain belief and solidarity despite this barrage of hostile propaganda, the Kingdom employed the tactics of the religious sect. It was selective in recruitment; it demanded a complete change of life and enforced this demand with public scrutiny; it isolated members from the "world" and forced them to proclaim the public stigma of their affiliation. Ethically disciplined deviance resulted. The price of affiliation was very high by worldly standards, but those who were willing to pay this price thereby created on a voluntary basis the kind of fanatic solidarity that made possible their cooperation in matters of business and social welfare. Except for the Depression, Father Divine would never have obtained the following he did. Even with the help of the Depression, Father Divine was able to enroll only a tiny minority of urban blacks in his "expression." Had he been less selective in recruitment and less taxing in the demands made on adherents, his movement would have been able to appeal to more

[45] "A Prophet and a Divine Meet," *Life*, September 28, 1953, pp. 103-04; "Cosmic Lubritorium," *Time* 62, September 21, 1953, p. 79.

people; but this broader appeal would have undercut the fanatical zeal of sect members and so have deleteriously affected Divine's capacity to operate a small-business empire and autonomous social welfare institutions.

To be sure, Father Divine's movement is an extreme case even among black cults in that it was communistic and modeled its social relations on those of God and his Heavenly Host, a *ne plus ultra* of moral community. But his community was unique only in its scope and intensity, not in its results. With the exception of Bishop Grace's flock, all other black cults of the period also achieved notable success in small business and virtual independence of public welfare.[46] The Black Jews and the Nation of Islam are current examples of the connection between religious sectarianism and bourgeois behavior in the black communities. As Howard Brotz has observed, "an ideology together with an organization can do things which individual entrepreneurship among Negroes cannot achieve."[47]

These sectarian achievements suggest the lengths to which blacks found it necessary to go in order to establish on a voluntary basis the kind of solidary moral communities which immigrant Orientals achieved on the basis of Old World social ties. These communities came spontaneously to Orientals, but blacks had to become religious fanatics to develop them on a voluntary basis. To make the pill more bitter, the general public and public officials accused blacks of being insufficiently business oriented and too dependent on relief. They compared them invidiously with Chinese and Japanese, whose self-reliance urban blacks were encouraged to emulate. Yet, the white public also condemned the sectarian black zealots who took their

[46] Fauset, *Black Gods*, pp. 75, 121.

[47] Howard Brotz, *The Black Jews of Harlem* (Glencoe, Ill.: Free Press, 1964), p. 104. Also see Erdmann Doane Beynon, "The Voodoo Cult Among Negro Migrants in Detroit," *American Journal of Sociology* 43 (May 1938): esp. p. 905; C. Eric Lincoln, *The Black Muslims in America* (Boston: Beacon, 1961), p. 93; E. U. Essien-Udom, *Black Nationalism* (Chicago: University of Chicago Press, 1962), pp. 104–20; Nathan Glazer and Daniel P. Moynihan, *Beyond the Melting Pot*, pp. 82–83; Charles E. Silberman, *Crisis in Black and White* (New York: Random House, 1964), pp. 158–59; "Black Capitalism in the Muslim Style," *Fortune* 81 (January 1970): 44. For an excellent discussion of black religion and capitalism with particular reference to the Nation of Islam, see Ofari, *Myth of Black Capitalism*, pp. 49–65.

advice and created on a voluntary basis solidary communities analogous to those of Orientals. The white public did not like Negroes
very much no matter what they did.

# From Mutual Aid
# to Insurance Enterprise

# 8

As the strongest black organization to emerge from slavery, the church naturally recommended itself as the principal vehicle for effecting the transition from enslaved dependency to free labor. In the small rural churches of the South, congregants organized church beneficial societies to provide "sickness and burial" relief for one another.[1] These church beneficial societies represented the first "insurance" operations among southern Negroes even though they were operated on a nonactuarial, mutual-aid basis. Church beneficials met regularly. Their meetings were social occasions, for the members knew one another personally. At the meeting the parson or someone who could read collected a sum of money from each member. The total collected was held in reserve against the sickness or burial of any member. Members also called upon the sick and bereaved, offering presents in money and kind. Women members took over the household chores in stricken families. "Practically every church of any size throughout the country had one or more such benevolent organizations attached to it."[2] Membership in a church beneficial was open to church members on a voluntary basis.

In addition to the congregationally based "sickness and burial" societies, blacks also organized mutual-aid assessment societies. These local organizations were independent of any religious congregation but were, nonetheless, strongly moralistic in tone. The earliest

[1] E. Franklin Frazier, *The Negro in the United States*, pp. 375–76; Monroe N. Work, "Secret Societies as Factors in the Social and Economical Life of the Negro," in *Democracy in Earnest*, ed. James E. McCulloch (Washington, D.C.: Southern Sociological Congress, 1918), pp. 342–45.

[2] W. J. Trent, Jr., "Development of Negro Life Insurance Enterprises," p. 16. Also see George W. Hines and George W. Cook, "Negro Insurance," *Howard University Record* 9, no. 6 (December 1915): 8.

mutual-aid society was the Free African Society which was formed in Philadelphia in 1787. Two ministers, Absolom Jones and Richard Allen, established the Free African Society "without regard to religious tenets, provided the persons lived an orderly and sober life, in order to support one another in sickness and for the benefit of their widows and fatherless children."[3] In addition to its benevolent and welfare activities, the Free African Society scrutinized the life conduct of members and expelled many for loose living. "Thus the first insurance enterprise among Negroes had the rather large and difficult task of fostering the advance in morals as well as the economic advancement of the group."[4] This unsteady alliance of insurance and moral scrutiny fell apart when Allen founded the African Methodist Episcopal Church. In 1810 the African Insurance Company of Philadelphia began to insure Negro lives without attempting to influence how the policyholders lived them.[5]

Church beneficials and mutual-aid societies dominated black insurance until 1880. Thereafter, both congregational and mutual-aid societies gave way to fraternal orders which offered insurance "features."[6] The church beneficials never recovered their earlier importance. Black migrants in the urban North did not reestablish these religiously affiliated insurance associations,[7] but mutual-aid societies of a sort regained some temporary stature at the turn of the century with the waning of fraternalism. Some mutual-aid societies were able to convert to stock or mutual companies, and thereby to gain a permanent place in Negro insurance; for example, the Pilgrim Benevolent Society became the Pilgrim Health and Life Insurance

[3] W. E. B. DuBois, ed., *Economic Cooperation Among Negro Americans* (Atlanta, Ga.: Atlanta University Press, 1907), p. 21. Also see Work, "Secret Societies," p. 342; E. Franklin Frazier, *The Negro Church in America*, p. 35.

[4] Trent, "Development," p. 5. A similar group was the Brown Fellowship Society of Charleston, S.C. Organized among "free brown men" in 1790, the group exerted itself to relieve widows and orphans "in the hour of their distress."

[5] James B. Browning, "The Beginnings of Insurance Enterprise Among Negroes," pp. 417–18; Hines and Cook, "Negro Insurance," p. 8.

[6] M. S. Stuart, *An Economic Detour* (New York: Wendell Mailliet, 1940), p. 6; Trent, "Development," p. 60; August Meier, *Negro Thought in America* (Ann Arbor: University of Michigan Press, 1963), p. 137.

[7] Frazier, *Negro Church*, p. 48. In the South they persisted longer. See Hylan Lewis, *Blackways of Kent* (Chapel Hill: University of North Carolina Press, 1955), pp. 258–59, 274.

Company and the Mutual Aid Association became the Atlanta Life Insurance Company.[8] In all such cases the transition from mutual-aid society to commercial company was purely technical in that none of the later societies had ever been nonfinancial in character.

Between 1880 and 1910 the fraternal orders experienced their "Golden Age." The expansion of fraternalism in this period was largely attributable to the discovery of insurance features. The older fraternal orders "added insurance to the other benefits they offer their members." And in the last two decades of the nineteenth century, at least 490 new fraternal orders were established.[9] Most of the fraternal orders organized in this period were little more than assessment insurance companies in which the lodge system of organization, ritual, and charitable-benevolent purpose were largely formalities. Nonetheless, by 1900 and as late as 1915, fraternal insurers accounted for the largest amount of insurance held by Negroes.[10]

Unlike the earlier church beneficial societies, the fraternal insurers were regional and national in scope. Fraternal orders integrated local chapters into a national organization. Thus, the True Reformers were organized into local fountains, regional fountains, and the Grand Fountain (national). Mass organization permitted the fraternal orders to pay higher benefits than those possible in purely local organizations such as the church beneficials.[11] Members paid a

[8] Stuart, *Economic Detour*, pp. 35–36.

[9] Booker T. Washington, *The Story of the Negro* (New York, 1909), 2:161–62; Charles H. Wesley, *History of the Improved Benevolent and Protective Order of Elks of the World* (Washington, D.C.: Association for the Study of Negro Life and History, 1955), p. 20. Also see David Abner III, "Some Aspects of the Growth of Negro Legal Reserve Life Insurance Companies, 1930–1960" (Ph.D. diss., Indiana University, 1962), p. 21; Howard W. Odum, *Social and Mental Traits of the Negro* (New York: Columbia University Press, 1910), esp. pp. 99–108.

[10] Hines and Cook, "Negro Insurance," p. 9; W. P. Burrell, "Report of the National Negro Insurance Association," in National Negro Business League, *Annual Report of the Sixteenth Session and the Fifteenth Anniversary Convention* (Nashville, Tenn., 1915), pp. 121–22; Robert H. Kinzer and Edward Sagarin, *The Negro in American Business*, p. 71; Trent, "Development," p. 76. Among whites, fraternal insurance in force amounted to approximately three-fourths of legal reserve insurance in force between 1900 and 1905. See R. Carlyle Buley, *The American Life Convention, 1906–1952* (New York: Appleton-Century-Crofts, 1953), p. 129.

[11] Work, "Secret Societies," pp. 346–47; Trent, "Development," p. 46. Also see Frazier, *Negro in the United States*, p. 376; Monroe N. Work, "The Negro in Business and the Professions," *Annals* 140, no. 229 (November 1928): 142; Hortense Powdermaker, *After Freedom* (New York: Viking, 1939), pp. 122–23; Odum, *Traits*, pp. 108–09.

premium to the national order, and the national order provided individual members with insurance protection. Impersonal administration replaced face-to-face mutual aid. This administration required technically sophisticated officials. Uneducated lodge moguls were incompetent to administer actuarial insurance plans: "Thorough organization and . . . up-to-date business methods became still more necessary when these fraternal organizations tended to emphasize less and less the ancient mysteries and developed more largely than ever into societies paying sick benefits and burial expenses."[12] The businesslike organization of fraternal insurance tended to shift the basis of operation from assessment to actuarial insurance and from noncontractual to contractual obligation. Actuarial insurance encouraged the passive participation of persons whose only connection to the lodge was the premium payment. Diffuse, affectively charged social obligations to persons gave way increasingly to specific contractual obligations to an organization. The fraternal community took on the characteristics of a *Gesellschaft*.[13]

The economic rationalization of fraternal insurance provoked a lively debate,[14] which separated Negroes along socioeconomic lines. Educated and religiously liberal Negroes pushed consistently for a more businesslike conduct of fraternal insurance. They favored sophisticated actuarial techniques, and they charged lodge insurance officials with graft and corruption and argued that the lodges' economic and welfare roles had been superseded by legal reserve "old-line" companies. In reply, supporters of fraternal insurance claimed that progress had been made in the control of administrative corruption. They excoriated the heartlessness of the old-line insurance companies which did not, for example, send letters of sympathy to beneficiaries on the occasion of an insured death. The fraternal spokesman emphasized the role of fraternalism in stimulating Negro-owned small business. Finally, they accused their educated critics of

[12] Carter G. Woodson, "Insurance Business Among Negroes," *Journal of Negro History* 14 (April 1929): 209.

[13] Stuart, *Economic Detour*, p. 11; Robert C. Puth, "Supreme Life: The History of a Negro Life Insurance Company, 1919–1962," *Business History Review* 43 (spring 1969): 23.

[14] See, for example, *Minutes of the "Silver Jubilee" and Twenty-Fifth Annual Meeting of the National Negro Business League and Affiliated Organizations* (Nashville, Tenn., 1924), pp. 73–86.

being "too high brow" because of nonliteral interpretations of the Bible.

## THE INSURANCE JUNGLE

The discovery of insurance "features" involved the social welfare of the black population in the interorganizational rivalries for membership. Competitive pressures induced many fraternal organizations to develop insurance programs in order to attract new members or prevent the defection of existing ones. The proliferation of insurance schemes tended, in turn, to exacerbate the membership competition.[15] In their social capacity, fraternals did, after all, differ qualitatively from one another; but in their capacity as insurers, they differed only in respect to insurance protection provided per dollar of premium paid. Competition over membership in rival insurance plans placed the fraternal orders in the role of business competitors with one another. Competition in these terms tended naturally to devalue the fraternal ties and ritual from which the orders had developed. If the basis of the many-sided competition was to be simply comparative insurance benefits, then a brother could switch his loyalties from church beneficial to fraternal order or from fraternal order to commercial enterprise in response to the vicissitudes of the market.

Highly touted insurance schemes encouraged many blacks to join fraternal orders solely for the purpose of enrolling in fraternal insurance plans. Such persons were uninterested in the social and moral purposes of the fraternal orders;[16] they did not care to participate actively in lodge activities. Remaining aloof from full social and intellectual commitment to an insuring fraternal order, such persons were impervious to organizational efforts to subject them to an ethically disciplined life style. The orders might have attempted to force active participation by making insurance conditional upon such membership activity; but such requirements would only have depleted the ranks of the fraternal orders, since insurance-minded blacks took their business elsewhere rather than bend to organi-

15 J. H. McConico, "The Business Side of Fraternal Orders," in National Negro Business League, *Report of the Fifteenth Annual Convention* (Nashville, Tenn., 1914), pp. 85–89.

16 Charles H. Brooks, *A History and Manual of the Grand United Order of Odd Fellows in America* (Philadelphia, 1893), p. 204.

zational demands for ethically disciplined deviance. Indeed, the proliferation of insurance schemes forced many bona fide fraternals to reduce the social and moral obligations of membership in order to encourage the brothers and sisters to remain affiliated. As a result, the increasing availability of cheap fraternal insurance without taxing membership requirements made it easier for the less committed to withdraw from any fraternal lodge whose ethical discipline they found too onerous.

Since fraternal insurance schemes were more laxly regulated than were the reserve companies, the world of fraternalism (black and white) was invaded by greedy, often hypocritical fortune seekers. These huckstering scoundrels rang up one of the most sickening, disgraceful performances in the sordid repertoire of Gilded Age capitalism. The conduct of fly-by-night white-operated fraternal insurers was a "notorious scandal" in which embezzlement vied with actuarial illiteracy to produce "numerous ultimate failures." Although they could afford them less than could the whites, black Americans had their share of fraternal insurance frauds in this buccaneering era. "The [insurance] success of not a few fraternals attracted some more or less unscrupulous men and women and it is a sad fact that too many of the fraternals . . . were organized by individuals whose sole aim was to make money by duping their constituency and to get out as quickly as possible with the spoils."[17] Insurance benefits provided an obvious means for such persons to achieve their unscrupulous objectives. Extravagant claims attracted many poor blacks; unscrupulous fraternal officers were thus in a position to attract a substantial paying membership by making impossible claims on behalf of their order's insurance benefits. The worst offenders never intended to pay off the insurance claims whose premiums they simply pocketed. Others found it necessary to abscond when embarrassing irregularities in bookkeeping were brought to light. In general, fraternal insurance failures resulted less from frank venality than from technical incompetence linked with a desire to attract membership by publicizing very low rates of insurance cover-

[17] Trent, "Development," p. 35. For an account of fraudulence in white fraternalism, see W. S. Nichols, "Fraternal Insurance in the United States," *Annals* 70 (March 1917): 110–111.

age.[18] Competitive pressures induced many untrained fraternal officers to make claims which they later found themselves unable to fulfill because assessments had not been collected on a sound actuarial basis. In such cases, ignorance rather than frank venality accounted for official defalcations and the failure of fraternal insurance plans. But those deprived of their savings were inconvenienced quite as much by incompetence as by venality.

Intensely competitive conditions in the insurance industry did not allow small Negro operations a wide margin for error or the opportunity to learn by doing. "Fraternals, benefit associations, and insurance companies were flying at each others' throats."[19] White industrial firms invaded the Negro market. For example, in the black wards of Philadelphia, Du Bois found thirty-one "petty insurance societies" doing business in 1896/97. For the most part conducted by whites, these fly-by-night insurance enterprises depended on lapses in payment and "bold cheating" to fleece their often illiterate customers.[20] To survive in the face of this unscrupulous competition, even the most cautious of the Negro-owned insurers had to teeter on the margins of insolvency. "In order to get the business of white companies, the common attempt was to make a rate lower than that charged by the white companies, and to pay more benefits."[21] Since the fraternals in general had more than their share of ignorant, incompetent, and sometimes venal administrators, ruthless competition tended constantly to weed out the fraternal beneficials. Rampant failures and defaults occurred. Coupled with the rationalized competition of old-line insurance companies (the fraternals called them "old lying" companies), these failures precipitated a decline of public confidence in fraternal insurance.[22] Only the old-line legal-reserve companies were able to survive this ruinous competition.

In 1921 the surviving commercial companies founded the National

---

[18] Woodson, "Insurance Business," pp. 208–09. Trent, "Development," p. 37.

[19] Trent, "Development," p. 78. See also Odum, *Traits*, pp. 114–118.

[20] W. E. B. DuBois, *The Philadelphia Negro*, p. 186.

[21] Work, "Secret Societies," pp. 347–48.

[22] McConico, "Business Side," pp. 85–89; James Jackson, "Fraternal Societies Aid Race Progress," *Crisis* 45 (July 1939): 235; Robert Austin Warner, *New Haven Negroes* (New Haven, 1940), pp. 208–09; Edward Nelson Palmer, "Negro Secret Societies," *Social Forces* 23 (December 1944): 211; Allan H. Spear, *Black Chicago*, p. 108.

Negro Insurance Association. This organization was able to introduce an era of cooperation and consolidation in Negro insurance. The commercial companies increased their hold on the market, and the fraternal beneficials were driven out, despite the efforts of the hastily formed Federation of Negro Fraternals to introduce a parallel organization in fraternal insurance.[23] By 1940 the forty-two member companies of the National Negro Insurance Association accounted for 98.9 percent of all insurance written by Negro-owned operations. Of these companies, only the Supreme Camp of American Woodmen was fraternal in organization. However, the proportion of all Negro-held insurance written by Negro-owned companies was small. In 1927 the thirty-two largest Negro-owned companies together accounted for about 85 percent of all Negro-held insurance written by Negro companies. These companies had but $316 million of insurance in force on Negro lives, whereas *one* large white commercial was reputed to have $900 million of insurance in force on Negro lives. In 1940, one large white commercial wrote more insurance on Negro lives than the forty largest Negro companies combined, and the relative position of Negro-owned insurance companies has deteriorated since that date.[24]

In the legal-reserve insurance companies, the "social and moral" element was entirely suppressed. The commercial insurers made no attempt to influence the conduct of those who paid their premiums regularly. This businesslike attitude obviously precluded the development of moral solidarity among those insured by a particular company. On the other hand, the complete elimination of moral ties and the rationalization of the enterprise were highly conducive to success in competitive business. Unrestricted competition among fraternal insurers had paved the way for the success of the commercial companies by secularizing the fraternal tie and by engaging in price competition in order to attract new members. The capitalistic orga-

23 Trent, "Development," pp. 78–79.
24 *Ibid.*, pp. 82–84. See also A. T. Spaulding, "Negro Insurance," *Best's Insurance News* 44 (December 1943): 42; Leonard Broom and Norval D. Glenn, *Transformation of the Negro American* (New York, 1965), p. 140; Kinzer and Sagarin, *Negro in American Business*, pp. 92–98; Abner, "Aspects," p. 8; Alex Poinsett, "The Economics of Liberation," *Ebony* 24 (August 1969): 152; Theodore L. Cross, *Black Capitalism* (New York, 1969), pp. 211–12.

nization of the insurance industry simply perfected and brought out into the open the latent competition for membership in which churches and fraternal orders had always engaged.

The triumph of the old-line legal-reserve companies represented, by all accounts, the Negro's greatest business achievement. This success permitted blacks to obtain insurance from a number of conservatively operated, reliable Negro-owned firms. These rationalized voluntary associations are major institutions of social welfare. Thanks to these firms, many thousands of black policyholders have been able to achieve a sense of personal security against the vicissitudes of life in urban ghettos. But the triumph of actuarial insurance paralleled the complete destruction of traditional, mutual-aid insurance among urban blacks. Neither churches nor fraternal orders in the urban North offered mutual-aid insurance on a pragmatic nonactuarial basis.[25] For protection against sickness, old age, and death, the black migrant in the North had perforce to buy insurance or go entirely unprotected.

MUTUAL-AID INSURANCE AMONG ORIENTALS

In fong, clan, and kenjinkai, provision for social welfare took the form of nonactuarial mutual aid. When a member was in trouble, others helped him with goods in kind, services, and money.[26] In these respects, the Chinese and Japanese welfare institutions resembled the church beneficial more than any other Negro institution. Unlike blacks, however, Chinese and Japanese operated mutual-aid institutions of this type in the urban North. Their traditional mutual-aid organization did not advance toward rationalization. Their moral communities remained intensely solidary and mutually supportive.

Mutual aid had characteristic advantages and disadvantages relative to actuarial insurance plans. Because the groups were small, Chinese or Japanese in need of help could not anticipate windfall rewards. Insurance policies provided much greater money payments than one could receive on a mutual-aid basis from fong, clan, or kenjinkai. On the other hand, some benefits of mutual aid were

[25] St. Clair Drake, "Churches and Voluntary Associations," p. 211; Frazier, *Negro Church*, p. 48.
[26] See Robert E. Park and Herbert A. Miller, *Old World Traits Transplanted* (New York, 1921), esp. pp. 124–32.

extremely valuable. If sick, a member could expect friends to operate his store or get him into a hospital for treatment; but the insurance company would not provide similar services for policyholders. If he were unemployed, a member's friends would help him to find a job; but the commercial insurance company provided no such service. The insurance company could provide the wherewithal to purchase goods and services; but friends could provide goods in kind and services for free. Obviously, there could be no question of chiseling benefits from fong or kenjinkai, because one did not chisel from friends and friends were sure to know when one claimed benefits one did not deserve. On the other hand, fraudulent insurance claims did not affect friends directly, and the insurance company did not automatically know which claims were fraudulent. In this sense, mutual aid was cheaper than commercial insurance, in that a beneficiary did not have to pay for fraudulent claims, a chronic problem of actuarial insurers.[27]

Operating a mutual-aid system did not require actuarial or technical skills. As insurance agencies, extended families, clans, fongs, kenjinkai, and the like operated themselves with only minor interference by administrative officials. There were no overhead costs, no educated, white-collar officials, and no official venality. In an era of lax state regulation of insurance plans, these advantages were most valuable. Negro-owned commercial insurers and fraternal beneficial societies experienced chronic difficulties in attempting to recruit technical experts to administer their insurance plans.[28] The lack of such people caused many fraternal and commercial operations to collapse, leaving the impoverished policyholders without group protection against the vicissitudes of life.

Mutual-aid insurance did not require the investment of a legal reserve in profitable securities. There was no legal reserve. Unfortunately, Negro insurers, like Negro-owned banks, needed to make profitable investments of their reserve funds. Negro-owned insurance companies showed a deplorable "tendency to lend money on church

[27] Stuart, *Economic Detour*, p. 18.
[28] Joseph R. Houchins, "Causes of Negro Insurance Company Failures," pp. 2–3. Also see Woodson, "Insurance Business," p. 220; Gunnar Myrdal, *An American Dilemma*, 1:317.

and lodge properties greatly in excess of the true valuation of these properties."[29] Such disastrous investments caused the failure of many black firms. Lacking a reserve with its survival need for profit, Oriental brotherhoods could not suffer the same harsh fate.

Poor blacks were covered by most industrial insurance policies only as long as they paid regular premiums. With the momentary cessation of income, policyholders lost their insurance protection. If they happened to take sick or die at that inopportune moment, they and their dependents were out of luck. Many blacks lived on the margin of poverty; their incomes were unreliable. Rates of insurance lapsation were, accordingly, very high among blacks.[30] Mutual-aid insurance precluded this chronic problem of the Negro insurance industry; so long as one's friends or relatives were alive, one could depend on their help in a crisis.

Church beneficial societies had no need of a technically skilled management to oversee investment of a reserve; nor did a person forfeit his claims just because he failed to make a premium payment. In these respects the church beneficials were similar to the kinship and regional groupings among Orientals. Both forms of mutual aid were distinguishable from commercial insurance on all these counts. Nevertheless, church beneficials and legal-reserve companies were both voluntary associations. On the other hand, immigrant brotherhoods ascribed membership to people on the basis of birth, and one had to choose *not* to belong. As voluntary organizations, church beneficials and insurance companies protected only those who joined them. In contrast, ascribed protection automatically covered every Chinese or Japanese.

In the church beneficials the membership's obligation to help one another was purely voluntary. Apart from the friendships produced by active participation and a public way of life, members of the church beneficials had no special bond to one another. In the South, church beneficials more easily attained moral solidarity on a voluntary basis, since the churches were rural and the population rela-

[29] Houchins, "Insurance Company Failures," p. 10.
[30] Trent, "Development," pp. 94–95. Also see Puth, "Supreme Life," pp. 9–10; Julian H. Nixon, "The Changing Status of the Negro: Some Implications for Savings and Life Insurance," *American Behavioral Scientist* 6 (May 1963): 82.

tively permanent. But in the North, voluntary associations could not rely on the traditional religiosity of an isolated population. Storefront churches could recapture some of the interpersonal intensity of religious experience in the South, but they were characteristically unable to develop the total membership commitment required for the operation of mutual-aid insurance. Competition for membership persistently broke down the internal solidarity of the storefronts. Because they were based on ascribed social ties, Oriental regional groupings were immune to this sort of competition. As a result, Oriental groupings retained the high levels of internal solidarity necessary for mutual aid.

In fong, clan, and kenjinkai, members helped one another because of their belief that people from the same place or of the same clan were morally obliged to help one another. This belief interfered with insurance rationalization by discouraging utilitarian calculations of personal advantage, and cost-benefit analysis. For example, Japanese kenjinkai extended (grudging) help to kenjin who were in difficulties but who had not theretofore actively participated in ken life and so "earned a right" to help. In this activity the kenjinkai recognized moral obligations which overruled actuarial science. Insurance companies recognize no transcendent moral obligations to persons who have not paid premiums. Even in the least rationalized, most moralistic of Negro insurance organizations, the church beneficial, the membership recognized only collective obligations to other paying members. This principle of equity was also that of the insurance enterprise. In both, equity involved helping those who had paid— and no one else. In principle, then, there was no internal barrier to actuarial rationalization in the church beneficial. Criticisms of the assessment plan based themselves on a principle of equity (to each according to his contribution) that was at least implicit in the church beneficials themselves. This particular principle of equity, the strictly actuarial insurance enterprise later proved better able to institutionalize than the church beneficial.

Where actuarial insurance made inroads into the Chinese and Japanese communities in the United States, it did so as a result of cultural assimilation. After 1924 assimilation increasingly attacked the traditional social structure and created needs for personal insurance protection on the actuarial plan. In the Orient, the basic old-age protection had been provided by having many sons and drilling them well in the principles of filial piety, familism, and mutual aid.[31] These principles had religious sanction through Buddhist and Confucian ethics which stressed the veneration of elders and ancestor worship. Instead of an annuity or pension, a Japanese or Chinese parent could rely on the pious support of his respectful sons. This sort of insurance had only hidden costs. Everything depended on maintaining in the youth a lively sense of familism and mutual aid.

In the United States, properly filial sons were hard to rear. The Japanese and Chinese immigrants resurrected the traditional family system but experienced great difficulty in its intergenerational perpetuation. Through mandatory attendance at the public schools, Japanese and Chinese youth acquired a Westerner's perspective on family relations and insurance. This perspective is decidedly immoral from the point of view of Oriental tradition. Filial obligations came to be viewed as a burden rather than a strict moral obligation and a "privilege."[32] Insurance companies offered cheap contractual protection which did not obligate a beneficiary to live a strict archaically righteous life under the scrutiny of tradition-bound elders. Japanese or Chinese immigrants who could not rely on their Americanized offspring for support in sickness and old age were perforce obliged to make private insurance provisions for these contingencies or risk a pauper's grave. A Japanese-American insurance agent remarked:

> Unlike the American community, everybody . . . in the Japanese community has taken out some kind of a life policy. . . . While in Japan these same people would have had security in simply belonging to a

[31] S. S. Huebner, "Life and Casualty Insurance in Japan and China," pp. 392–94; idem, "Insurance in China," pp. 105–08; Betty Lee Sung, *Mountain of Gold*, p. 153; William J. Goode, "Perspectives on Family Research and Life Insurance," *American Behavioral Scientist* 6 (May 1963): 58; Ch'eng-K'un Cheng, "Familism, the Foundation of Chinese Social Organization," *Social Forces* 23 (October 1944): 57.

[32] Fumiko Fukuoka, "Mutual Life and Aid Among the Japanese of Southern California," pp. 60–61; Jitsuichi Masuoka, "Changing Moral Bases of the Japanese Family in Hawaii," *Sociology and Social Research* 21 (November-December 1936): 158–69; Wen-Hui Chung Chen, "Changing Socio-Cultural Patterns of the Chinese Community in Los Angeles," pp. 213–14; Paul C. P. Siu, "The Chinese Laundryman: A Study of Social Isolation" (Ph.D. diss., University of Chicago, 1953), p. 268; Stuart H. Cattell, "Health, Welfare, and Social Organization in Chinatown, New York," p. 59.

certain family group, here the family system has broken down and there is no one to turn to in case of death of the breadwinner. . . . Thus, while there was at first a general disinterestedness in insurance policies . . . about the latter part of the [First World War] period we had an unusual boom in the insurance business.[33]

Although tendencies toward the Americanization of the youth were widely observed and bewailed by spokesmen of the Japanese and Chinese communities, the spirit of traditional filial piety and familism could not be revived; social pressures were able, however, to restrict the manifestation of the pestiferous individualistic canker.

The progress of rationalized insurance among Orientals is suggested by the increasing percentage of Chinese and Japanese employed as insurance agents and officials (Table 10). Between 1910 and 1930, this percentage increased nearly thirtyfold. In both 1910 and 1930, a higher percentage of Negroes were represented in this occupation than the average percentage of Chinese and Japanese combined, although their rate of increase was less dramatic. Comparison of Chinese and Japanese in 1930 shows that the two Oriental groups differed substantially in their propensity to become insurance agents and officials. The rate of Japanese participation was eight times higher than that of Chinese. The Japanese percentage alone was also substantially higher than that of Negroes in 1930.

These differences between Chinese and Japanese in 1930 may reflect underlying differences in attitudes toward insurance, as well as the true rate of personal insurance in the respective populations. Japanese were probably more favorable to commercial insurance than were Chinese and probably more highly insured than the Chinese in 1930. The persistence of the clan among the Chinese would tend to explain why they were willing to place greater confidence in traditional mutual aid than were the Japanese, among whom the lineage clan system perished under the Tokugawa regime. It is also tempting to suppose that the greater Japanese proclivity to become

[33] Shotaro Frank Miyamoto, *Social Solidarity Among the Japanese in Seattle*, p. 97. See also Kian Moon Kwan, "Assimilation of the Chinese in the United States: An Exploratory Study in California" (Ph.D. diss., University of California, Berkeley, 1958), p. 123; Sung, *Mountain*, p. 121; Kim-Fong Tom, "Function of the Chinese Language School," *Sociology and Social Research* 25 (July–August 1941): 557–61.

## TABLE 10

*Percentage of Oriental, Negro, and All Males 10 Years of Age or Older Gainfully Employed in Nonagricultural Pursuits and Engaged in Selected Commercial Occupations, 1910 and 1930*

| | Oriental | Negro | All Males |
|---|---|---|---|
| *1910*[a] | | | |
| Number of males 10 years of age or older engaged in non-agricultural pursuits | 89,074 | 1,336,311 | 19,239,862 |
| *Percentage occupied as:* | | | |
| Retail dealers | 7.43 | 1.55 | 5.87 |
| Bankers, brokers, and money lenders | .08 | .02 | .53 |
| Insurance agents and officials | .01 | .11 | .49 |
| Real estate agents and officials | .02 | .05 | .64 |
| *1930*[b] | | | |
| Number of males 10 years of age or older engaged in non-agricultural pursuits | 68,346 | 2,170,338 | 28,515,745 |
| *Percentage occupied as:* | | | |
| Retail dealers | 9.48 | 1.63 | 5.97 |
| Bankers, brokers, and money lenders | .24 | .01 | .74 |
| Insurance agents and officials | .27 | .38 | .95 |
| Real estate agents and officials | .10 | .23 | .84 |
| *1930*[b] | Chinese | Japanese | Negro |
| Number of males 10 years of age or older engaged in non-agricultural pursuits | 42,291 | 26,055 | 2,170,338 |
| *Percentage occupied as:* | | | |
| Retail dealers | 8.74 | 10.67 | 1.63 |
| Bankers, brokers, and money lenders | .07 | .52 | .01 |
| Insurance agents and officials | .08 | .57 | .38 |
| Real estate agents and officials | .01 | .31 | .23 |

[a] U.S. Department of Commerce, Bureau of the Census, Bulletin 127, *Chinese and Japanese in the United States, 1910,* (Washington, D.C., 1914); idem, Bulletin 129, *Negroes in the United States, 1910* (Washington, D.C., 1915); idem, *Thirteenth Census of the United States, 1910. Population, 1910,* vol. 4, *Occupation Statistics* (Washington, D.C., 1914).

[b] U.S. Department of Commerce, Bureau of the Census, *Fifteenth Census of the United States, 1930. Population,* vol. 5, *General Report on Occupations* (Washington, D.C., 1933), Table 3, p. 82, and Table 6, p. 95.

insurance officials reflected more favorable attitudes toward Westernization. In any event, the higher degree of Japanese involvement in commercial insurance is highly congruent with their generally more loose-knit social organization.

The same conclusions cannot be drawn with regard to the differences between Japanese and Negroes. Possibly a higher proportion of Japanese than Negroes in 1930 were actually subscribing to commercial insurance. But the figures pertaining to insurance agents and officials give no indication of the percentage of all insurance which was arranged by white insurance brokers. This figure was probably rather low for the Japanese, and it certainly was quite high for Negroes.[34] Hence, one cannot deduce the differences in rate of insurance from the proportion of the respective populations employed as insurance brokers. It does, however, seem likely that a higher proportion of both Japanese and Negroes subscribed to commercial insurance than did Chinese.

Although cultural assimilation naturally tended to reduce the differences between Orientals and Negroes, these differences were still very pronounced in 1930. On the one extreme, Chinese residents, especially the poorer ones, were quite uninvolved in any commercial insurance schemes.[35] The poorer Chinese were more or less completely dependent on mutual aid and filial piety for any social security. On the other extreme, informal mutual aid among Negroes had by 1930 given way to rationalized insurance policies. Especially in the urban North, such individual provision for the future was the black wage earner's largely exclusive source of social security. Between both of these extremes, the Japanese apparently maintained both a traditional mutual-aid system of social security and commercial insurance policies. Japanese were expected to make private insurance provision for the future, but the destitute uninsured were still in 1930 able to secure assistance from *ko*, kinsmen, and kenjin.

Among Orientals and Negroes alike, educated, wealthy, and higher status persons preferred the insurance policy to traditional insurance practices. The impact of Western education appears very clearly

---

[34] "Unless the agent happens to belong to the right *ken* group, it is very difficult for him to sell insurance." Miyamoto, *Social Solidarity*, p. 79.

[35] California State Emergency Relief Administration, "Survey of the Social Work Needs of the Chinese Population of San Francisco, California," p. 24.

among the native-born Orientals. The members of that generation also tended to be more interested in Western insurance concepts than were poorer foreign-born Japanese and Chinese. In all three groups, the poor and uneducated migrants were most resistant to the rationalized insurance policy and most likely to favor some traditional and collectivity-oriented means of achieving social security. But the availability of traditional welfare services was much greater among the Orientals than among urbanized Negroes.

Naturally, the poor and uneducated are precisely those most likely to require some form of social assistance and to need this help very badly when they need it. Traditional forms of mutual-aid insurance were, therefore, of greatest significance to those segments of the Oriental and Negro populations otherwise most likely to become public welfare clients. Among Orientals and Negroes, as among Americans in general, those most likely to purchase an insurance policy were also those otherwise least likely to stand someday with hand outstretched at the threshold of the public welfare department.[36] Hence, it is of capital significance that the blacks' traditional forms of mutual aid did not survive in the cities whereas those of the Chinese and Japanese did.

In times of prosperity, blacks did not notice too much the disappearance of their own traditional style of mutual aid, but the Great Depression of the 1930s produced mass awareness of vulnerability to the business cycle and unavailing attempts to reconstitute mutual aid. For example, in 1931 the Relief Bureau of the Abyssinian Baptist Church in Harlem raised funds to feed the unemployed; other churches followed suit. But the need was too great for the churches to succeed. Through the Harlem Division of the Emergency Unemployment Relief Committee, Harlem authorities made repeated calls for employed blacks to share their income with an unemployed person: "The aim of this division is to urge upon the community the necessity for the majority of workers who have been able to

[36] Frequency of insurance coverage and average annual premium paid vary directly with income in the United States. See Institute of Life Insurance, *Life Insurance Fact Book* (New York, 1959), p. 16; Fabian Linden, ed., *Market Profiles of Consumer Products* (New York: National Industrial Conference Board, 1967), *passim*.

retain their places as wage earners, to share their earnings with less
fortunate brethren, who have been unable to find work and are left
stranded."[37] However, old-fashioned mutual aid could not be sud-
denly resurrected on a mass scale in response to unprecedented need.
Had this pattern survived among lower class blacks, then they would
have been able, like the Orientals, to employ these informal resources
for the relief of the Depression-spawned unemployed.[38]

[37] New York *Age*, November 14, 1931, p. 4.

[38] Cf. Clyde Vernon Kiser, *Sea Island to City*, p. 210; Ruth S. Cavan and
Katherine H. Ranck, *The Family and the Depression* (Chicago: University of
Chicago Press, 1938), pp. 90–94; Albert K. Cohen and Harold M. Hodges, Jr.,
"Characteristics of the Lower Blue-Collar Class," *Social Forces* 10 (spring 1963):
esp. pp. 305–07.

# Voluntary Association and Immigrant Brotherhood

# 9

Moral community is a state of shared moral values. Both voluntary association and the tribal, clan, or territorial (ascriptive) brotherhood may attain a state of moral community. In this sense, a willed, noncompulsory moral community which one has voluntarily chosen is a structural equivalent of an unchosen, automatic moral community in which one's membership is simply ascribed. Family and sect have this quality in common. On the other hand, the meaning and dynamics of a moral community based only on voluntary ties differ from those of a community based only on ascriptive ties.

The ascriptive brotherhood institutionalizes two patterns of social conduct. One pattern applies to contacts between members of the ascribed in-group. They are expected to be brotherly, helpful, and trusting. A second pattern applies to contacts between brothers and aliens. These contacts do not take place within the normative framework of the ascriptive brotherhood, since the moral principle of the brotherhood is coterminous with the ascriptive ties. Moral obligations are owed to others because of their ascriptive relationship. Hence, when unrelated persons interact, their social relations are competitive, instrumental, and mistrustful. Brotherhood extends no further than the ascriptively defined circle: "Tribal practice is exclusive; a man is either one of the group or an alien, and there is little or nothing to choose among different kinds of aliens."[1] The ascriptive brotherhood militates against experiments in voluntary association beyond the boundaries of the in-group. Such experiments require mutual trust based on shared moral principles, but there can be no shared

[1] Michael Banton, "Social Alignment and Identity in a West African City," in *Urbanization and Migration in West Africa*, ed. Hilda Kuper (Berkeley and Los Angeles: University of California Press, 1965), p. 139.

moral principles among ascriptively unrelated persons when the moral principle itself is coterminous with the ascriptive tie.[2]

Voluntary associations in general (church, sect, insurance company) introduce unrelated persons who must interact on a universalistic basis. The relationship of members to one another is stipulated in impersonal rules which set down the rights and duties of membership. Anyone fulfilling the prescribed duties of membership obtains a right to the benefits of membership. The point of view of the voluntary group to nonmembers is an impersonal extension of the principles of the group. This impersonal group view treats all ascriptive ties as equal. Hence, as a member of a voluntary association, an individual cannot favor his own tribe or kin against aliens; but precisely such a preference is the basis of ascriptively bounded morality. Hence, as a voluntary member, one must divorce oneself from traditional moral ties to kinsmen.

The tension between the point of view of the voluntary association and that of the ascriptive brotherhood is maximal when the voluntary association is avowedly moralistic. Under these circumstances, the voluntary group explicitly claims moral universalism. This moral universalism directly attacks the moral particularism of ascriptive brotherhoods. When a voluntary association is not moralistic, this implicit conflict of principle is less pronounced. In a church, impersonal morality may coexist with practical moral behavior which extends no further than the boundaries of the ascriptively defined group. Thus, in Freetown, Michael Banton found that most Moslem tribes had "their own mosques or praying rooms," so unpleasant did tribesmen find worship in the presence of ethnically unrelated coreligionists. Congregants of ethnically Irish or Italian Catholic churches in the United States have worshipped separately in quite the same spirit as the Freetown Moslems.[3] Demanding only a modicum of assent to moral universalism, churches do not police daily conduct —even in the church building itself. But in the religious sect the

[2] Benjamin Nelson, *The Idea of Usury* (Princeton, 1949); Max Weber, *The Sociology of Religion* (Boston: Beacon, 1956), pp. 250–51; idem, *Ancient Judaism*, pp. 343–55.

[3] Michael Banton, *West African City* (London: Oxford University Press, 1957), p. 137; Herbert J. Gans, *The Urban Villagers* (New York: Free Press, 1962), pp. 112–13.

believer is swallowed by the voluntary group and radically isolated from ascriptive ties. Conduct is subject to the critical scrutiny of peers who enforce an ethical discipline in the rounds of daily life. Thus, it is precisely in the voluntary religious sect that the moral conflict between traditional particularism and moral universalism attains its maximal intensity and has the greatest likelihood of influencing conduct in daily life.

In this sense the religious sect and the ascriptive brotherhood are in pure competition for members. The particularist morality of the ascriptive brotherhood conflicts with the universalist morality of the religious sect. But there can be no compromise between religious sect and ascriptive brotherhood, because both require members to manifest in their daily life a particular life style. Individuals cannot simultaneously lead the outward and visible life style approved by a religious sect while continuing to lead their ethnic life style.[4] The moral conflict between church and ascriptive brotherhood is generally less flagrant, since the church does not require adherents to lead a deviant life style under ethical discipline. Hence, the church makes possible a compromise between ascription and universalism—intellectual assent to its moral principles but practical behavior in accordance with traditional morals. The radical conflict between religious sect and ascriptive brotherhood suggests the preeminence of the sect as opposed to the church in the overthrow of ascriptive traditionalism.

### THE POLITICS OF BROTHERHOOD

The competition of urban voluntary associations for membership is also a competition of elites for followers. Since the proliferation of voluntary associations in black neighborhoods made this competition particularly intense, autonomous black leaders found it eternally necessary to scurry for popular support by adjusting their

[4] In contemporary Africa, the number of religious sects is rapidly increasing. But these sects tend to enroll only members of one tribe or another. Their religious principles are in such cases largely coterminous with tribal customs. Hence, members of such sects experience little conflict between sectarian life style and ethnic life style. These tribally specific religious sects "make little or no progress when they come to tribal frontiers." David Barrett, *Schism and Renewal in Africa* (Nairobi: Oxford University Press, 1968), pp. 59–60, 275.

publicly espoused plans or positions to their reading of the constituent mood.[5] Preachers, lodge officers, bankers, educators, and politicians all strove with one another to achieve success by giving the black public the kind of leadership it wanted to support. Protests of white racism were always applauded in black communities; and black spokesmen or would-be spokesmen tried to outdo one another by articulating ever more popular protests. Naturally, different social strata preferred different types of protest and different ideological emphases. Also, when the popular mood changed, the style of protest favored by leaders had also to change. Hence, there was always ample diversity of community opinion to support widely differing leaderships and programs.

Northern blacks have nowhere sustained a single organization whose leadership could authentically claim to speak for the entire black population of a major city or state. As one result, television programs desiring to portray a black view during the racial crisis of the 1960s had typically to take the form of panel discussions among various black leaders—with immense diversity of philosophy and personal life style represented on the panel. The so-called default of leadership in the black communities has actually arisen from the chronic inability of any single leadership to acquire the support of all sectors of the black public. Although this diversity made black protests harder for authorities to deal with, the democratic condition simply mirrors the divided opinions of the black population. If Negroes lack a single, universally acknowledged spokesman organization, the reason is the democratic, popular, and fluid quality of black American urbanism.

Until quite recently, Chinese and Japanese communities have lacked any vocal politics of militant protest even though, like the blacks, the Orientals have had much to protest in the treatment American society has accorded them. In the popular view, the noteworthy reticence of Orientals is attributed to their traditional family-centered values. This view has considerable merit; and Lyman has convincingly explained some differences between Chinese and Jap-

---

[5] James Wilson, *Negro Politics*, pp. 306, 311. Also cf. Joseph A. Schlesinger, "Political Party Organization," in *Handbook of Organizations*, ed. James G. March (Chicago: Rand McNally, 1965), pp. 764–801.

anese by reference to the Japanese immigrants' speedier establishment of a domestic life in America.[6] On the other hand, the Chinese and Japanese populations have been large enough to harbor some diversity of opinion and outlook. The past half century has also been a period of violent and painful social change in Asia. The conservative homogeneity of social-political conduct among Asian Americans in this period is unmatched in Asia itself, where people also have traditional family-centered values.

Unlike blacks, Chinese and Japanese have historically supported unitary organizations of community spokesmanship. Before World War II, the spokesman organizations were the Japanese Association of America and the Chinese Six Companies. The most successful businessmen became the leaders of these organizations. Business class leaders encouraged their people to work hard, to save money, and to avoid unfriendly publicity. Their views in this respect were similar to those of Booker T. Washington. But unlike the Tuskgeegean, established Oriental leaderships were able to exert decisive, conservative influence on local politics. The influence of these leaders is, therefore, of at least supplementary importance in explaining the striking absence of politically directed protest among Orientals.[7]

Especially before 1940, established Oriental leaderships simply did not approve of popular protest, whether directed against them or against the whites. Traditional family-centered values certainly colored their views, but there were other influences. For one thing, leaders of the Chinese Six Companies and of the Japanese Association of America saw nothing morally wrong in many nonviolent forms of ethnic and racial discrimination. They themselves discriminated

[6] Stanford M. Lyman, *The Asian in the West*, pp. 27–31, 61.

[7] John Modell, "A Different Color Line: The Japanese-American Response to Racism, 1900–1940" (paper prepared for 1970 meetings of the Organization of American Historians). Of 98 eminent Chinese listed in Van Norden's *Who's Who*, 91 were listed as businessmen. Only 17 of the 98 reported a bachelor's or higher degree. See Warner M. Van Norden, *Who's Who of the Chinese in New York* (New York, 1918). Cf. also Clifford Jansen, "Leadership in the Toronto Italian Community," *International Migration Review* 4 (fall 1969): 25–41; J. Gottfried Passche and Clifford J. Jansen, "Unity and Disunity in Two Ethnic Groups in Toronto" (paper presented at the 1969 meetings of the Canadian Sociology and Anthropology Association, York University, Toronto, Ontario, Canada). J. Max Bond ("The Negro in Los Angeles," pp. 302–18) provides an insightful but widely overlooked comparison of Japanese and blacks.

against out-groups in housing and employment, and they expected out-groups to discriminate against them. For another, they believed the whites to be so numerous and ruthless that the best policy was one of patient accommodation. Finally, business class leaderships had an interest in preserving the economic status quo. For their part, most sojourning immigrants wanted only to be left alone to accumulate as much money as possible as quickly as possible. Many had families to support in Asia. Laboring men rarely experienced a strong desire to protest against the whites; protests against their own leaders were rare but more common.

Business class leaders were usually in a position to squash serious dissenters by depriving those who made trouble of employment opportunities. Purges of radicals and trade unionists were fairly common among both Chinese and Japanese during the 1930s. By virtue of discrimination in the American labor market, Chinese and Japanese wage earners depended on ethnic businesses for employment. Therefore, blacklisting and expulsion from this sector was a serious personal disaster for a Chinese or Japanese employee. Even a self-employed businessman needed the goodwill of powerful leaders to stay in business. This dependency was particularly strong among the Chinese whose very title to property depended on licenses obtainable only from the Six Companies and district associations. Much less restrained in this direct sense, Japanese businessmen in most trades depended on the cooperation of ethnic retailers or wholesalers. The Japanese Association was often in a position to deprive an obnoxious troublemaker of this cooperation.

To get a job or run a business in the ethnic economy, a man needed to belong to an influential territorial or clan group. Each of these various groups tended to favor its own sort in business matters. Hence, ouster from a territorial or clan organization was tantamount to ouster from the ethnic economy. Even displeasing a man influential in so critical an organization was quite likely to have deleterious economic consequences. Accordingly, the established leaders of territorial and clan organizations were in a strong position to deter moral or political behavior of which they disapproved.

So long as they were locked into exclusive village, territorial, and family groupings, Chinese and Japanese workers were unable to shift their membership support to any leadership that pleased them. Hence, the rank and file could not readily control unresponsive territorial elites by playing them off against one another. Moreover, so long as the Old World loyalties remained lively, mutual distrust tended to prevent disgruntled people of differing immigrant backgrounds from making common cause against conservative elites. Regularly characteristic of private governments, oligarchy becomes especially powerful and durable when ordinary members do not have the ability to form or join rival organizations. In this sense, the mutually exclusive immigrant brotherhoods of the sojourning generation endowed business class leaders with an enormous capacity to mold developing Chinatowns or Little Tokyos in the image of their conservative social and economic philosophy.

This system of social control could not easily accommodate the native-born generation. Unlike their immigrant parents, native-born, American-educated Chinese and Japanese could muster scant loyalties to Old World villages or provinces. These places they had never seen and never expected to visit. The home dialect their elders had to teach them in gloomy classrooms. Therefore, many native-born youth found the moral solidarity of the immigrant brotherhoods archaic, sentimental, and parochial.[8] As sectional differences receded in subjective importance, generational differences increased. To most native-born Orientals, the important question was not what family or village was in a person's background, but whether a person was native born or foreign born. The native born often considered themselves to have more in common with other native-born young people than they did with foreign-born persons from the same village or province or even with foreign-born kinsmen. The generational consciousness was particularly strong among the Japanese whose generational nomenclature (issei, nisei, sansei) is the basic sociology of the group.

Voluntary associations met the needs of educated, native-born

---

[8] Cf. Maurice Freeman, "Immigrants and Associations: Chinese in Nineteenth Century Singapore," and Marjorie Topley, "The Emergence and Social Function of Chinese Religious Associations in Singapore," both in *Immigrants and Associations,* ed. L. A. Fallers (The Hague: Mouton, 1967), pp. 41, 56.

Orientals estranged from Old World social categories. Unlike the exclusive territorial and family brotherhoods, these voluntary associations were formally open to all irrespective of immigrant background. The first of these secular voluntary associations developed before World War II, but their social influence has become more visible since the war. The two prototype organizations are the Chinese American Citizens' Alliance (CACA), and the Japanese American Citizens' League (JACL).

The CACA has waged a legal and electoral battle against segregation and discriminatory treatment of Chinese since its incorporation in 1895. All Chinese are eligible for membership in the CACA. In fact, its charter explicitly forbids members to entertain clan or sectional prejudice against one another. On the other hand, the CACA is exclusive in other respects. Membership is by invitation only. Every new member requires two sponsors. Native-born college-educated professionals have been disproportionately numerous and influential. The CACA introduced fraternal insurance benefits in 1912 when many educated Chinese felt that American insurance companies discriminated against them. The insurance option attracted new members, and the CACA added additional benefits in 1920. But the CACA abruptly dropped all of its insurance programs in 1947, and membership began to decline. By 1965, the CACA's San Francisco membership had dropped to 600—less than one-third the pre-1940 figure. According to Tan, "insurance was apparently a major attraction of the association."[9] Most college age Chinese now regard the CACA as overly conservative and in league with the Six Companies establishment. Those San Francisco Chinese professionals who join any Chinatown organization are more likely to select the Chinese American Democratic Club or Gordon Lau's Concerned Chinese for Action and Change. However, most native-born Chinese live in suburban areas and return to Chinatown only

[9] Mély Giok-Lan Tan, "Social Mobility and Assimilation," p. 212. Also see Betty Lee Sung, *Mountain of Gold*, pp. 639–40; Linda Matthews, "New Oriental Immigrants Seen Cut off from Prosperity, Hopes" *Los Angeles Times*, May 6, 1968, sec. 2, p. 1; Wen-hui Chun Chen, "Changing Socio-Cultural Patterns of the Chinese Community in Los Angeles," pp. 292–95; Ching Chao Wu, "Chinatowns: A Study of Symbiosis and Assimilation" (Ph.D. diss., University of Chicago, 1928), pp. 187–88.

to lay in grocery supplies on Sunday. The majority are apathetic and join no Chinatown associations. But for the family name associations, most native-born Chinese would have no link at all with Chinatown.

Membership in the Japanese American Citizens' League is available to "all Americans 18 years of age or older," but most of those who join are of Japanese descent. The JACL deplores civic apathy and welcomes applications for membership. Nonetheless, its membership is disproportionately native born, higher status, and urban. In 1970, the JACL claimed a national membership of 25,000, its largest ever. This membership is only a fraction of the 464,332 Japanese who were in the United States in 1960. But, the membership is absolutely and proportionately much larger than any counterpart organization among Chinese Americans. Of course, only a handful of people in the various JACL chapters are really active in the organization: "the vast majority of members join only for insurance."[10]

When the JACL and the CACA first appeared, their immediate problem was to establish a modus vivendi with the territorial and family organizations whose leaders considered them both secular and dangerous. After all, these new civic voluntary associations were new centers of power. These centers the established leadership did not control. Moreover, the civic associations emphasized insurance rather than mutual aid and filial piety, the traditional virtues. They considered the moral solidarity of the immigrant brotherhood both stifling and parochial. They tried to attract new members and did not care about the Old World origins of those they admitted. The presence of these centers created new options for people who were secretly critical of established leaders. They provoked dissent and stirred up people who had previously been acquiescent. They were, in sum, provocative, "amoral," and democratic influences.

In Japanese communities, the "relocation" of 1942 brutally resolved the rivalry. The relocation and the uncompensated confiscation of property laid the axe to the old Japan-oriented issei-dominated prefectural clubs as well as to the Japanese Association. In the 1930s, the immigrant generation had shaken heads gravely over the "nisei

[10] Raymond Okamura, "One Man, One Vote in JACL," *Pacific Citizen*, October 23, 1970, p. 6.

problem," but in 1942 the nisei-run JACL took over spokesmanship for the incarcerated Japanese. The alien generation was in no position to contest this leadership, although many members privately complained of the war-spawned status inversion.[11] The accommodationist role of the JACL during the relocation is still a matter of controversy in the Japanese community, whose youth in particular would have preferred the JACL to have struck a more heroic posture of defiance. Nonetheless, the JACL remains the acknowledged spokesman for Americans of Japanese descent.

The only opposition to the JACL comes from vocal segments of the militant youth. Espousing ideologies of "yellow power" or even Third World solidarity, these leftist groups are open to any person of Asian descent who approves of their views and distinctive life style.[12] The same sectarian group can, therefore, have Korean, Samoan, Chinese, Japanese and Filipino members. In the late 1960s activist youth of Japanese descent joined such groups rather than or in addition to the JACL. Militants found the JACL too respectable, parochial, and reformist. Largely in response to its sansei critics, the nisei-dominated JACL launched a successful lobbying effort to secure repeal of Title II of the hated Internal Security Act of 1950. This act authorized the mass detention of potentially troublesome citizens in time of national emergency. The JACL has also appointed to a paid staff position the leading college-age radical in the frank expectation that his appointment would mollify the "increasing number of young leaders" who have begun to question the "viability" of JACL. On the other hand, the JACL cannot make too many concessions to the vocal youth without offending the already antagonized majority of self-employed businessmen, some of whom say that social workers and school teachers have too much influence in the organization.[13] In order to retain its spokesmanship for all segments of Japanese opinion, the JACL has to squeeze under one

[11] Shotaro Frank Miyamoto, "Immigrants and Citizens of Japanese Origin" *Annals* 223 (September 1942): 11; T. Tanaka, "History of the JACL" (unpublished manuscript in Bancroft Library, University of California, Berkeley, 1944?), ch. 2.
[12] Amy Uyetsuma, "The Emergence of Yellow Power in America," *Gidra* 1 (October 1969): 8–11.
[13] Raymond Uno, "In Diversity We Must Find Unity," *Pacific Citizen*, October 9, 1970, p. 6.

organizational roof people who are virtually at opposite ends of the American political spectrum. The remarkable capacity of the JACL to preserve the façade of ethnic unity seems authentically to reflect a culturally derived Japanese preference for face-saving harmony over public rancor and vilification. Also, since the JACL does not control anyone's livelihood, only the ideologically committed youth have a motive for attempting to break up its claim to community spokesmanship.

In America's Chinatowns, civic voluntary associations have not replaced the immigrant brotherhoods. The Six Companies still retain control of and spokesmanship for American Chinatowns. In part, however, this traditional authority prevails because the constituent district associations were willing to share power with some emergent voluntary associations. In the nineteenth century only the district associations had any voice in the Six Companies. But the district associations now share formal decision-making authority with clans, tongs, and a variety of all-Chinese voluntary associations including newspapers and womens' clubs. In New York the Six Companies now includes the representatives of about sixty Chinatown organizations.[14] However, the Six Companies extend recognition only to those voluntary associations deemed respectable and firmly anti-Communist. Some dissident Chinese claim that the shared power is only a façade behind which the district associations and the powerful tongs continue to rule Chinatowns. Even if this charge is true, the illusion of shared power has undoubtedly facilitated the Six Companies' continued monopoly over spokesmanship for American Chinese.

Yet disaffection has grown to the point where the Six Companies' thick walls are no longer able to muffle Chinatown's internal disputes and power rivalries. Operating in the English language outside of the Chinatown establishment, educated activists are openly critical of the Six Companies. They condemn that organization's "do nothing" and "reactionary" policies. They also accuse the Six Companies of being a "closed" organization which excludes Chinese who are

[14] Sung, *Gold Mountain*, p. 136; Tan, "Social Mobility," pp. 210–11; Bell Gale Chevigny, "The Harmonious Fist of Radical Chinatown," *Village Voice*, September 10, 1970, p. 12.

"not members" of its constituent bodies.[15] Therefore, they find the Six Companies unrepresentative of Chinatown and unworthy of continued spokesmanship. In sum, they reject the Six Companies' ancient claim to universality of membership and treat this private government as though it were just another voluntary association on the American model.

Exacerbating this debate is a wave of new immigration from Hong Kong. Since the Naturalization and Immigration Act of 1965 struck down the old national origins quota system, the population of San Francisco's overcrowded Chinatown has doubled. Like earlier immigrants, those from Hong Kong have obvious problems of social adjustment. In 1968, the San Francisco Department of Social Services reported that 41 percent of families in Chinatown census tracts had family incomes of $4,000 or less whereas only 21 percent of all San Francisco families had incomes so low. The Department also classified 27 percent of Chinatown housing as substandard; only 10 percent of all San Francisco housing units were declared substandard. Tuberculosis is endemic in Chinatown. The district also contains a high proportion of persons 65 years of age and older among whom rates of suicide are unusually high. Yet despite the poverty and health problems of these heavily Chinese census tracts, the 6.6 percent of San Franciscans living in them contributed only 2.3 percent of the city's welfare recipients under Aid to Families with Dependent Children (AFDC) programs, and 7.5 percent of welfare recipients under Old Age Security (OAS) programs.[16]

The position of the Six Companies is still that immigrant brotherhoods ought to oversee the social welfare of members. After years of decline, the family name associations have, in fact, begun to reassert their old function in Chinatowns. So, for example, the Lee Family Association in New York City opened a credit union for Lee family members. In 1970, the new credit union's assets were almost one million dollars. The Six Companies encourage the revival of traditional welfare institutions—and oppose demands for more tax-

---

[15] Tan, "Social Mobility," p. 209; "Choy Blasts Six Co. for Cop Out," *East/West*, October 7, 1970, p. 1; Lyman, *Asian in the West*, p. 113.

[16] *Report of the San Francisco Chinese Community Citizens' Survey and Fact Finding Committee*, abridged edition (San Francisco: H. J. Carle, 1969), pp. 10–16, 75.

supported welfare services in Chinatown.[17] The President of Citizens for Youth in Chinatown, a Six Companies auxiliary, even advises immigrant youth to achieve success by showing "a little determination." In maintaining this conservative position, the Six Companies have to confront liberal Chinese who feel that traditional welfare measures are leaving human needs unmet. In addition to this indigenous opposition, the Six Companies have also, for the first time, to joust with Asian American federations whose adult membership includes non-Chinese Asians.

The Council of Oriental Organizations (COO) is a Los Angeles-based federation of Asian American voluntary associations. In 1970 the COO drafted a plan for a Los Angeles County Asian Community Service Center intended to serve the social work needs of 250,000 Japanese, Chinese, Koreans, Samoans, Filipinos, and other Asians in the county.[18] The social workers who drafted and presented the plan claim that the mutual aid of family, clan, and ethnic charity is no longer adequate to cope with burgeoning problems of unemployment, drug abuse, delinquency, medical care, family planning, and gerontology. Respect for the aged and for authority are hardly more characteristic of young Asian Americans than of any other young Americans. They argue that Los Angeles has no right to expect Asian Americans nobly to deprive themselves of welfare services accorded other poor Americans.

Should the country actually fund the all-Asian service center, Chinese would be among the beneficiaries. Even though the Hong Kong people have been extremely reticent in seeking tax-supported welfare services, they would probably be grateful to the COO for helping them obtain benefits they do need. Grateful people would be naturally tempted to switch their ideological and political support

[17] Lyman, *Asian in the West*, pp. 115–16; Bill Moore, " 'No Real Problems:' One Chinatown View," San Francisco *Chronicle*, August 15, 1969, p. 8; idem, "The Facts About Life in Chinatown," San Francisco *Chronicle*, August 11, 1969, p. 1; San Francisco Planning and Urban Renewal Association, "Babel in Bagdad by the Bay" (San Francisco: San Francisco Planning and Urban Renewal Association, 1970); Daryl Lembke, "Chinese Influx Taxing S.F., Committee Says," *Los Angeles Times*, February 24, 1971, part 1, p. 20. Murray Schumach, "Waves of Uncertainty Roil Future of Chinatown," *New York Times*, November 19, 1970, p. 45.

[18] *Pacific Citizen*, October 9, 1970, p. 3. Also see Linda Matthews, "Chinatown: Booming but Worried," *Los Angeles Times*, May 5, 1968, sec. C, p. 1; idem, "Chinatown's Young, Old Suffer," *Los Angeles Times*, May 7, 1968, sec. 2, p. 1.

to voluntary groups supporting the COO—and away from the Six Companies which did nothing for them. In this sense, attempts by an Asian American federation of voluntary associations to obtain new welfare services for all Asians tend to force the Chinese Six Companies to wonder about the loyalties of the Chinese poor.

### BROTHERHOOD AND ETHNIC HONOR

Max Weber made an important distinction between cities of the Oriental type and cities of the Occidental type. Basically, a city of the Oriental type is one in which rural migrants to the urban areas retain hinterland tribal, territorial, and clan identities. Town residents then think of themselves as rural people who are temporarily living in the city. A city of the Occidental type is one in which migrants shed hinterland identities and affiliations in favor of a civic "voluntary" association. When they do, a melted down status group of city people emerges; and the city people differentiate themselves from country people.[19] Chinese and Japanese immigrants to American cities followed the Oriental pattern of rural-urban migration. American blacks followed the Occidental pattern. But American cities in the twentieth century were neither Occidental nor Oriental in type. Rather, the American cities contained some rural migrants (especially the foreign born) whose settlements tended to follow the Oriental pattern. They contained other migrants (principally the native born) whose migration was more on the Occidental pattern.

When city populations are internally divided into mutually hostile, mutually exclusive groups, the progress of voluntary association is both integrative and democratic. Hence, voluntary associations tend to reduce the despotism, ethnic hostility, and insularity characteristic of the Oriental type of city. Weber arrived at his favorable evaluation of civic voluntary association on these grounds. But, actually, the civic communes of late medieval Occidental cities were by no means

[19] Max Weber, *Economy and Society*, 3:1236–65. Also see Vatro Murvar, "Some Tentative Modifications of Weber's Typology: Occidental vs. Oriental City," *Social Forces* 44 (March 1966): 381–89; Bert F. Hoselitz, "The City, the Factory, and Economic Growth" in *Comparative Perspectives on Industrial Society*, eds. William A. Faunce and William H. Form (Boston: Little Brown, 1969), pp. 72–90. Works of related interest are Robert E. Park and Ernest W. Burgess, *Introduction to the Science of Sociology* (Chicago: University of Chicago Press, 1921), pp. 507, 613–14; F. L. K. Hsu, *Clan, Caste, and Club*, pp. 207–15, 224–25, 245.

voluntary. "Within the city, the mass of burghers was forced to join the sworn confraternization." Those who refused the civic oath were "forced into exile."[20] Therefore, Weber never confronted a condition of urban society in which a plurality of competing voluntary associations constituted the exclusive basis of social solidarity. However, the heavy reliance of migrant blacks on noncompulsory associations approximates this condition. There is accumulating evidence that, when socioeconomic status is held constant, proportionately more blacks than whites participate in voluntary associations.[21] Despite these high rates of participation, urban blacks have historically suffered unusually severe problems of atomization and demoralization. This black experience implies that voluntary association evidences a regular tendency to atomize and demoralize the poor. In turn, this conclusion suggests that voluntary association causes some social problems even while it tends to resolve those of the Oriental type of city.

The first and most serious limitation of voluntary association, ignored by Weber, is its capacity to enroll only those who voluntarily join. In general, the poor and uneducated do not join voluntary associations; hence, such associations have everywhere tended to enlist only the middle and upper classes. When tribal, clan, territorial, and extended family ties are strong, the urban poor are automatic members of these solidary groups even though they do not join voluntary associations. On the other hand, when these ascribed ties are weak or nonexistent, then the poor and other nonmembers of voluntary associations wind up entirely lacking group memberships. Under these infelicitous conditions, the poor turn into an atomized mass. The poverty-stricken atomized mass falls prey to all forms of social pathology, from contagious disease to narcotics. Because it is atomized, the poverty-stricken mass cannot help itself. Therefore, treatment of social pathology in this class becomes the responsibility of civic-minded voluntary associations of the middle class or of the welfare state. "Community action programs" attempt to resolve the problem by establishing self-help organizations for

20 Weber, *Economy and Society*, 3:1253.
21 See Marvin E. Olsen, "Social and Political Participation of Blacks," *American Sociological Review* 35 (August 1970): 682–97.

the poor. This scheme proves regularly abortive—because the poor do not join voluntary associations![22]

Even when the poor do join voluntary associations, the ones they join are usually led by people interested in expanding the membership size. Scurrying for ever broader support, the organizational elite is in no position to impose stringent life style rules on their transient and calculating followers. On the contrary, they must work persistently to reduce the ratio of organizational demands to benefits in order to maintain fickle loyalties of persons already supporting them and to court the favor of those supporting some rival organization. These requirements are conducive to organizational rationalization, but they tend to institutionalize a cosmopolitan "what's-in-it-for-me" attitude on the part of the members.

Ultimately this process develops into the supermarket situation, where individuated housewives respond on the basis of personal utilities to the urgent claims of rival grocery chains. The housewives' separate decisions do affect the planning of distant grocery store executives; and in this sense, rival grocery elites compete for their transient favor. On the other hand, housewives who bump carts every day in the same supermarkets are ordinarily incapable of organizing a car pool for mutual advantage because they lack any social organization. The supermarket is, or course, a *ne plus ultra* of rationalized competition for membership. Nonetheless, its example applies (albeit in milder degree) to political parties, churches, vacation resorts, houses of prostitution, and any other voluntary association which takes seriously the problem of increasing the membership size. Rationalized membership competition erodes internal solidarity. Hence, the most successful competitors are least capable of social control or social solidarity.

To avoid supermarket solidarity and to retain an organizational capacity to subject members to social control, a voluntary organization needs to remain "exclusive" in some sense. Being exclusive involves an unwillingness to water down organizational demands in the interest of increasing the membership size. There are many exclusive voluntary associations. Yet in the long run, as Weber under-

[22] Edward C. Banfield, *The Unheavenly City* (Boston: Little, Brown, 1968), p. 130.

stood, this exclusionist decision tends to emerge only when a voluntary association can make a successful claim to social prestige, so that organizational elites are in a position to subject the voluntary membership to the demands of the organization regarding their life style and to exclude those who do not measure up. Thus, in the black ghettos the voluntary organizations most capable of enforcing mundane discipline in daily conduct were those snobbish social clubs and Greek letter fraternities which were able to claim social prestige. In such associations the circle was able to pressure "strivers and strainers" to "keep up" with their fellows in terms of conspicuous displays of consumer goods, status symbols, educational and occupational prestige, and, of course, in terms of conspicuous absence from jail registers, welfare rolls, hysterical domestic fights, and gossip columns. No snobbishly exclusive voluntary association admits the poor. In fact, the prestige of any snobbish club depends on keeping the poor out. In general, then, voluntary associations maintain internal solidarity and discipline by excluding "undesirables," that is, the poor.

Revolutionary cells, thieves' dens, delinquent gangs, elite military units, and world-denouncing religious sects are exclusive voluntary associations that admit the poor. Save for the military, these groups are at war with the established system of social stratification. Their central ideological principal is rejection of snobbery and inequality. In radical religious and political associations, the poor man finds his best opportunity for strictly voluntary membership in solidary, morally disciplined groups. Loyalties to such groups are typically intense; ideologies are firm. If all poor people joined one radical sectarian body, then all poor people would be members of a morally disciplined, solidary group. But, in ordinary times, only a minority of the poor join voluntary associations at all; and of this original minority only a minority join radical sectarian ones. Most of those who join anything at all join the membership-seeking nonexclusive associations. These associations offer tangible benefits, and worldly ideologies, but they are not mutually supportive moral communities.

In general, then, voluntary associations tend to atomize the poor, the uneducated, and the "undesirable." A direct result of such atomization among the poor is the loss of group-defined standards of achievement and personal conduct capable of motivating individuals to attempt to measure up to the standard. The drive for achievement derives from membership in groups which subject members to demands and standards. Apart from such a group context, there can be no persistent and disciplined drive for achievement in the face of the inevitable daily frustrations. Atomization of the poor implies, in this sense, the demoralization of the poor as well. Bourgeois society emphasizes individual social mobility and voluntary associations; but there is a contradiction between the two, since voluntary association tends to create among the poor social conditions unconducive to respectable ambitions or disciplined work. These qualities, in turn, are prerequisites of upward social mobility. Horatio Alger characters do not need solidary groups in which to acquire mobility values or discipline; real people do.

Tribal, clan, territorial, and extended family groupings organize all strata of a population. These ascriptively bounded groupings also uphold a sense of ethnic, tribal, clan, territorial, and family honor. They thereby provide all strata of a population with group standards to which individuals are expected to conform. Ethnic honor is exclusive. When a sense of ethnic honor is joined to an ascriptive associational framework, the maintenance of ethnic honor becomes a demand capable of disciplining individual conduct. Such a situation is, for example, signaled when children are told not to do something lest they bring disgrace and shame to their ethnic group. This sort of social control is actually quite analogous to the social controls employed in purely status-based groups. Unlike a purely status-based honor, the "sense of ethnic honor is the specific honor of the masses, for it is accessible to anybody who belongs to the subjectively believed community of descent."[23] Hence, the sense of ethnic honor is capable of penetrating even the lowliest home, no member of which joins any voluntary association. Among the "poor white trash" of the American South, the sense of racial honor was a very ugly social characteristic, involving as it did, their interest in the caste subordination of blacks. Racial honor among Nazis was similarly sordid. Weber quite properly called attention to the vicious implications of this "specific honor of the masses." Yet, there is a sense in which

[23] Weber, *Economy and Society*, 1:391.

Weber's analysis of the sense of ethnic honor and of the integrative significance of urban voluntary association overlooked possible contributions of ascriptive brotherhood and ethnic honor to the well-being of the lowest strata of bourgeois society—within a context of humane social values.

Among Chinese and Japanese in the United States, a sense of ethnic honor was joined to the ascriptive basis of social association. As a result, individuals, irrespective of social status, were amenable to group controls over their behavior in the interest of maintaining an unsullied ethnic honor. A shared sense of ethnic honor resulted in group standards of everyday conduct which kinship and territorial associations carried into every corner of Oriental-American society. Such demands made their appearance particularly in cases involving interactions with the white majority. Chinese and Japanese rarely confronted the whites as individuals; instead, such contacts took place under the careful scrutiny of group surveillance in the interests of ethnic honor.

For example, in commercial relations with whites, Orientals were at pains to trade with the utmost circumspection instead of, as Weber would have expected, with a double standard of economic morality devoted to cheating and fleecing outsiders. These practices resulted in a very favorable popular image of Oriental honesty, especially that of the Chinese. To be sure, honesty was the expedient best policy in the light of the Orientals' minority status and vulnerability. Nonetheless, such a development is indicative of the manner in which traditional social controls could be employed to create very untraditional outcomes.

The extraordinary success of children of Oriental descent in the public schools can, in a similar sense, be traced to a sense of ethnic honor. Oriental children are enjoined to study hard and achieve scholastic eminence in order to bring credit to their family and to their ethnic group. School performances are evaluated by circles of significant persons who praise and blame the youth in terms of their impersonal achievements in school.[24] These circles enforce the in-

[24] William Petersen, "Success Story, Japanese-American Style," in *Cities in Trouble*, ed. Nathan Glazer (Chicago: Quadrangle, 1970), pp. 158–71; Tan, "Social Mobility," p. 193 ff.

junction to study hard and thus to be a credit to one's ethnic group, and they discipline individuals. In this manner, the sense of ethnic honor and the ascriptive forms of social association characteristic of Oriental communities combine to develop ambitious young people who are highly qualified in their fields of endeavor by any standard of performance.

The sense of ethnic honor thus harnessed to impersonal achievement is not the pristine pure, inner-directed ethnic honor which Weber typologized. It is not comparable to the status honor of a *Junker* aristocracy. Instead, this sense of ethnic honor has been importantly Americanized so that, for example, the current conceptions of ethnic honor held by American-born Chinese differ markedly from those held by their immigrant forebears. The old dichotomy of Chinese or barbarian has broken down, and the Chinese have taken an interest in the good opinion of whites and in high standards of personal achievement by their youth in order to validate their group's sense of ethnic honor. Such a need implies a degree of cultural assimilation in that the good opinion of non-Chinese is desired in order to support the group's good opinion of itself. Weber did not conceive of status or ethnic groups thus haunted by a desire to validate their sense of honor by impersonal achievements able to win the good opinion of aliens. Hence, he overlooked this sense in which, under special conditions, ethnic honor and the ascriptive brotherhood supporting it might eventuate in strong drives for impersonal achievement and long-range planning to that end. Such a development is naturally most important in social strata not penetrated by voluntary associations.

Caste subordination of Negroes involved shared black-white conceptions of the proper place of blacks in a white society. This view did not assign to Negroes a separate ethnic honor but rather deprived them of any valued ethnic identity. So long as these conceptions were shared, there was obviously no room for social conflict between blacks and whites. But this heritage carried with it manifest disadvantages in the urban North. Unlike Orientals, black migrants could not be disciplined by reference to ethnic honor, since Southern-born migrants did not conceive of themselves as having any honor. Especially among the lowest stratum of urban Negroes, peers could rarely induce a fellow to actually refrain from some line of personally advantageous activity lest it discredit or shame blacks in general, nor were there persisting grouplets able to encourage impersonal achievements in the interest of ethnic black honor. Hence, social contacts took place outside of a framework of this normative control. Blacks were free to act as individuals quite apart from group approval of the impact of their actions on black honor. The rampant individualism contributed to the disorganization of social life in the slums.

Of course, black racism is no prettier than white racism. Yet the lack of an assertive sense of ethnic honor among lower class, slum-dwelling blacks was no unmixed blessing for American society. Lower class blacks were not mobilized by all-black voluntary associations, and white racial prejudice excluded them from the larger society. A sense of ethnic or family honor might have been capable of reaching into lower class black homes which were isolated from all other forms of community control.[25] Such a sense of honor would have provided a social standard against which poor blacks might collectively have measured individual conduct. This discipline would have permitted lower class blacks to mobilize themselves as a group in the interests of impersonal achievements capable of wringing respect from the most unsympathetic whites. It would certainly have curtailed the highly individualistic social relations which in fact emerged. But to make this argument is to point out that ascriptive ties and a sense of ethnic honor may have consequences quite different from those Weber enumerated. These forms of social association and control certainly fill social lacunae which voluntary association systematically creates.

[25] Charles Hamilton, "How Black Is Black?" *Ebony* 24 (August 1969): 47.

# Appendix

ESTIMATIONS OF FAMILY SIZE AND RELIEF POPULATION OF
INDIVIDUALS BY RACE AND COLOR, 1933

The Federal Emergency Relief Administration (FERA) report
of October 1933 provided only the number of relief families and of
all persons of Chinese and Japanese descent in the selected cities.[1]
The report did not provide information concerning the number of
Chinese or Japanese families in a given city or the number of persons
receiving relief. To arrive at the latter figures, it was accordingly
necessary to estimate the mean size of the average Chinese and Japanese casework family receiving relief. The 1930 census provided
no information concerning the mean size of Chinese or Japanese
casework families. However, the California (State) Emergency Relief Administration's survey of San Francisco Chinese on relief provided appropriate information for May 1933 and March 1934. In
these two months combined, there were 413 separate Chinese relief
cases in San Francisco, and these cases involved a total of 2,104
persons (adults and children). Each Chinese casework family thus
included, on the average, five persons.[2] This figure (5.0) was employed as the basis for estimating both the Chinese and Japanese
relief populations.[3] Thus, in Chicago the FERA reported twenty-
three Chinese relief families, and seven Japanese relief families.
Estimating each relief family to include 5.0 persons, the Chinese and
Japanese relief population was estimated at 116 and 35, respectively.
The same procedure was applied to each of the selected cities.

For the cities of Los Angeles and San Francisco, the FERA report omitted the number of white and Negro persons on relief. These
were estimated on the following basis: The ratio between relief per-

---

[1] Federal Emergency Relief Administration, *Unemployment Relief Census: October, 1930.*

[2] California State Emergency Relief Administration, "Survey of the Social Work
Needs of the Chinese Population of San Francisco, California," p. 40.

[3] Cf. Betty Lee Sung, *Mountain of Gold*, p. 166; Harry H. L. Kitano, *Japanese
Americans*, p. 169.

sons and relief families was computed for whites and Negroes in Chicago, New York, and Philadelphia (see table, below). This ratio

*Ratio of Relief Persons to Relief Families by Race for Three Cities, October 1933*

|              | White | Negro |
|--------------|-------|-------|
| Chicago      | 3.4   | 3.2   |
| New York     | 4.0   | 3.4   |
| Philadephia  | 4.4   | 3.6   |

expressed the mean number of persons per casework family in each of the separate cities. In each city, Negro families on relief included fewer persons than did white families on relief. But for both whites and Negroes, the mean number of persons per casework family was smallest in Chicago. Accordingly, the Chicago means were used to estimate the relief populations of whites and Negroes in San Francisco and Los Angeles. Thus, the FERA listed 19,437 white and 261 Negro relief families in San Francisco, and these figures were multiplied by 3.4 and 3.2 respectively to yield an estimate of the white and Negro relief population of San Francisco. Employment of the Chicago means tended to minimize the white and Negro relief populations of the California cities and, accordingly, to reduce the discrepancy between whites and Negroes, and Orientals in terms of percentage of the total population receiving relief. The estimates should not be taken as accurate counts, but they do permit an appreciation of the typical rank ordering of the various populations with respect to relief and the magnitude of the differences involved.

# Works Cited

INSTITUTIONAL AUTHORSHIPS

*United States Government Publications*

Federal Emergency Relief Administration. *Unemployment Relief Census: October, 1930, Report no. 1, United States Summary.* Washington, D.C.: Government Printing Office, 1934.

*Report of the National Advisory Commission on Civil Disorders.* Washington, D.C.: Government Printing Office, 1968.

United States Industrial Commission. *Reports,* vol. 15, pt. 4, "Chinese and Japanese Labor in the Mountain and Pacific States." Washington, D.C.: Government Printing Office, 1901.

United States Senate, 61st Congress, 2d Session, Document No. 633, Reports of the Immigration Commission. *Immigrants in Industry,* pt. 25, *Japanese and Other Immigrant Races in the Pacific Coast and Rocky Mountain States,* vol. 1, *Japanese and East Indians.* Washington, D.C.: Government Printing Office, 1911.

*California State Publications*

California State Emergency Relief Administration, Project No. 156. "Survey of the Social Work Needs of the Chinese Population of San Francisco California." Mimeographed. San Francisco: State Emergency Relief Administration, May 1935.

State Board of Control of California, Report to Governor William D. Stephens. *California and the Oriental: Japanese, Chinese, and Hindus.* Sacramento, 1920.

State of California. *Annual Report of the Superintendent of Banks.* Sacramento: State Printing Office, 1900–1940.

*Other Official Publications*

Chicago Commission on Race Relations. *The Negro in Chicago.* Chicago: University of Chicago Press, 1922.

National Negro Business League. *Reports of Annual Sessions.* Nashville: National Baptist Publishing Board, 1914–1924.

National Urban League. *Fortieth Anniversary Yearbook, 1950*. New York: National Urban League, 1951.

San Francisco Chinese Chamber of Commerce. "San Francisco's Chinatown: History, Function, and Importance of Social Organizations." Mimeographed. San Francisco: San Francisco Chinese Chamber of Commerce, 1953.

INDIVIDUAL AUTHORSHIPS

Ardener, Shirley. "The Comparative Study of Rotating Credit Associations." *Journal of the Royal Anthropological Institute* 94, pt. 2 (1964): 201–29.

Banfield, Edward C. *The Moral Basis of a Backward Society*. New York: Free Press, 1958.

Barnett, Milton L. "Kinship as a Factor Affecting Cantonese Economic Adaptation in the United States." *Human Organization* 19 (spring 1960): 40–48.

Barth, Gunther. *Bitter Strength: A History of the Chinese in the United States, 1850–1870*. Cambridge, Mass.: Harvard University Press, 1964.

Bascom, William R. "The *Esusu*: A Credit Institution of the Yoruba." *Journal of the Royal Anthropological Institute* 82, pt. 1 (1952): 63–69.

Bendix, Reinhard. *Work and Authority in Industry*. New York: John Wiley, 1956.

Berger, Peter L. *The Sacred Canopy: Elements of a Sociological Theory of Religion*. Garden City, N.Y.: Doubleday, 1967.

Berk, Richard. "Doing Business in the Ghetto: Retail Merchants." In *Racial Attitudes in American Cities*, edited by Angus Campbell and Howard Schuman, pp. 125–131. Supplemental Studies for the National Advisory Commission on Civil Disorders. Washington, D.C.: U.S. Government Printing Office, 1968.

Bond, J. Max. "The Negro in Los Angeles." Ph.D. dissertation, University of Southern California, 1936.

Brimmer, Andrew F. "The Banking System and Urban Economic Development." Paper presented before a joint session of the 1968 annual meeting of the American Real Estate and Urban Economics Association and the American Finance Association, December 28, 1968, Palmer House Hotel, Chicago, Illinois.

————, and Terrell, Henry S. "The Economic Potential of Black Capitalism." Paper presented at the 82d annual meeting of the American Economic Association, December 29, 1969, Hilton Hotel, New York, N.Y.

Browning, James B. "The Beginnings of Insurance Enterprise Among Negroes." *Journal of Negro History* 22 (October 1937): 417–32.

Cather, Helen Virginia. "The History of San Francisco's Chinatown." Master's thesis, University of California, Berkeley, 1932.

Cattell, Stuart H. "Health, Welfare and Social Organization in Chinatown, New York." Mimeographed. New York: Community Service Society of New York, 1962.

Chen, Wen-hui Chung. "Changing Socio-Cultural Patterns of the Chinese Community in Los Angeles." Ph.D. dissertation, University of Southern California, 1952.

Condit, Rev. Ira M. *The Chinaman as We See Him.* Chicago: Fleming H. Revell, 1900.

Coolidge, Mary Roberts. *Chinese Immigration.* New York: Henry Holt, 1909.

Daniels, Roger. *The Politics of Prejudice: The Anti-Japanese Movement in California and the Struggle for Japanese Exclusion.* University of California Publications in History, vol. 71. Berkeley and Los Angeles: University of California Press, 1962.

Davison, R. B. *West Indian Migrants.* London: Oxford University, 1962.

Drake, St. Clair. "Churches and Voluntary Associations in the Chicago Negro Community." Mimeographed. Chicago: Work Projects Administration, 1940.

————, and Cayton, Horace R. *Black Metropolis.* 2 vols, 2d ed., rev. New York: Harper and Row, 1962.

Du Bois, W. E. Burghardt. *The Philadelphia Negro.* Philadelphia: University of Pennsylvania Press, 1899.

Embree, John F. *Suye Mura: A Japanese Village.* Chicago: University of Chicago, 1939.

Fei, Hsiao-tung. *Peasant Life in China.* London: Routledge & Kegan Paul, 1939.

Foley, Eugene P. "The Negro Businessman: In Search of a Tradition." *Daedalus* 95 (winter 1966): 107–44.

Frazier, E. Franklin. *Black Bourgeoisie.* New York: Free Press, 1957.

———. *The Negro Church in America.* Liverpool: Liverpool University Press, 1964.

———. *The Negro in the United States.* 2d ed., rev. New York: Macmillan, 1957.

Fukuoka, Fumiko. "Mutual Life and Aid Among the Japanese in Southern California, with Special Reference to Los Angeles." Master's thesis, University of Southern California, 1937.

Geertz, Clifford. "The Rotating Credit Association: A 'Middle Rung' in Development." *Economic Development and Cultural Change* 10 (April 1962): 241–63.

Glazer, Nathan, and Moynihan, Daniel Patrick. *Beyond the Melting Pot.* 2d ed., rev. Cambridge, Mass: M.I.T. Press, 1970.

Harris, Abram L. *The Negro as Capitalist.* Philadelphia: American Academy of Political and Social Science, 1936.

Harris, Sara, with the assistance of Crittenden, Harriet. *Father Divine: Holy Husband.* Garden City, N.Y.: Doubleday & Co., 1953.

Heyer, Virginia. "Patterns of Social Organization in New York City's Chinatown." Ph.D. diss., Columbia University, 1953.

Herskovits, Melville J. *The Myth of the Negro Past.* 2d ed., rev. Boston: Beacon, 1958.

———. *Trinidad Village.* New York: Alfred A. Knopf, 1947.

Houchins, Joseph R. "Causes of Negro Insurance Company Failures." Mimeographed. Washington, D.C.: U.S. Department of Commerce, Bureau of Foreign and Domestic Commerce, Negro Affairs Division, Bulletin 15, April 1937.

———. "Negro Chambers of Commerce." Mimeographed. Washington, D.C.: U.S. Department of Commerce, Bureau of Foreign and Domestic Commerce, Negro Affairs Division, Bulletin 8, August 1936.

———. "Negro Trade Associations." Washington, D.C.: U.S. Department of Commerce, Bureau of Foreign and Domestic Commerce, Negro Affairs Division, Bulletin 13, November 1936.

Hoy, William. *The Chinese Six Companies.* San Francisco: Chinese Consolidated Benevolent Association, 1942.

Hund, James M. *Black Entrepreneurship.* Belmont, Ca.: Wadsworth, 1970.

Hsu, Francis L. K. *Clan, Caste, and Club.* Princeton: D. Van Nostrand, 1963.

Huebner, S. S. "Insurance in China." *Annals of the American Academy of Political and Social Science* 152 (November 1930): 105–8.

————. "Life and Casualty Insurance in Japan and China." *Proceedings of the Casualty Actuarial Society* 14 (May 25, 1928): 392–93.

Hyndman, Albert. "The West Indian in London." In *The West Indian Comes to England,* edited by S. K. Ruck, pp. 65–151. London: Routledge & Kegan Paul, 1960.

Ichihashi, Yamato. *Japanese in the United States.* Stanford: Stanford University Press, 1932.

Iwata, Masakazu. "The Japanese Immigrants in California Agriculture." *Agricultural History* 36 (January 1962): 25–37.

Johnson, James Weldon. *Black Manhattan.* New York: Alfred A. Knopf, 1930.

Kataoka, W. T. "Occupations of Japanese in Los Angeles." *Sociology and Social Research* 14 (September-October 1929): 53–58.

Katzin, Margaret. " 'Partners': An Informal Savings Institution in Jamaica." *Social and Economic Studies* 8 (December 1959): 436–40.

Kinzer, Robert H., and Sagarin, Edward. *The Negro in American Business: The Conflict Between Separation and Integration.* New York: Greenburg, 1950.

Kiser, Clyde Vernon. *Sea Island to City.* New York: Columbia University Press, 1932.

Kitano, Harry H. L. *Japanese Americans: The Evolution of a Subculture.* Englewood Cliffs, N.J.: Prentice-Hall, 1969.

Kraar, Louis. "The Wealth and Power of Overseas Chinese." *Fortune* 83 (March 1971): 78 ff.

Kulp, Daniel H., II. *Country Life in South China.* 2 vols. New York: Columbia University Press, 1925.

Lee, Rose Hum. *The Chinese in the United States of America.* Hong Kong: Hong Kong University Press, 1960.

Little, Kenneth. *West African Urbanization: A Study of Voluntary Associations in Social Change.* New York: Cambridge University Press, 1965.

Lyman, Stanford M. *The Asian in the West.* Reno and Las Vegas: Desert Research Institute, University of Nevada, 1970.

————."Contrasts in the Community Organization of Chinese and Japanese in North America." *Canadian Review of Sociology and Anthropology* 5 (May 1968): 51–67.

————. "Marriage and the Family Among Chinese Immigrants to America, 1850–1960." *Phylon* 29 (winter 1968): 321–30.

————. "The Structure of Chinese Society in Nineteenth-Century America." Ph.D. diss., University of California, Berkeley, 1961.

McKay, Claude. *Harlem: Negro Metropolis.* New York: Dutton, 1940.

Matsui, Schichiro. "Economic Aspects of the Japanese Situation in California." M.A. thesis, University of California, Berkeley, 1922.

Mays, Benjamin E. *The Negro's God.* Boston: Chapman & Grimes, 1938.

————, and Nicholson, Joseph W. *The Negro's Church.* New York: Institute of Social and Religious Research, 1933.

Miyamoto, Shotaro Frank. *Social Solidarity Among the Japanese in Seattle.* University of Washington Publications in the Social Sciences, vol. 11, no. 2. Seattle: University of Washington Press, 1939.

Modell, John. "The Japanese of Los Angeles: A Study in Growth and Accommodation, 1900–1946." Ph.D. dissertation, Columbia University, 1969.

Myrdal, Gunnar. *An American Dilemma.* 2 vols. New York: Harper & Brothers, 1944.

Nodera, Isamu. "A Survey of the Vocational Activities of the Japanese in the City of Los Angeles." M.A. thesis, University of Southern California, 1936.

Ofari, Earl. *The Myth of Black Capitalism*. New York: Monthly Review Press, 1970.

Pierce, Joseph A. *Negro Business and Business Education*. New York and London: Harper & Brothers, 1947.

Reid, Ira De A. *The Negro Immigrant*. New York: Columbia University Press, 1939.

Scanland, J. M. "Chinese Business Methods in San Francisco." *Business* 17 (1904): 1069–81.

Spear, Allan H. *Black Chicago: The Making of a Negro Ghetto, 1890–1920*. Chicago: University of Chicago Press, 1967.

Strickland, Arvarh E. *History of the Chicago Urban League*. Urbana, Ill.: University of Illinois, 1966.

Sung, Betty Lee. *Mountain of Gold*. New York: Macmillan, 1967.

Tan, Mély Giok-Lan. "Social Mobility and Assimilation: The Chinese in the United States." Ph.D. dissertation, University of California, Berkeley, 1968.

Trent, W. J., Jr. "Development of Negro Life Insurance Enterprises." Master's thesis, University of Pennsylvania, 1932.

Watson, J. J. "Churches and Religious Conditions." *Annals of the American Academy of Political and Social Science* 49 (September 1913): 120–28.

Weber, Max. *Ancient Judaism*. New York: Free Press, 1952.

———. *Economy and Society*. 3 vols. New York: Bedminster Press, 1968.

———. *The Protestant Ethic and the Spirit of Capitalism*. New York: Charles Scribner's, 1958.

———. *The Religion of China*. Glencoe, Ill.: Free Press, 1951.

Wilson, Bryan R. "An Analysis of Sect Development." *American Sociological Review* 24 (February 1957): 3–15.

Wilson, James Q. *Negro Politics*. Glencoe, Ill.: Free Press, 1960.

Woodson, Carter G. "Insurance Business Among Negroes." *The Journal of Negro History* 14 (April 1929): 202–26.

# Index

Absentee ownership: in West Indies, 41; in the United States, 41–42
Abyssinian Baptist Church, 168
Achievement, drive for, 187, 189
Active participation: Japanese, 65, 66; Chinese, 89; Urban League, 109, 110; Business League, 115, 117; role fusion, 130; Father Divine, 148; insurance, 155, 156, 159; voluntary associations, 184, 185
Africa: esusu, 30–31; local origins of slaves, 37; attitudes toward, 104
African Insurance Company, 153
African Methodist Episcopal Church, 153
Agriculture: Japanese, 9, 10, 16, 48, 73–78, 99; Chinese, 72, 91; black, 8, 38–43
Aid to Families with Dependent Children (AFDC), 181
Alien land laws, 9, 73–74
Allen, Richard, 153
Ancient Order of Forresters, 129
Angels, 142–143. See also Father Divine Peace Mission Movement
Anomalies, 22
Anti-Jap Laundry League, 71, 72
Apparel stores, 3, 15, 119, 123
Ascriptive brotherhood: Orientals, 98; blacks, 107, 150; and voluntary associations, 170–172
Asia: attitudes toward, 103
Asian community service center, proposed, 182
Asiatic Exclusion League, 10, 70
Assessment societies: in American South, 152; criticized, 163. See also Insurance
Assimilation, 163, 164
"Asu," 32. See also Esusu
Atlanta Life Insurance Company, 154
Automotive stores, 15, 16

Bahamas, the, 32
Bank of Canton, the, 47
Banks: discrimination, 19–20, 29, 36; Oriental, 29, 45, 46, 47, 48, 50; Negro-owned, 45–58; administrative problems, 48–51, 54, 55; economic problems, 51, 52, 53, 54, 55, 56–58; and rotating credit, 45, 48, 50–51, 55, 56, 57, 58, 61
Baker, George, 142. See also Father Divine
Banquets, 24, 143, 146. See also Father Divine Peace Mission Movement; Hui
Barbados, 32, 42
Barbers, Negro, 14, 119
Beauticians, 14, 119
Bidding system, 24, 25, 26, 27, 28
Binga, Jesse, 52
Binga State Bank, 46, 50, 52
Blacks, American: business proprietorships, 2–6, 10–14, 19–22, 33, 43, 118–119, 125–126, 144–156, 148, 150; welfare dependency, 87, 88, 113; black power, 190. See also Negroes in the United States
Board of Control of California: Oriental business, 10; Japanese banks, 47–48; Japanese agriculture, 75
Boardinghouses: Japanese, 66, 74–75; Chinese, 86; Father Divine, 143, 144
Boss, agricultural, 74–75
"Boxi money," 32
Brothers and Sisters of Love and Charity, 139
Browne, Rev. W. W., 53
Brown Fellowship Society, 153n
Buddhists, 28, 164
Bumpkins, country, 106, 183
"Buy black," 116

California: Oriental retail commerce, 5–10, 14–18; Oriental banks, 29, 45–48, 50; Japanese agriculture, 9, 10, 16, 48, 72–78, 99; Chinese agriculture, 72; blacks in, 101
California Banking Act, 46, 50
California Farmers' Cooperative Association, 75
Canneries, 9, 78
Canton, China, 81
Canton Bank, 47
Capitol Savings Bank, 50
Carnegie, Andrew, 115

Caseworkers, 108–110
Cathay Bank of Los Angeles, the, 47n
Chan family, 91
Chee Kung Tong, 96
Cheese, Mr., capitalist, 69
Chee Tuck Sam Tuck Family Association, 83
Chew Yut, 84, 97
Chiang family, 91
Chicago, Illinois: retail dealers, 13; Chinatown, 83; relief population, 88; locality clubs, 101, 102; black businesses, 118; black churches in, 137
Chin family, 91
China Steamer Day, 6
Chinatown: pillaged, 6; tourists, 16, 99, 100; clans in, 83–84; dialects, 84, 97, 99, 100; and Japantowns, 98, 99, 100; white businesses in, 122
Chinese American Citizens' Alliance (CACA), 177–178
Chinese American Democratic Club, 177
Chinese Chamber of Commerce, 97
Chinese Consolidated Benevolent Association. See Chinese Six Companies
Chinese Exclusion Act, 7
Chinese Hand Laundry Alliance, 94
Chinese in the United States: discrimination, 5–6, 174–175; nineteenth century, 6–7; retail dealers, 7, 12–16; business partnerships, 18, 93; hui, 25–27, 86; social organization, 81–86; clans, 83–87; dialects, 84, 92, 97, 99, 100; welfare, 84–89, 163–168, 177, 181–182, 191–192; institutional rules, 89–91, trade guilds, 91–94; tongs, 94–98, 100; and Japanese, 98–100
Chinese Peace Society, 97
Chinese Six Companies: name, 81, 82; organization, 81–82, 180; and Japanese Association, 82; community leadership, 81, 174, 180; welfare activities, 84–85, 87–88, 181–182; Great Depression, 87, 88; sanctions, 89–91, 175; consumer credit, 123; venality, 140; criticized, 181
"Chiselers, relief," 88
Chop suey, 18
Church beneficials, 152–154, 160, 162, 163
Churches, black: membership, 127, 128, 129; storefronts, 128, 129; moral

communities, 130, 131; active participation, 130, 141; and immigrant brotherhoods, 131, 139, 140, 141; ethical discipline, 132, 135, 138; social mobility, 136, 137; competition among, 136–139, 163; beneficial societies, 152, 153, 154, 160, 162
Churches, Japanese, 28
Church of God, 141
Cigar making, 7
Citizens for Youth in Chinatown, 182
Citizenship, U.S., 105
City Market of Los Angeles, 76
Clans, Chinese: hui, 26, 86; settlement, 83; occupations, 86, 92, 95, 124, 175; welfare activities, 106, 111, 160, 161, 163, 165, 181; and Urban League, 109, 110, 111, 114; competition among, 139–140, 175–176; honor, 187
Colored Merchants' Association (CMA), 125, 126
Colorless skin, 5
Community action programs, 184
Competition, interorganizational: Urban League, 112–113; white businessman, 118; fraternal orders, 136, 138, 139, 156, 158–160; churches, 136, 137, 138, 139, 160; ethnic elites, 139–140, 172–183; insurance, 158, 159, 160; and life style, 185
Concerned Chinese for Action and Change, 177
Consolidated Slave Acts, 38
Consumer demands, 10–18
Contract labor system, 75
Cooks, Chinese, 7, 91
Council of Oriental Organizations (COO), 182, 183
"Cousins," clan, 83, 89, 118
Credit, consumer: blacks, 57, 119–121; Orientals, 122–123. See also Banks; Debt collection
Credit, rotating. See Rotating credit associations
Crime: white-collar, 49–50, 51, 140, 155, 157–158; other, 94–98, 100
Curio stores, Chinese, 8, 16–17, 99–100

Dashi, 30. See also Esusu
Dear family, 91
Debt collection: banks, 57; rotating credit, 58–60; consumer, 120; Japanese, 122–123

Depression, Great, the: Japanese in, 63, 70, 77, 88; Chinese in, 87–89; religious cults during, 141, 144, 146–149; welfare dependency during, 63, 87–88, 147–148, 149, 150, 168, 169

Deprivation, relative, 103

Detroit, Michigan, 2, 83

Deviance: in churches, 132, 133, 134, 135; Orientals, 133. See also Life style

Devine, Major J., 142

Dialects: Japanese, 62; Chinese, 84, 92, 97, 99, 100; black, 105

Diet: Oriental, 12, 14, 16, 18; black, 105

Disadvantage, social, 14

Discrimination: foreign-born whites, 5, 20; Chinese, 5–7, 20, 95, 175; Japanese, 5, 20, 29, 36, 80, 110, 175; West Indians, 35–36; American blacks, 6, 10, 19–20, 190

Disgrace, social, 64, 86, 95, 187

District associations: defined, 81; welfare activities, 84–85, 89; economic intervention, 91, 95; membership, 104; venality, 140; sanctions, 175; in Six Companies, 180

Divine, Father. See Father Divine

Divine Peace Mission Movement Co-operatives, 144, 145

Domestic service: Chinese in, 7; Japanese in, 9; blacks in, 8, 143

"Double duty dollar," 118, 119

Double standard, 9, 188

Douglass National Bank, 46, 50

Doyer Street, 96

"Draw," the, 32

Drayage, 14

Dry-cleaning, 17, 94, 119

Education: of foreign born, 4; of blacks, 48–49, 110, 155, 161; of Orientals, 110, 164, 167, 168, 188, 189

Elites: Negro, 48–49, 108, 115, 117, 155, 173, 186; venality, 49, 50, 54–55, 140, 155; Chinese, 81, 109–110, 114, 140, 174–183; Japanese, 82, 98, 109, 110, 114, 174–183; competition among, 139–140, 172–183

Elks, Negro, 129

Emergency Unemployment Relief Committee, 168

Esusu: defined, 31; in West Indies, 31–33, 37; American blacks, 36, 37, 43; and slavery, 37–44; cultural disappearance of, 37, 44

Ethical discipline, 132–134, 156–157, 172. See also Active participation

Ethnic honor, 187–190

Exploitation, white, 3, 119–121

Extortion, 94, 97

Faithful Mary, 145

Familism, 164, 165

Family: reputation, 59, 60, 86, 187–188; extended, 60, 64, 86, 118; nuclear, 100 and n, 148; black, 100, 106, 148, 190; Oriental, 100, 164, 165, 167, 182, 187–188; moral community, 170

Family associations: membership, 83; and district associations, 84, 85; welfare activities, 85–89, 113, 118; business activities, 90, 91; and native born, 178. See also Clans, Chinese

Family name associations. See Family associations

Father Divine: early years, 141–142; death, 149

Father Divine Peace Mission Movement: early years, 141–143; other cults, 141, 150; Angels in Heavens, 142–144, 149, 150; sex, 143, 149; banquets, 143, 146; businesses, 144, 145, 146; Kingdom names, 144, 149; employment practices, 146, 147; insurance, 147, 148

Federal Emergency Relief Administration (FERA): in Chinatown, 88; relief statistics, 191, 192

Federation of Negro Fraternals, 159

Filial piety, 164, 165, 167, 178

Fisherman, 17, 78

Fong. See Village association

Food stores: in ghetto, 3, 4, 33, 119; Oriental, 15, 16, 17

Foreign born: discrimination, 5; special consumer demands, 11–12; in business, 4, 5, 12, 14–15; Orientals, 164, 168, 176. See also Issei

Four districts dialect. See Sze Yap

Fraternal orders: banks, 45, 52–56; membership, 129, 130, 130n, 131, 139, 141; moral communities, 130, 131; ethical discipline, 135, 159; and Orientals, 139, 140, 141; competition, 138–139; 156, 158–159; and Father Divine, 147; Golden Age, 154; insurance, 154, 154n, 155, 157–159; venality in, 155, 157–158; leadership, 155,

157, 158, 161
Free African Society, 153
Furniture stores: in ghetto, 2, 3, 119; Oriental, 15, 16

Gambling, 94
Gardeners, 7
Garment industry: Chinese in, 7, 16
Garvey, Amy Jacques, 33
Gaut Sing, 95
General merchandise stores, 15, 16
General stores, 15–17, 89
"God, Incorporated," 145, 148
Gold Rush, 6
Good Samaritans, the, 129
Goodwill, business, 90
Grace, Bishop "Daddy," 141, 149
Grocery stores: Japanese, 10, 17; Chinese 12, 15–17; in ghetto, 3, 4, 119

Hakka, 91
Hamid, Sufi Abdul, 149
Harlem, New York: 1935 riots, 121; Colored Merchants' Association stores, 125; churches, 127; cults, 143, 146; Depression in, 168
Hatchetmen, 90, 92, 95–97, 100
Hawaii, 28, 123
Heavens, 142, 143, 149
Heterodoxy, 134, 135
Hip Sing Tong, 94, 97
Hok Shung, 84, 97
Holsey, Albon, 125, 126
Hong Ah Kay, 95
Hong Kong and Shanghai Banking Corporation, 47
Hong Kong immigrants, 181, 182
Honshu, southern, 103
Hoodlums, 6, 70, 97
Horatio Alger, 4, 187
Hotels: Japanese, 10, 17; Father Divine, 144, 145
Hui: in South China, 23, 24; in Britain, 25n; in the United States, 25–27; collateral, 57; size of group, 60, 61; membership in, 86

Ibo, 104
Illegal entry into United States, 90
Illinois, Negro businesses in, 16, 17
Immigration: Chinese, 6, 81; Japanese, 8, 62, 67; West Indian, 33, 34, 35;

and interstate migration, 102; from Hong Kong, 181
Incompetence: in banks, 48–50, 54; and rotating credit, 50, 51; insurance companies, 157, 158
Indigent: Japanese, 64, 65, 168; Chinese, 85, 86, 168. See also Welfare
Individualism, 98, 190
Industrial Bank of Fresno, 47
Insurance: Father Divine, 147; assessment societies, 152, 153; church beneficials, 152, 162; white fraternals, 154n, 157; venality, 155, 157; legal reserve, 155, 158, 159, 160, 161; old-line, 155, 158, 160; competition, 158, 159, 160; Negro share, 159; Oriental, 160–169; fraudulent claims, 139, 161; industrial, 162; agents and officials, 165, 167; tanomoshi as, 167; and income, 168; Chinese American Citizens' Alliance, 177; Japanese American Citizens League, 178
Internal Security Act, 179
Invisible man, the, 3
Irish: discrimination, 5; as hoodlums, 6; policemen, 90
Isolation, social, 132
Issei: agriculturalists, 72, 73, 74; and nisei, 79, 80; defined, 176; Japanese Association, 178
Italians, discrimination, 5

"Jackleg" revivalists, 137
Jamaica: "partners," 32–35; slavery in, 38
Jamaicans: in Britain, 35; in Harlem, 33–34
Japanese Agricultural Association of Southern California, 75
Japanese American Citizens' League (JACL), 76, 77
Japanese Association of America: and Six Companies, 82; community leadership, 174; sanctions 175, 178
Japanese Cooperative Farm Industry (JCFI), 76, 77
Japanese Fishermens' Association, 78
Japanese in the United States: discrimination, 5, 10; immigration, 8, 62, 100, 105; early years, 8–9, 66, 69, 71, 72; agriculture, 9, 72–78; retail stores, 11, 13, 14, 15, 16, 17, 122–124; produce distribution, 16, 17, 76; prefectural ties, 62, 66, 67; welfare dependency,

63, 66, 88, 167–169; fisheries, 78; industrial paternalism, 78, 79, 80; family, 100, 164, 165; relocation, 178
Japanese Shoemakers Guild, 68–69
Japantowns: ethnic clientele, 15; and Chinatowns, 98, 99, 100; white proprietorships in, 122
Jehovia, Father, 142
Jews: merchants, 2, 33, 120; discrimination, 5; Black, 141, 150
Jones, Absolom, 153
Jones, Prophet, 149
Jung family, 91

Kako Domei Kwai, 68, 69
*Ken*, defined, 62
*Kenjin*: defined, 62; boardinghouses, 66; settlement pattern, 67; occupational clustering, 66, 67, 118, 124; welfare activities, 66, 167
*Kenjinkai*: defined, 62; welfare activities, 63–65, 106, 111, 160, 161, 163; economic significance, 66, 67, 68; and Chinese district asociations, 90; membership, 104; and Urban League, 109, 110, 111, 114; and churches, 131; competition among, 139, 140
Kingdom, the. *See* Father Divine Peace Mission Movement
Kingdom names, 144
Kinship: credit, 60, 124; sects, 140, 170. *See also* Clans, Chinese; Family
Knights of Honor, 45, 129
*Ko*. See *Tanomoshi*
*Koden*, 70
Kwangtung province, 81, 103, 104
Kwong Duck Tong, 95

Labor, white: and Chinese, 6–7; and Japanese, 9–10, 70, 71
Lapsation of insurance, 162
Lau, Gordon, 177
Laundries: Chinese, 7, 16, 92–94; steam, 72
Lawson, Bishop, 149
Leadership. *See* Elites
Lee family, 91, 181
Legal reserve, 155, 158, 159, 160, 161, 162. *See also* Insurance
Leong family, 91
Life style: ethical discipline, 132–133; ethnic, 133, 172, 172*n*; organizational demands, 135, 136, 185, 186; of Negro

leaders, 173. *See also* Active participation
Lincoln, Abraham, 68
Little Pete, 97
Loans, 59, 60, 124. *See also* Rotating credit associations; Banks
Loan sharks, 121
Locality clubs, 101, 102, 112
Looters, 2, 3, 121, 122
Los Angeles, California: Watts rioting, 1; Japanese in, 10, 17; anti-Japanese manifestations, 71; produce markets, 76; relief population, 88; Negro population, 101, 174*n*; proposed Asian center, 182, 183
Louisiana Club, 101
Lumber: Japanese in, 9; Oriental retailers of, 15, 16
Lum Hip, 96
Lyman, Stanford M., 95, 100, 174

Manumission, 39
"Meeting," the, 32
Memberships, multiple, 139, 140, 149, 150, 171, 172
Militia, white, 40, 41
Mismanagement: in banks, 50, 54, 55; in rotating credit associations, 55–57; in insurance companies, 156, 157
Moi family, 91
Moneylender, town, 24
Moorish Science Temple of America, 141
Moral communities: blacks and Orientals, 130, 131, 150, 151; defined, 170; voluntary and ascribed, 170–172
Mortuaries, 14
Mosaic Templars of America, 129
Mt. Sinai Holy Church of America, 141
*Mujin*. See *Tanomoshi*
Mutual aid, 152, 153, 155, 162, 164, 167–169, 178, 182. *See also* Insurance; Welfare
Mutual Aid Association, the, 154

Natchez Club, 101
National Business League. *See* National Negro Business League
National Guard, 2
Nationalism, Japanese, 99, 178
National Negro Business League: membership, 115, 125; recruitment and training, 116, 117, 118; consumer credit, 119, 124; Colored Merchants

Association, 125, 126; voluntary association, 131
National Negro Insurance Association, 158, 159
National Urban League, the: origins, 107, 108; public relations, 108; professionalism, 108, 109; and Oriental welfare, 109, 110, 111, 114; educational activities, 111, 112; and black competitors, 112, 113; permanent objectives, 113, 114; and Business League, 115, 131
Nation of Islam, the, 150
Native born: white businessmen, 12, 13; Orientals, 29, 79, 80, 165, 176, 177; blacks, 11, 13, 14, 33, 36, 43, 44, 101–106. *See also* Nisei; Sansei
"Natural course of labor," 68
Naturalization and Immigration Act, 181
Nazis, 187
Negroes in the United States: riots, 1, 2, 3, 121; proprietorships, 2, 11, 13, 14, 17, 18, 118, 119; discrimination, 6, 10, 19–20, 190; West Indians, 33–34; rotating credit, 33–36; slavery, 36–42; postemancipation conditions, 42–44; banks, 45, 46, 48–55, 57, 58, 61; welfare dependency, 87, 88, 113; locality clubs, 101, 102, 112; migration, 101, 102, 106, 107; Urban League, 107–114; voluntary associations, 107, 112, 131, 184; Business League, 114–126; churches, 127–129, 131–133, 36–138, 152, 153, 160, 168; fraternal orders, 129, 130, 131, 132, 133, 135, 136, 138, 139, 153–160; Father Divine, 141–151; elites, 172, 173, 186
Neighborliness, Japanese, 98, 99
Newark, New Jersey, 2
"New order of life," 135n
New York, N.Y.: proprietorships, 13; relief, 88, 168
Ning Yeung Company, 81, 140
Nippon Bank, 47, 50
Nippon-California Farmers Association, 76
Nisei: savings habits, 29, 30; Alien Land Laws, 73; work attitudes, 79, 80; defined, 176; Japanese American Citizens' League, 178–179
Norris, Austin, 145
Nupe, the, 104

Oakland, California: retail proprietorships, 13; Chinatown, 83; Negro population, 101
Occidental type of city, 183
Occupational community, 132n
Odd Fellows, 129
Old Age Security (OAS), 181
Old-line insurance companies, 155, 158, 160. *See also* Insurance
"Old lying" insurance companies, 158
Oligarchs, 140, 176. *See also* Elites
Ong family, 91
On Leong Tong, 94, 97
Opium, 94
Order of St. Luke, 129
Oriental type of city, 183, 184
Overseers, 41, 42

Park-Frazier thesis, 104n
"Partners": in Jamaica, 32; in the United States, 33, 34; in Britain, 34, 35. See also *Esusu*
Partnerships, Chinese, 18, 93
Paternalism, industrial: Japanese, 67, 78, 79, 80; Chinese, 89, 93
Peculium, 39, 40
Pell Street, 96
Philadelphia, Pennsylvania: retail trade, 13; relief population, 88; churches, 127; fraternal memberships, 130n; insurance frauds, 138
Picnics, *kenjinkai*, 63
Picture brides, 100
Pilgrim Benevolent Society, 153
Pilgrim Health and Life Insurance Company, 153, 154
Planning, economic, 53
Poles, 5
Police: in Watts, 1; brutality, 2; in Chinatowns, 90
Poor white trash, 187
Pork chops, 18
*P'o tai*, 90
Postemancipation social conditions, 42, 43
Prejudice. *See* Discrimination
Prince Hall Masons, 129
Produce stores, 16, 17, 76
Prostitution, 94, 100
Protection racketeering, 97
Protests, social, 173–176
Public way of life, 130, 132, 133, 143–144. *See also* Life style; Active participation

Racism, 2, 70–71, 124, 173, 190
Railroads: Chinese labor, 6; Japanese labor, 9
Real estate: West Indian, 35; banks, 52
Regional associations: Japanese, 62 (see also *Kenjinkai*); welfare activities, 63–66, 84, 85, 109, 113; Chinese, 81, 82 (*see also* District associations *and* Chinese Six Companies); blacks, 101, 102, 128, 129; and Urban League, 109, 110, 111, 114; occupational contacts in, 118; competition among, 140, 175, 176; sanctions, 175
Regional loyalties: in credit, 60, 124; of American blacks, 101–106; of native-born Orientals, 176; and social control, 187, 188
Relief: Japanese on, 63, 66, 88; blacks on, 87, 88, 113; Chinese on, 87, 88, 181; Divine Angels on, 147, 148. See *also* Welfare; Insurance
Relocation of Japanese Americans, 178
Reputation: family, 59, 60, 86, 187, 188; merchants' in ghetto, 121
Restaurants: Chinese, 7, 15; Oriental, 15, 17; black, 16; Japanese, 16, 17
Retail trade: in ghetto, 2, 3, 11, 14, 33, 118–122, 124, 125, 126, 145; Chinese, 7, 8, 11, 12, 13, 14, 15, 16, 94, 122; Japanese, 10, 11, 14–16, 17, 29, 68, 72, 76, 122, 123; of whites, 11–14; in six cities, 13
Rice, 72
"Roads," 31
Rotating credit associations: defined, 22, 23; Chinese 23–26; Japanese, 27–30; West African, 30–35; American blacks, 36; and slavery, 36–44; and banks, 50, 51, 55–58; decentralized operations, 55; fraternal, 55, 56; overhead, 56; advantageous, 58; mutual trust, 58; 59; family reputation, 59, 60; size, 60; as insurance, 167. See also *Esusu*; *Hui*; *Tanomoshi*
Rural-urban migration, Negro, 106, 107

St. Bishop the Vine, Rev., 142
Sam Yap, 84
San Francisco, California: hoodlums, 6, 96, 97; earthquake and fire of 1906, 63, 87; Japanese in, 67, 69, 72, anti-Japanese manifestations, 71; Chinese clans, 83; relief population, 88, 181; Sam Yup, 91; Negro population, 101; Hong Kong immigrants, 181
*Sansei*: defined, 176; and Japanese American Citizens' League, 179
Sayville, Long Island, 142, 143, 144
Seattle, Washington, 10
Sects: defined, 134n; and immigrant brotherhoods, 131, 132, 140, 150, 151; in ghetto, 141; and ascription, 170, 172; in Africa, 172n
Secularism, 127
Service proprietorships, black, 2, 14, 119
Seven Wise Men, 129
Sex in Heavens, 143, 149
Sharecropping, 43
Shoemakers' Union, 69
Shoplifting, 121
Sib, Cantonese, 83
Skin color, 5
Slavery: *esusu*, 31, 32, 37; African origins of blacks, 37; slaves' economy, 38, 39, 40; administration, 41, 52
Small business: financing, 19, 20, 21; recruitment and training, 116, 117, 118. See also Rotating credit associations; Retail trade; Service proprietorships
Social mobility: real estate, 52; of clergy, 136; in fraternal orders, 138, 139
Social movements, 135n
Sojourners, 103, 104, 105, 106, 175–177, 183
Soul brothers, 1, 121
South, the: slavery in, 38–42; postemancipation conditions, 42, 43; black-owned banks, 52–55; emigration of blacks, 101, 105; emigrant whites, 105; black attitudes toward, 103, 104, 105, 106; cultural homogeneity, 105; Negro churches in, 127, 128, 137, 152; sickness and burial relief, 152, 162
Southern California Flower Market, 76
Special consumer demands: evidence, 10–15; criticized, 15–18
Stigma, 134
Storefront churches, 128, 129, 163
Strikebreaking, Japanese, 9
"Strivers and strainers," 186
Success symbols, business, 21
Suey Sing Tong, 95
Sugar plantations, 38, 42

"Suit *tanomoshi*," 123
Sumitomo Bank, 47, 48
Supermarket solidarity, 185
Supreme Camp of American Woodmen, 159
Surname associations. *See* Family associations
*Susu*, 32
"Swat the Jap" crusade, 70
"Symbol of opportunity," 4
Sze Yap, 82, 84

Taiji, 78
*Tanomoshi*: in Japan, 27, 28; in the United States, 28–30, 48; costs, 56; collateral, 57; size of restricted, 60, 61; consumer credit, 123, 124; as insurance, 167. *See also* Rotating credit associations
Terminal Island, East San Pedro, 78
Territorial associations. *See* Regional associations; *Kenjinkai*; District associations; Chinese Six Companies
Third World, 179
Three districts dialect, 84
Toi-shan, 81, 83, 133, 140
Tokugawa shogunate, 165
Tom family, 91
Tongs: enterprises, 94; enforcers, 95–97; wars, 100; in Chinese Six Companies, 180
Tourists, in Chinatowns, 16, 99, 100
Trade associations: Negro, 125
Trade guilds: Japanese, 68–72, 75, 90, 98; Chinese, 91–95, 98
"Tradition-of-enterprise" hypothesis, 21, 36
Tribal honor, 187
Trinidad, 32, 36
True Reformers: Savings Bank, 50, 53–55; insurance, 154
Trust, social: and credit, 58–60, 122, 123, 124; fraternal orders, 139; ascription, 170–171
Tsao family, 91
*Tsu*, Cantonese, 83, 86
Tsukamoto, Mr. (steam laundry operator), 72
Tsung Tsin Company, 91

Unemployment: of Orientals, 11, 63, 88; of blacks, 88, 149, 168–69
United House of Prayer for All People, 141

"Uplift" philosophy, 109
Urban League. *See* National Urban League

Venality: in banks, 49, 50; rotating credit, 51; in Six Companies, 140; in fraternal orders, 155; in insurance companies, 157, 158
Vicksburg Club, 101
Village associations: welfare activities, 85, 86, 106, 160, 161, 163; and churches, 131; membership competition, 139, 140
Voluntary associations: banks as, 60; among blacks, 107, 112, 131, 150–151, 184, 186; participation in, 112, 115, 127–129, 131, 152, 184; and regional associations, 133, 150–151; and ascriptive brotherhood, 170–172; defined, 171; of Orientals, 176–182; in cities, 183–187; problems of, 184, 185; exclusive, 185, 186
Voluntary chain, 125

Washington, Booker T.: popularizes success symbols, 21; National Negro Business League, 114, 115; outlook, 174
Watts, California, 1, 2, 121
Weber, Max, 136, 183–185, 188–189
Welfare, social: Depression, 63, 88, 89, 141, 148, 150, 168–169; *kenjinkai*, 63–65, 66, 106, 111; Japanese on relief, 63, 66, 88; public, 63, 87, 88, 113, 147, 150, 181; district associations, 84, 85, 88, 111, 181, 182; Chinese village associations, 85, 86, 88, 89, 106, 111, 113, 181; Chinese on relief, 87, 88; Negro, 88, 101, 107–114, 147, 150; Negroes on relief, 88, 112, 113, 148; caseworkers, 108, 109; regional associations, 109, 113; vacuum, 112, 184. *See also* Insurance; National Urban League; Relief
West Indians: in the United States, 33–34; in Great Britain, 34–35; regional ties, 102
West Indies: whites in, 38; slaves' economy in, 38–42; postemancipation social conditions in, 42–43
White power structure, 2
Wholesale Terminal Market, 76
Wong family, 83
Work Projects Administration (WPA), 147

World War II: labor shortages, 8; Cantonese immigration, 81; Japanese
American relocation, 178

Yan Wo Company, 91
Yee family, 83, 91

Yellow power movement, 179
Yeung Wo Company, 91
Yokohama Specie Bank, 47, 48
Yoruba: *esusu*, 30, 31, 32; in West
Indies, 37; mentioned, 104
Yueh-woey, 26